ML

**Books are to be returned on or before
the last date below.**

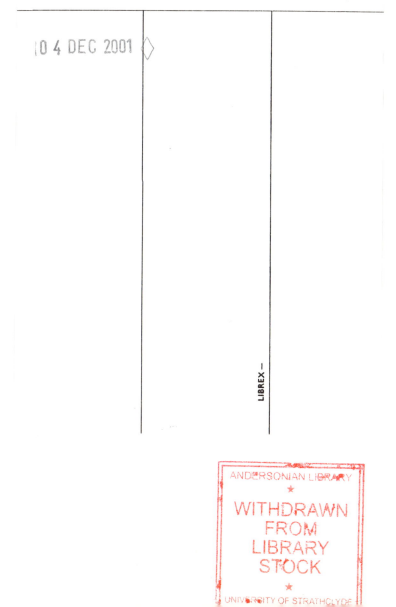

# MANUFACTURING RATIONALITY

# Manufacturing Rationality

*The Engineering Foundations*
*of the Managerial Revolution*

Yehouda Shenhav

OXFORD
UNIVERSITY PRESS

# OXFORD
## UNIVERSITY PRESS

Great Clarendon Street, Oxford OX2 6DP

Oxford University Press is a department of the University of Oxford.
It furthers the University's objective of excellence in research, scholarship,
and education by publishing worldwide in

Oxford  New York

Athens  Auckland  Bangkok  Bogotá  Buenos Aires  Calcutta
Cape Town  Chennai  Dar es Salaam  Delhi  Florence  Hong Kong  Istanbul
Karachi  Kuala Lumpur  Madrid  Melbourne  Mexico City  Mumbai
Nairobi  Paris  São Paulo  Singapore  Taipei  Tokyo  Toronto  Warsaw

with associated companies in  Berlin  Ibadan

Oxford is a registered trade mark of Oxford University Press
in the UK and in certain other countries

Published in the United States
by Oxford University Press Inc., New York

British Library Cataloguing in Publication Data

Data available

Library of Congress Cataloging in Publication Data
Shenhav, Yehouda A.
Manufacturing rationality: the engineering foundations of the
managerial revolution / Yehouda Shenhav.
p. cm.
Includes bibliographial references and index.
1. Management science   2. Industrial engineering.   I. Title.
T56.S413   1999   658.5—dc21   99–37909
ISBN 0 19 829630 4 (hb.)

1 3 5 7 9 10 8 6 4 2

Typeset by
Cambrian Typesetters, Frimley, Surrey
Printed in Great Britain
on acid-free paper by
Biddles Ltd
Guildford & Kings Lynn

# Acknowledgements

This book brings to a conclusion an intellectual journey that took place in several geographical locations over a period of five years. The empirical materials for this book were collected during my sabbatical stay at the University of Wisconsin-Madison between 1992 and 1993. Ann Miner, Pam Hoschild, and Marc Suchman provided useful suggestions in this crucial stage of research design. I am grateful for the assistance and services I received at the Wisconsin Historical Library and the Wendt Engineering Library in collecting the materials. They went out of their way to give me access to treasured documents. Thanks also to the Engineering Societies Information Center, Linda Hall Library East, in New York City, where I received complementary materials missing elsewhere.

Parts of this manuscript were written while I was a visiting professor in my *Alma Mater*, the Department of Sociology at Stanford University, between 1994 and 1995. Being at Stanford I benefited from the intellectual atmosphere in two research centers: SCOR and SCANSCOR. Three individuals exerted strong influence on this study there: John Meyer, Jim March, and Dick Scott.

A number of colleagues have read the manuscript, or parts of it, and provided useful substantial or editorial comments at various stages of the project: Kalman and Ingrid Appelbaum, Steve Barley, Barbara Czarniawska, Michal Frenkel, Mauro Guillen, David Hounshell, Alexandra Kalev, Adriana Kemp, John Meyer, Aviad Raz, and Ely Weitz. Aviad Raz gave me excellent advice on writing, content, and the interplay between them. I also benefited from discussions with a large number of colleagues in Tel Aviv and elsewhere: Nitza Berkovitz, Daniel Breslau, Yinon Cohen, Marie-Laure Djelic, Frank Dobbin, Eva Eillouz, Haim Hazan, Gideon Kunda, Rachel Lotan, Peter Mendel, Francisco Ramirez, Itzhak Saporta, Ora Setter, Ronen Shamir, David Strang, Marc Ventresca, David De-Vries, and Yuval Yonay. I am particularly indebted to the late Yonatan Shapiro, a senior colleague and a friend, who always had faith in the manuscript.

It was a pleasure to work with a wonderful group of graduate students at Tel Aviv University, students who provided me with a cozy environment on the one hand and intellectual challenge and criticism on the other: Daniel De-Malach, Michal Frenkel, Alexandra Kalev, Ori Landau, Anat Leibler, Ely Weitz (who is now a colleague), and Aviva Zeltzer. Dorith Geva, Alexandra Kalev, Shoham Melamed, Seffi Shteiglitz, and Aviva Zeltzer gave me technical assistance. I particularly want to thank Alexandra Kalev who helped with devotion, wisdom, and care. They all formed the intellectual context within which this book was written.

The research for this study was supported by grants from the Israel Foundation Trustees, Ford Foundation (1994), and from the Israel Academy of

Sciences and Humanities. Support was also received from the Faculty of Social Sciences, Tel Aviv University.

I would like to thank David Musson, the editor at Oxford University Press, and Sarah Dobson, Assistant Editor at Oxford University Press, for their sensitive and wise professional guidance throughout this process.

My special love goes to my partner Orna Ben-Dor, and my daughters Inbar and Noa, for being there for me.

Y. S.

# Contents

# List of Figures

# List of Tables

# Introduction

> Pangloss . . . proved incontestably . . . that things cannot be other than they are, for since everything was made for a purpose, it follows that everything is made for the best purpose. Observe: our noses were made to carry spectacles, so we have spectacles. Legs were clearly intended for breeches, and we wear them. Stones were meant for carving and for building houses, and that is why my lord has a most beautiful house . . . It follows that those who maintain that all is right talk nonsense; they ought to say that all is for the best.
>
> (Voltaire, *Candide*, 20)

Managerial rationality is a powerful mode of thought and code of conduct in the modern world.[1] Its emergence in the early twentieth century offered a clear vision of social order as a panacea for inefficiency and chaos, replacing former ideologies such as Social Darwinism, welfare capitalism, and religious discourses of labor. Common wisdom—in academic and popular circles alike—asserts that managerial rationality represents the American industrial way, a natural extension of economic progress, and the inevitable outcome of universal business practices. The managerial revolution (which pointed historically to the dispersion of corporate ownership) is, likewise, generally portrayed as a 'silent revolution' with no obvious protagonists or antagonists.[2] It is represented as a narrative of progression carried out by social agents for the benefit of all people.[3] Management guru Peter Drucker stated this position very clearly:

> Rarely, if ever, has a new basic institution, a new leading group, emerged as fast as has management since the turn of the century. Rarely in human history has a new institution proven indispensable so quickly; and even less often has a new institution arrived with so little opposition, so little disturbance, so little controversy. (Drucker 1986: 3)

This all-embracing view of management—an ideal, teleological, and not very factual view—is the product of historical reification. Drucker's observation, and organizational texts in general, tend to purge management history of its inherent conflicts and disputes.[4] After all, a 'revolution without revolutionaries' seldom involves conflict and tension. The non-conflictual view of the rise of management contradicts early historical discords between capitalist owners and their hired managers. Adam Smith already foresaw such discords in the late eighteenth century, with the ascendancy of the English industrial revolution. Smith expressed deep skepticism regarding the ability of salaried managers—rather than owners/capitalists—to manage industrial firms honestly and efficiently:

> Being the managers rather of other people's money than of their own, it cannot well be expected, that they should watch over it with the same anxious vigilance with which the

partners in a private copartnery frequently watch over their own. Like stewards of a rich man, they are apt to consider the attention to small matters as not for their master's honour, and very easily give themselves a dispensation from having it. Negligence and profusion, therefore, must always prevail, more or less, in the management of affairs of such a company. (Smith 1937: 700)

In Smith's view, the ability of owners to limit the involvement of salaried managers was a litmus test of the traditional capitalist vision.[5] Smith's conclusion, based both on his economic philosophy and on the historical experience of British industrialists, proved to be more than a mere anecdote (Pollard 1965). Salaried managers eventually did become a quintessential part of modern organizations, but this coming to power was plagued by conflicts and rather fierce confrontations with capitalist owners as well as with labor unions and unorganized workers. While Smith's *Wealth of Nations* is considered a cornerstone of modern economic and management thinking, his view on management has been discarded if not altogether forgotten.[6] This arguably reflects the appropriation of Smith by managerial historiography and its rationality. History, as the oft-quoted saying goes, is written by the winners.

A major objective of this book is to offer an alternative historical analysis of the evolution of managerial rationality as a contested ideology and practice. Mainstream management history likes to adopt the portrayal of managerial rationality as a natural and inevitable outcome of modernization (e.g. Chandler 1977), despite the fact that such a portrayal dismisses workers' resistance to the importation of management practices into their factories (e.g. Nelson 1974, 1975; Jacoby 1985; Montgomery 1987). In contrast I suggest that altogether management systems encountered vociferous resistance and were often promoted against the interest of industrial employers, against the interest of fellow engineers, and against the interest of workers. In the course of the analysis I unravel the multiple and contested meanings that managerial rationality assumed in early industrial and management history.

I offer to read this book simultaneously as a historical account of the birth of modern management, as a chapter in the history of American capitalism and industrial relations, as an ideological analysis of the rise of industrial engineering, and as a chapter in the sociology of (organizational) knowledge. By tracing the actual discourse of engineers in the United States between 1880 and 1932—the year that Berle and Means proclaimed the 'managerial revolution' with the appearance of their now classic book *The Modern Corporation and Private Property*—I expose the process by which managerial rationality crystallized to become the unquestioned pacemaker of modern social order. Management's dissemination proceeded at a rate faster than any other twentieth-century social ideology, and it played a critical role in diffusing repertoires of instrumental rationality worldwide. My aim will be to show how engineers had planted the seeds for the managerial revolution and how the managerial revolution, in turn, furnished business with its organizing principles.

Effecting this change presented no simple task for engineers, the main actors in this drama. Engineers sought ascendancy for their systems and themselves in a context where capital and labor were much more powerful. Engineers triumphed. By redefining industrial conflict as a mechanical problem rather than as a result of political struggles, engineers were able to universalize their particularistic interests, to depoliticize the conflictual nature of their rationality, and eventually to monopolize industrial discourse and almost completely silence alternative ideological voices. Consequently, the conflicts, objections, and struggles that actually took place left no marks on managerial historiography and on our collective consciousness.[7]

The institutionalization of management systems had several ramifications. First, it legitimized the engineers as managers and as propagators of managerial curricula in business schools. A new class of technocrats was crowned.[8] Its gospel gradually spread to include an administrative view of society whose practices eventually became a worldwide ideology.[9]

Second, it has succeeded in cleaving a sharp compartmentalization between politics and economics, blurring the fact that economic logic is politically and ideologically weighted. The institutionalization of management systems gave objective and universal status to value-laden assumptions such as economic maximization, efficiency, and standardization. These assumptions came to constitute a system of invisible domination defining what is legitimate and what is not in business, politics, law, art, culture, science, and religion. The snowball of bureaucratization became a scheme for interpreting and understanding private lives, personal experiences, leisure, love, and intimacy.

Third, the struggles of engineers were edited out of economic history and management historiography. Through reified concepts such as 'bounded rationality' or 'uncertainty reduction' academic texts reproduce instead the view of management as universal and politically or ideologically neutral. I suggest that contemporary social sciences were not only instrumentalized. They are themselves infused with the ideological and epistemological parameters born during the efforts to establish the legitimization of management. Management ideology has gradually become an inextricable part of established social scientific fields such as sociology, political science, and public policy.

I use three interrelated perspectives to analyze the complex phenomenon under study. The first perspective focuses on the most direct context of historical analysis. It is anchored in a particular time and place, relating to the (often messy and unpredictable) details of historical analysis. Using primary historical sources, I analyze where, how, and why everyday engineering practices became a dominant ideology.[10] The second perspective deals with the wider yet overlapping context of American ideology and politics. It shows how engineering practices and ideology were fuelled by broader political discourses that characterized the USA, particularly Progressivism and American Exceptionalism. The third perspective moves beyond these contexts to the more expansive discourse of social science. It uses the historical evidence to draw sociological, political, and moral conclusions about the dominant nature of rationality as ideology.

## 1. An alternative history of the managerial revolution

The concept of management was invented and developed in American industry during the period 1880–1932. The genealogy of the so-called 'managerial revolution' demands an analysis which goes back to the nineteenth century, to the time when engineers were carrying out extensive ideological work toward their own professional legitimization. The empirical analysis in this book makes substantial use of primary sources which are often missing in otherwise important studies of managerial history. I used data compiled from two periodicals, the *American Machinist* (established in 1877) and *Engineering Magazine* (established in 1891), the first magazines to provide a voice for industrial engineering when it evolved as an autonomous field. 'Systems' and 'systematization', perhaps the key ideological tropes of management, were constructed as such within the pages of these journals.

The textual part of this project began in the 1880s with an unprecedented outburst of management literature.[11] Between 1895 and 1917, the volume of management text ballooned by 400 percent. Such proliferation did not take place among contemporary European journals (Litterer 1986).[12] The American engineering literature, which contains the earliest known treatment of management as a separate domain of inquiry, established a very different language from the language of traditional capitalism.[13] It replaced 'individuals' with 'systems' and 'labor'; 'free initiatives' with 'planning'. Most importantly, this logic of 'organized capitalism', a term coined by Lash and Urry, sought to eliminate 'oversight' and 'confusion' through 'standardized system' (Lash and Urry 1987). It was the birth of a new epistemology, the creation of objects of knowledge, and a transition of world-views, the generation of images through which industrial reality was filtered. These language conventions became instruments which formulated the consciousness of the American nation and beyond, during these years (Locke 1996: 13). There would have been no room for the twentieth-century managerial revolution without the widespread readiness to accept the spirit of these arguments. This was the ideological phase of the managerial revolution forged in a specific historical context: that of American Exceptionalism, the dominance of the 'robber barons' in industry, a continuous industrial struggle, and the rise of the Progressive vision.

The empirical analysis upon which this study is based offers a non-evolutionary and conflictual history of rationalization and rationality. It challenges the simplistic view which claims that the systematization of organizations between 1880 and 1930 was the result of employers' efforts either to rationalize production (e.g. Chandler 1962, 1977) or to control labor (Marglin 1974; Stone 1974; Edwards 1979) as it falls short in explaining the dynamics of management historiography.

Therefore, the so-called 'managerial revolution' will not be viewed as a linear exten-sion and natural organ of the capitalist order, as it often is by class-based analysis (e.g. Braverman 1974).

## 2. The idiosyncratic nature of American managerial thought

The dissemination of the American model of management worldwide entails an intriguing paradox as it was both unique and universal. It is widely believed that 'management' is an American term and that modern management is an American creation (Locke 1996). Indeed, this belief is well grounded. At the turn of the century, the USA had the largest proportion of administrative staff to industrial workers, indicating that in the US economy the separation of owner-ship from control in industrial firms was the strongest (Guillen 1994). It was in the USA that the new class of salaried management first emerged in significant numbers, and set the blueprint for American management practices. Furthermore, it was in the United States that an independent discourse on management emerged.[14] The American scientific justification of management practices and organizational ideas sets it apart from European countries where more importance was attached to religious, nationalistic, and culture-specific ideas determining human relations in the workplace. American management theory was presented as a scientific technique administered for the good of soci-ety as a whole without relation to politics. This ostensibly apolitical stance was the legacy of the political ideology of Progressivism, which aspired to establish a 'neutral' and 'efficient' administrative state (Merkle 1980). The 'non-political', and 'ahistorical' agenda of management replaced explicit political discourse and decontextualized culture, politics, and history.

During the first half of the twentieth century, American management started a universal career by attracting pilgrimages from Europe. The economic and military supremacy of the USA was attributed to its unique managerial and productivity spirit. As Robert Locke put it: 'Winston Churchill, looking at Fortress Europe, had proclaimed the invincibility of the "American clear-cut, logical, large-scale, mass production style of thought" which he correctly saw preparing the powerful Normandy landings' (Locke 1996: 12). Nevertheless, while the logic of managerial vision was adopted worldwide, its justification varied across space (see Djelic 1998). At the risk of oversimplifying, it can be said that European countries such as Britain, France, and Germany developed differ-ent indigenous models and justifications of management. For example, in the USA the application of management was justified 'scientifically'. The debates over its legitimacy were anchored only in terms of its potential to provide 'scien-tific' solutions in industrial practice. The debates about management in Britain, however, were moral and ideological discourses, and were not couched in scien-tific terms. Likewise, the adoption of Human Relations programs in the United States was linked to workers' productivity and was justified with scientific (i.e.

'non-ideological') reasoning. In Britain, by contrast, the main rationalization for the introduction of Human Relations programs was 'ideological': to enhance democracy in the workplace (Guillen 1994). Whereas the techniques may now be similar or even identical across countries, the logic of their justification was at its inception substantially different and culturally bound. This will be further discussed below.

## 3. Meta-analysis of the managerial revolution

At the broader, meta-analytical level, I focus on the relationship between institutionalization, reification, and 'social amnesia'. Organizational history tells us that the engineers were the forerunners of management but it does not tell us about their struggles and conflicts. Following the 'institutional' theoretical tradition I propose that institutionalization reifies our reality to the extent that it seems uncontested despite its conflictual roots. Reification makes us forget that the 'final version' of a certain aspect of our reality seems natural only because of its dominance. Peter Berger and Thomas Luckman (1966), who were most concerned with that phenomenon, suggested that 'reification is a modality of consciousness, more precisely, a modality of man's objectification of the human world' (Berger and Luckmann 1966: 89). For phenomena to be taken as objects of social scientific explanation, they must first be stripped of the natural and concrete immediacy in which they appear to everyday consciousness. This is true for the social sciences as well. In his *History and Class Consciousness* (1923/1971), Georg Lukács provides a cultural critique of reification, arguing that Weber's sociological analysis of rationality was incomplete since he did not include sociology and social sciences themselves in its scope. To Lukács, society, and the social sciences that study it, are no more 'rational' than they are totemistic. He proposed to include the formal rationality of the social sciences themselves under critical scrutiny. Rationality, in other words, should be perceived as cultural logic that was reified, and not as a transcendental epistemological condition. In line with these two observations, I advance the view that most ideas, facts, and claims held at present and considered self-evident (in the social sciences, management sciences, or in everyday mundane reality) may be problematized by exposing the oppositions and struggles they encountered during their formation. At those junctures of opposition, history could have taken different routes. Weber's 'objective possibilities'—the historical options that were never realized[15]—can be used as a vantage point from which to espy the perils associated with dogmatic institutions that legitimize themselves with the functional logic of the inevitable. It is our role as sociologists to examine the manner in which reality was constructed and to give voice to the squashed options that were never materialized.[16]

Managerial efficiency, for instance, is a taken-for-granted universal concept, and its legitimacy today is beyond question. However, if we went back in time to the formative years of the concept we would find that it was quite controversial. Familiarity with the arguments against the acceptance of efficiency—and with the various unrealized alternatives that existed—in early years is crucial in order to unravel the process of its institutionalization and its arbitrary aspects. In essence, I attempt to 'rewind' well-known and widely accepted institutionalized facts back to their starting points, to unwind the variety of pathways these ideas might yet have taken prior to institutionalization. Some of these pathways are not part of our reified collective memory, and they are not discussed in our history books. It is this method of taking ideas and practices back in time to their original breeding ground, to isolate their meanings and to search for existing alternatives and objecting voices, that I employ in this book.

'Rewinding' is not merely an intellectual game. The historicization and politicization of accepted realities is a crucial moral and political task for a democratic society. More specifically, I hold that the institutionalization of management practices—dominated by instrumental managerial rationality—can pose a real danger to an open civil and democratic society. Consider the following two cases.

In 1995, the Israeli military occupation in the Gaza Strip implemented TQM (Total Quality Management) techniques in its administration. The idea was imported by high-ranking military officers who had recently obtained MBA degrees in Europe and at Ivy League universities in the USA. This was considered a calculated rational decision. After all, TQM is highly fashionable worldwide and had been adopted by all manner of organizations including schools, prisons, churches, art museums, and the USA Department of Defense. The documents prepared by the Israeli military officers depicted the administrative apparatus of the military occupation as a firm, while the Palestinians under occupation and the Jewish settlers in the occupied territories were likened to customers of the enterprise. Principles of 'quality control', 'Just in Time', and other statistical analyses were then naturally implemented. Needless to say, this bizarre characterization of reality, once institutionalized, depoliticized the military occupation and neutralized its language to simple business events. It legitimized the adoption of deeper control mechanisms and blurred the political and human meaning of the officers' and soldiers' actions.

Management ideology was assigned a similarly supreme role by Robert McNamara in the Pentagon of the 1960s (see Waring 1991, citing Gibson 1986). In implementing operations research techniques, which were growing in popularity during and after the Second World War, McNamara fostered the misconception that America was winning the war in Vietnam. Under his influence, and that of his 'whizz-kids', American political leaders viewed the conflict in managerial terms, by the use of figures, numbers, charts, and mathematical analyses. They aspired to use resources efficiently and defined their efficiency as kill-ratios. As Gibson suggested: '[The] American defeat in Vietnam was inherent in the managerial thinking that was institutionalized in the Pentagon and American society. Managerial techniques were perfectly applied, but to problems for which they were unsuited, and that was why America lost' (quoted in Waring 1991: 33). The question, of course, is not whether America lost or won. The issue at hand is the omnipresence of the managerial thinking at the time, and the precedence managerial rationality was given over other modes of thought. These examples, among many others (see for example Bauman 1989), shed light on the dangers of legitimizing the possession of unlimited authority by a 'universal' managerial rationality without introducing political, cultural, and moral balances. For these reasons I suggest that managerial rationality should be considered not as a neutral endpoint without moral and political consequences, but as a means bearing a clear moral and political responsibility that requires constant scrutiny.

## 4. Rationality in chains: the instrumentalization of American management

The moral critique of management and the idiosyncratic nature of American systems converge in the example of how Weber's concept of bureaucracy was domesticated in the United States. In its original intent, Max Weber's work in Germany conveyed a strong political message to those who study organizations. He perceived bureaucracy first and foremost as a form of domination (*Herrschaft*), an institution that is embedded in the history of conflict in Western societies. Whereas earlier forms of domination were based on either charismatic or traditional legitimization, bureaucratic domination was based on legal rationality. Weber did not distinguish between the management of political apparatuses and of industrial firms. His analysis was both political and historical. Weber was intrigued by the strength of bureaucracy but he also cautioned his readers about the unexpected consequences of instrumental rationality (see Sheleff 1997).

In the United States, Frederick Taylor was struck, as Weber had been, by the omnipotence of bureaucracy, but, contrary to Weber, Taylor sent a strong apolitical message to those who studied and operated in organizations. He perceived bureaucracy as an end in and of itself. Rather than warning the community about the unexpected consequences of bureaucracy, Taylor offered it as a solution to ideological cleavages, as an engineering remedy to the war between the classes. To Taylor, rationality was instrumental: a lathe is a lathe is a lathe. To Weber, a lathe is not always the same lathe: its identities change as the contexts of its use change. At times it shapes the product, at times it shapes the operators. The strength of American organization and managerial theory was based on reversing Weber's perspective and excluding 'domination' from its scope.[17] This was an act of instrumentalization. There is nothing alarming about instrumental rationality *per se*. Only when it tends to authorize 'purposive' action, and when it trivializes other spheres of actions, does it become troubling (R. Pippin, 'On the Notion of Technology as Ideology', in Feenberg and Hannay 1995: 43–61).

It is this worrisome nature of instrumental and rational managerial ideology that motivates my inquiry into its historical and sociological roots. The ideology of rationality authorizes a scientific scheme which legitimizes pure instrumentalism and replicates teleological assumptions. It reifies objects of knowledge to assume a reality-like status while repressing other forms of knowing. It creates multiple closed systems which are not in dialogue with each other, and which truncate our reality into incommensurable modes of thought. It allows for scientific compartmentalization in which no one authority takes responsibility for consequences. My main goal is to unfold the development of these practices and to deconstruct their nature.

The book is structured as follows: in Chapter 1 mechanical and industrial engineers—the prophets of the managerial revolution—are under the spotlight. The chapter situates management rhetoric and practice within its engineering breeding ground, presents the historical conditions that shaped its development, and grounds the discussion within two political and cultural perspectives which dominated American society during the period 1880–1932: Progressivism and American Exceptionalism. The chapter conceptualizes engineers, their associations, and their periodicals as central agents of the ideological phase of the managerial revolution and introduces the sources upon which the empirical analyses in subsequent chapters are based.

Chapter 2 traces the origin of the two engineering projects, 'systematization' and 'standardization', and defines them as social practices and cultural images which formed the backbone of management. These images and practices then migrated from the technical domain to other spheres of human action, including organizations.

Chapter 3 empirically examines how management differentiated itself from engineering, and how the notion of 'system' was 'translated' from the technical field to become a dominant paradigm in the world of organizations. It focuses on the logic and rhetoric employed by the early systematizers and the manner in which they justified the introduction of systems to the management of organizations.

Chapter 4 focuses on the opposition to 'management systems'; on the objection of manufacturers, engineers, and employee representatives. The chapter argues that management systems were not promoted by capitalists or their representatives, but rather by a group of engineers—a new class of salaried technocrats—wishing to carve out their own domain within industrial organizations.

Chapter 5 describes the relationship between engineering rationality and labor politics prior to 1900. Quantitative empirical data presented in the chapter show that while labor unrest intensified over time, its coverage in engineering literature gradually declined. The chapter further argues that the severity of industrial unrest was overlooked within the bounds of American Exceptionalism. Strikes were considered foreign to the American experience, anarchism was attributed to European subversive philosophies, and the possibility of class struggle was denied.

Chapter 6 extends this analysis to the Progressive era. During this period the severity of industrial unrest was recognized, and engineers established themselves as arbiters of industrial conflicts. They perceived themselves as gatekeepers situated at the junction between politics and economics and offered management systems—to manufacturers and the public at large—as a solution to political instability. The chapter shows how system discourse gradually replaced the explicit ideological discourse, the process resulting in the depoliticization of the labor struggle.

Chapter 7 summarizes the genealogy of management ideology from the Civil War until the Great Depression, and emphasizes the conflictive biography of management rhetoric and practice. The chapter further points to the cultural idiosyncrasy of American management and provides an international comparative framework. The chapter ends with the argument that much of management and organization theory is epistemologically infused with the ideological parameters that were born during the efforts to establish the legitimization of management. This is illustrated with a discussion of three key managerial concepts, 'system', 'rationality', and 'uncertainty', and their canonization in organization theory.

## Notes

1. The concept of 'rationality' is heavily discussed and debated in philosophical, sociological, and historical literature. For critical discussion on rationality see Toulmin 1990; for a critical discussion of 'modernity' see Albrow 1996; Pippin 1991; Foucault 1977. Throughout this book I tend to avoid an a-priori definition of 'rationality', and rather treat it as a cultural and historical product (i.e. artifact), a version that evolved and developed empirically in engineering and managerial texts. See Chapter 7 for discussion on the institutionalized version of managerial and organizational rationality.

2. The cradle of the concept 'managerial revolution' can be found in the 1932 publication of *The Modern Corporation and Private Property*, a book that was hailed by the *New York Herald Tribune* as 'the most important work bearing on American state craft between the publication of the immortal Federalist and the opening of the year 1933' (Stigler and Friedland 1983: 241). The authors of this book, Adolph Berle and Gardiner Means, made two novel observations that challenged economic theories of capitalism in America in the late 1920s. First, they observed a dispersion of ownership and the greater prominence of financial institutions. In other words, the control of family capitalism—which was fairly strong in American corporations until the early 1900s—was gradually being eroded. Second, they observed that a new group (some would say 'class') of professional people succeeded in developing an autonomous agenda that was significantly different from that of owners (Berle and Means 1932: 124; see also Berle 1959; Sklar 1988). They envisioned business-school educated professionals—rather than owners—in the role of corporate managers, 'relegating "owners" to the position of those who supply the means

whereby the new princes may exercise their power'. However, Berle and Means were not explicit about a managerial revolution, nor did they coin the term. A decade later, in 1941, James Burnham, rising from a different ideological tradition, was more straightforward in making a similar observation. His thesis can be understood within the context of the so-called 'New Class' theory (or theories). Burnham identified 'a drive for social dominance, for power and privilege, for the position of ruling class, by the social group or class of the managers' (Burnham 1941/1960: 71). Since the 1940s, the observation made by Berle and Means has converged with the term coined by Burnham to become 'the managerial revolution' (see for example: Larner 1970; Mizruchi 1987; for an alternative thesis rejecting the significance of the managerial revolution, see Zeitlin 1974; Schwartz 1987). It set the tone for the formulation of a new perspective that generated awareness of the role of managers as an autonomous class in modern capitalist America. Despite its divergent ideological sources, the 'managerial revolution' was understood in the USA as a natural development of capitalist and democratic society (for a counter-argument see n. 3).

3. It is quite intriguing, and usually overlooked, that the thesis about the managerial revolution was stimulated simultaneously by scholars from heterogeneous ideological positions. Early in the century, socialist thinker Thorstein Veblen believed that the capitalist class impairs the expansion of production because of the greed for profit which characterizes its members (the robber barons such as Rockefeller and Vanderbilt). He perceived engineers as the real and true promoters of 'equitable, efficient and progressive' production (Veblen 1919/1963). Neoclassical Austrian economist Joseph Schumpeter observed that the rise of the large corporations—headed by the Vanderbilts, Carnegies, and Rockefellers—brought capitalist entrepreneurship to destruction. In his view, the placement of control in the hands of managers would result in the transformation of capitalism into socialism (Schumpeter 1943/1966). According to Burnham, Schumpeter, and others, the distinction between socialism and capitalism became more blurred. Both economies became operated by a new social formation known as 'managerialism' representing the so-called 'managerial revolution'. (See also Sutton et al. 1956.) Enteman (1993) and Lash and Urry (1987) provided additional explanations. Enteman argues that 'managerialism' evolved in the face of the breakdown of capitalism and socialism, and in the vacuum created by the fact that intellectuals have not constructed an alternative ideology with a moral justification. Lash and Urry attribute the rise of the new class to the emergence of 'organized capitalism'. They argue that the growth of this class and its ideology took place within the context of capital–labor conflict.

4. To be sure, Drucker was not blind to the political processes underpinning the emergence of modern management. He was a keen observer with a wide political and intellectual perspective. Following the European intellectuals and particularly German philosopher Friedrich Stahl (about whom he wrote his first book), Drucker searched for a method capable of integrating freedom and power that would also address Schumpeter's concern with the decline of entrepreneurship in capitalist society (Schumpeter 1943/1966). In his famous *Management by Objectives*, Drucker attempted to formulate a synthesis between the collective spirit of European corporatist political theory and the extreme individualism of American business. He believed that such a synthesis would soften industrial conflict and inefficiency, espe-

cially among 'knowledge workers'. See Waring 1991 for a careful analysis of Drucker's epistemological position.

5. A similar concern was expressed by neoclassical economist Joseph Schumpeter who argued that the salaried manager tends 'to acquire the employee attitude and rarely if ever identifies itself with the stockholding interest even in the most favorable cases' (1943/1966: 141). Capitalists 'would find themselves in much the same situation as generals would in a society perfectly sure of permanent peace . . . the management of industry and trade would become a matter of current administration, and the personnel would unavoidably acquire the characteristics of a bureaucracy. Socialism of a very sober type would almost automatically come into being. Human energy would turn away from business' (1943/1966: 131).

6. Admittedly, 'agency theory' in organizations (e.g. Fama 1980; Fama and Jensen 1983; Kaufman and Zacharias 1992; Kaufman, Zacharias, and Karson 1995) attempts to conceptualize antagonistic relationships between managers and owners/principals. This stream of literature, however, uses non-conflictual and ideologically neutral language which buys into most of the assumptions of economic or management theories. For example, authority relationship and corporate control are defined as mere economic contracts. It provides no room for workers to organize collective action and reject the assumptions of corporate capitalism. Moreover, it employs language such as uncertainty, maximizing utilities, rewards, efforts, employment contracts—concepts which became legitimized in organizations during the time-period that this study addresses. All these are taken for granted (see Perrow 1986). Likewise neo-Marxist analysis of organizations (e.g. Braverman 1974; Clawson 1980; Clegg and Dunkerley 1980; Edwards 1979; Marglin 1974; Stone 1974) is considered in 'agency theory' as foreign to the mainstream canonical narrative of organizational evolution.

7. Strikingly enough, several attempts to provide sociological accounts of the transformation of work under capitalism have overlooked the managerial revolution altogether. See for example Tilly and Tilly 1998.

8. New Class theory (or theories) has a long tradition in the social scientific literature. The first phase of this theory was promoted by 19th-century anarchist critics of Marx, such as Mikhail Bakunin. They referred to the power of the communist intelligentsia which seemed to form a basis of power above the proletariat. The second phase of the theory took place during the 1940s and 1950s and promoted the managerialist thesis. In the West, this thesis identified technocrats, experts, and trained managers as new agents of the economic order replacing private owners (see n. 2). In the East it referred to the power of bureaucrats who gained independent power to control the economy politically. The third phase refers to the 'knowledge-class' theories of the 1970s and to the work of scholars such as Daniel Bell's *The Coming of Post-industrial Society* (1973) and Alvin Gouldner's *The Future of Intellectuals and the Rise of the New Class* (1979). See Szelenyi and Martin 1988 for elaboration on this genealogy.

9. In his seminal work *Work and Authority in Industry*, Reinhard Bendix was the first to apply the term 'ideology' to management practices. He was unclear, however, with regard to its exact definition. Here, I follow Stuart Hall (1982), who draws a connection between the Geertzian perception of ideology as a 'system of meanings'

and the concept of 'power' which is absent in Geertz but is pronounced in neo-Marxist discourse and especially in Gramsci's analysis of hegemony (1971). Following Hall, ideology will be defined as a system of meanings and metaphors, embodied in everyday practices of human beings. Unlike the humanist tradition in which meaning is subjective, in Hall's conceptualization the system of meaning is created and attributed in the course of a political struggle. By successfully identifying itself with symbols or signs, a group can render its interpretation dominant in public discourse. Such definition of the term 'ideology' avoids two difficulties prominent in the idealist and neo-Marxist conceptualizations of the concept. The idealist approach, similarly to the functionalist tradition in sociology, has tended to view ideology as a closed system of ideas subjected to its internal logic. On the other hand, neo-Marxist theorists have identified the term ideology with the concept of 'false consciousness', a distorted image of reality. The present definition avoids such conceptualization by simply underlining the nexus between the way reality is grasped by those who experience it, and the interests of groups who successfully shape this reality. Since there is no presumption of true consciousness, a false one is meaningless. Furthermore, this definition avoids a dichotomy between ideology and practice. Ideology is analyzed as everyday practice of industrial engineering (see n. 10).

10. Several important books in management and organization historiography fail to treat ideology as practice, among them the classic books by Braverman (1974) and Edwards (1979). Furthermore, most organization texts treat ideology as embedded in the history of ideas. These approaches are interested in the unfolding of intellectual history as a 'great chain of ideas'. Scholars attempting to trace the evolution of management and organization thinking go back to 19th-century classical social thought (Hassard 1993; Morgan 1986). Hassard, for example, examined the writings of Auguste Comte, John Stuart Mill, Herbert Spencer, and Emile Durkheim to expose those aspects in their work 'which underpin the development of a systems theory orthodoxy in organizational analysis' (Hassard 1993: 16). Hassard believed that these 19th-century European ideas offered the basis for characterizing organizations as 'systems'. He further argued that systems ideas from functional sociology were juxtaposed with general systems theory, which was developed following the Second World War in various scientific disciplines (which included Ludwig von Bertalanffy and his biological concept of 'open system'; Norbert Wiener's formulation of cybernetics; Ross Ashby's work on machines; Shannon's work on information and communication theory; Williams's operations research in England; the Games theory of von Neumann and Morgenstern, among others; see Lilienfeld 1978). In accordance with the definition of ideology described earlier, my approach is to leave this intellectual discourse aside and to focus on the everyday production of ideas and ideology.

11. Most historians agree that there was little literature on organizations in the United States before the 1870s (e.g. Bendix 1956/1974; Chandler 1977; Nelson 1975). An exception is the literature that emerged in the railroad industry from the 1850s (Yates 1989). This literature, however, was not readily accessible until the first decade of the 20th century (Jenks 1961). In addition to the railroad literature, and additional sporadic work of economists particularly regarding wages, there were

frequent but not systematic reprints of materials written in Europe. Known in particular are the study of work, motion, and fatigue by French engineers and the study of factory economics by English economists. See Litterer 1986; Doray 1988; Rabinbach 1990.

12. Similarly, Americans tended to circulate published information on management issues more widely than any of their European counterparts. See: 'American Mechanics from an English Point of View', *American Engineer*, August 1889: 78.

13. The only portion of this literature that had roots earlier was cost accounting, which can be traced to the early days of commercial capitalism in Europe and industrial capitalism in England. See Litterer 1986.

14. American creation of management grew out of engineering practices that were different from the European experience. The US engineer-managers were very much attuned to the economic constraints of the enterprise and the management of production processes. This was not the case with European engineers, especially with the French and Germans, who were more concerned with technical variables in line with their scientific traditions (Locke 1984; Gispen 1989). Germany's economy was organized around 'rational lines' and bureaucratic ideas about order and duty that were borrowed from the German army and state administration (Guillen 1994). But it did not enjoy the professional discourse that developed in the United States during the Progressive era. In the United States the professional discourse emerged within engineering circles and was then diffused in industry. In Germany, the bureaucratic model was formed in state apparatuses. To the extent that managerial thought developed in Germany to its modern form, it was an American influence. American management techniques arrived in Germany a few years before the First World War (Merkle 1980; Rabinbach 1990). In the mid-1920s Germany's acute economic problems drove engineers, manufacturers, academics and intellectuals to make pilgrimages to the United States in order to unravel the American romance with modern management. Every serious business and engineering magazine in Germany regularly covered American success stories, usually not without mention of Fordism, Scientific Management, or Sears, Roebuck, and Company (Nolan 1994). Economic historians estimated that in the mid-1920s there were 600 private organizations, 85 state offices, and 67 research institutes that dealt with issues related to rationalization (Guillen 1994). This was, to a large degree, an American influence. See the concluding chapter for additional discussion.

15. See 'The Logic of Cultural Sciences', in Weber (1949). Weber developed 'a "model" of what "ought" to exist to be carefully distinguished from the analytical construct, which is "ideal" in the strictly logical sense of the term' (Weber 1949: 91–2). Whereas the former is a normative concept, the latter is a construct 'which our imagination accepts as plausibly motivated and hence as "objectively possible" and which appear[s] as adequate from the nomological standpoint' (ibid.).

16. Roy (1997) as well as Yonay (1998) provide two recent examples for 'objective possibilities'. Roy examines the rise of the modern industrial corporation and argues that it is a social creation, not a natural entity, which was developed from a pre-existing form of the public corporation designed by state officers. The corporate form retained many of the privileges given to the public form. This analysis enables us to avoid deterministic explanations and entertain historical alternatives to existing

social constructs. Yonay examines the struggle between neoclassical and institutional economics and the manner in which the latter was edited out of the canon of economic theory and history. His analysis provides room for institutional economics as a viable possibility that was suppressed in both economic practice and economic historiography.

17. This peculiar interpretation of Weber in the USA has to do with the nuances of Talcott Parsons's translation of Weber into English (Cohen, Hazelrigg, and Pope 1975; Weiss 1983). Parsons gave his own interpretation to Weber mostly in line with the theoretical perspectives existing in the USA in the 1930s and 1940s. Parsons's translation presented Weber as more concerned with value consensus and effective functioning than with the role of conflicting material interests in domination (Weiss 1983). The best-known difference between Parsons's translation and those of other scholars is over the interpretation of the term *Herrschaft*. Several scholars translated the term as 'domination' (e.g. H. Gerth and C. W. Mills, 1958), while Parsons translated it first as 'imperative coordination' and later as 'leadership'. Weber did not develop a model for effective functioning as Parsons implied, but rather worked on historical modes of domination. The crux of Parsons's misrepresentation of Weber is his overweening emphasis on the normative and the nomological dimension which led him to expand what is but a part of Weber's sociology and make it very nearly the whole (Cohen, Hazelrigg, and Pope 1975: 240). For example, he interpreted Weber's instrumentally rational action as normative because means and ends are normatively selected (i.e. actors use 'efficient norms'). By so doing, Parsons abandoned a crucial aspect in Weber's dualistic framework, and expanded the normative (which indeed existed in Weber's analysis) to become his entire scheme. Nobody would claim that Parsons was intentionally distorting Weber's meaning. It is the result of his attempt to provide conceptual consistency, not very apparent in the original, since Weber was a careful observer of ambivalence.

# 1

# Prophets of Management: American Engineers between Industrial Growth and Labor Unrest

*The Spirit of Management*
We've done with the days of 'hit or miss'
When we blundered along in careless bliss,
In frantic hurry and foolish haste
With useless labor and senseless waste;
We've done with the days of 'more or less'
When we worked by chance and we planned by guess
For we've learned there's more to a workman's job
Than putting him down where the shop athrob,
With lathes and presses in vast array,
And letting him blindly feel his way!

For now we study and now we plan
The work and effort of every man,
The reason 'Why' and the manner 'How,'
To lessen the sweat of his back and brow,
Relieve his muscles of stress and strain
And lighten the task of his harried brain;
To give him leisure for rest and fun
While swelling the sum of the work that's done!

We must show the Worker the work to do,
The Way to do it, until he KNOWS;
We must give him the mighty spirit, too,
By which the World in its wonder grows;
For the Spirit of Modern Progress comes
From men with bodies and minds kept strong . . .
And it's our concern in a selfish light
For men work best when they're full fit,
With minds untroubled and calm eyes bright,
And bodily vigor and clear, keen wit!

That's first class gospel, because it's fair
Because it's good for the human race,
Because it moves us to do and dare
And quickens the world on its forward pace,
Because it brings us to better ways,
And so,—in the long, long run—IT PAYS!
    (Berton Braley. Written expressly for *American Machinist:*
    1 January 1914: 34)

The emergence of professional management, with salaried managers, business schools, and formal theoretical foundations, is a recent phenomenon. The New York Public Library did not have a single title on management prior to 1881, whereas in 1910 it already carried 240 titles. The first school of industrial management was established in Pennsylvania in 1881,[1] but it was only at the beginning of the twentieth century that additional schools of business were instituted nationwide.[2] In the late 1890s the language of industrial management was identified, and its first maxims were formalized. Litterer, who reviewed the literature on management until 1900, used the metaphor of an automatic pilot to describe its feat. The pilot selects the course and feeds this information into the automatic pilot. The automatic pilot then directs and oversees a myriad of operations, insuring that they are performed to keep the plane on course. Litterer's 'automatic pilot' metaphor is loyal to the linear, evolutionary, and 'automatic' image of the unfolding of management and corporate structure, yet is blind to the conscious efforts of the actual pilots.

In practice, American engineers had to navigate the aircraft of management through stormy and rough conditions. These travails are absent from management theory and its official historiography.[3] But this is not the only fallacy associated with management historiography. In the history of ideas, ideological revolutions are often attributed to single individuals, the great thinkers of their time. Liberalism is attributed to Locke, communism to Marx, and psychoanalysis to Freud. In this vein, management ideology is attributed to Frederick Taylor. Most management textbooks begin with Taylor's Principles of Scientific Management as the first chapter of modern management theory. Students of organizations are taught to believe that these principles—a set of abstract and contextless maxims—were necessitated by the logic of economic growth and the imperatives of industry. It is almost as though the Principles of Scientific Management were divinely ordained the way the Ten Commandments were handed down to Moses.[4] This form of presentation overrates the role of individuals in determining ideological transitions.

The acceptance of Taylor's principles of management as a functional, unquestioned necessity was not a one-man project, nor were his principles formulated altogether peacefully. They came at the end of turbulent transformations, bitter struggles, and processes of delegitimization. The following chapters situate management ideology within its breeding ground: a network of engineers who struggled to establish themselves as legitimate social actors in the industrial arena. This puts mechanical and industrial engineering—the prophets of the managerial revolution—under our spotlight.

As early as the 1860s, engineers perfected their technical skills and led an industry-wide project of standardization and systematization. In the 1890s this project was extended into a public political campaign. Engineers publicized their project by monopolizing the liberal discourse about rationality, human nature, progress, equality, and moral standings. They created a new discourse which became not only the underpinning ideology of management, but a prism through which social and cultural issues were interpreted and determined. Through this campaign engineers were able to transform their technical view of mechanical objects into a grand theory of society. The engineers elaborated ideas about political economy, government, international relationship, gender, race, war, and peace. Their views were expressed in newspapers, magazines, and professional meetings, thereby preparing the groundwork for the managerial revolution. This was thus an ideological phase preceding and enabling the 'managerial revolution' declared by Berle and Means in 1932.[5]

Prior to the 1880s, engineers played only a minor role in the traditional capitalist order. Firms were by and large controlled by family capitalism. The large corporations had not yet emerged. The so-called 'robber barons' exercised centralized control over production, marketing, and organization (see for example Burton 1919; Josephson 1934/1995; Jones 1968). Smaller manufacturers personally supervised their enterprises. In the power structure of this industrial order, there was little place for autonomous engineers. Lacking their own means of production, engineers could only offer their engineering principles in order to gain a respectable position in the industrial order. Moreover, they encountered opposition from manufacturers who were apprehensive about the introduction of management methods. Manufacturers viewed the attempt to invent management practices as a strategy employed by engineers to expand their professional territory. To them, management systems were costly and superfluous. At the other pole of the capitalist order, the proletariats were forming their interests, strategies, and representatives. They, too, rejected engineering-based managerial ideas.

The political context in which management first emerged was a violent and bloody period in US industrial relations, when labor (occupational groups and craft unions) and capital (manufacturers and owners) were fighting a bitter war. In the initial opposition of both many employers and employees to the rise of management, labor unrest was introduced as a leverage to gain legitimacy for management practices. Engineers entered this conflict as purportedly interest-free mediators. They eventually played a significant role in redefining it (after 1900) from a war of attrition between owners and crafts to a mere tension between 'management', 'employees', and 'professionals' (Jacques 1996). They did so by colonizing the discourse and monopolizing industrial know-how. Mechanical engineers, later known as 'production engineers', designated management as a branch of engineering, likening organizations to mechanical systems. They became the priests of organizational rationality, mobilizing business ideology around secular engineering ideals rather than previously dominant religious, philanthropic, paternalistic, or Social Darwinist philosophies (Bendix 1956/1974; Barley and Kunda 1992; Guillen 1994). 'Systems', as a metaphor for mechanics, and 'systematization', were conceptualized as ideological tropes. Engineers' efforts reproduced the ideological assumption that human and non-human entities are interchangeable and can be equally subjected to engineering manipulation.

The triumph of these practices as well as their rational discourse placed engineers in the position of a new middle class of professionals at the epicenter of the stratification system of their time. They replaced earlier ideologies of 'unscrupulous' and 'chaotic' capitalism with a modern, 'benevolent', liberal terminology. The natural, objective, and 'apolitical' image of management rationality was used to legitimize its direct political application. Yet, rationality is culturally embedded, self-serving, and hegemonically imposing. It has become an invisible trope, an accepted epistemological assumption, one which has infused other disciplines such as sociology, psychology, history, and political science, not to mention economics.

Following this realization I argue that the written history of management is an 'authorized version', produced by early management activists themselves, and not an independent inquiry. In other words, the history of management, as well as management and organization theories, is infused with the ideology of management activists. Thus, it is not surprising that conflictual elements are edited out of its history. Management ideology is presented as linear, an inevitable extension of capitalist democratic order. Peter Drucker, whose observations are presented in the Introduction, is a representative of this narrative. It strips management history of its inherent conflicts and often bloody disputes.

This historiographical bias calls for a genealogical analysis of management history and its ideology.[6] It requires a close focus on the 'shift' from machine standardization to organizational systematization. Since engineering literature served as a primary forum of management from the 1880s until the 1920s, I use data from two engineering periodicals popular at that time: *American Machinist* (established in 1877) and *Engineering Magazine* (established in 1891). These magazines were the first specialized periodicals to give voice to industrial management as it evolved as an autonomous field. These are primary sources, missing in many other studies of nineteenth-century organization practices.[7] The magazines were not only sources of information, they were also actors in the political field, contributors to the goal of establishing the legitimacy of management.

The current chapter focuses on the engineers, their associations, and their periodicals, as central agents of the ideological phase of the managerial revolution. Two major processes underpin the historical background of the rise of engineers: industrial growth on the one hand, and labor unrest on the other. In describing these two factors I will be navigating between economic historiography and labor historiography. The former regards management as a functional necessity of industrial growth and modernization. The latter counters this evolutionary view by stressing the political role of management in regard to the 'labor problem'.

While citing historical data that may supplement the mainstream narrative of the instrumentality of management, my analysis also criticizes the mainstream narrative by stressing the political and historical embeddedness of management ideology. My argument is therefore framed between the 'doxa' of management and organization theory and the 'heterodoxa' of a history 'from below'. It is offered as a genealogical project rather than a historical projection. With this in mind, I proceed with the exposition of industrial growth *vis-à-vis* labor unrest, and then present the empirical materials for the genealogical analysis. Finally, I ground my discussion of the rise of management ideology within two political ideologies which dominated that period: American Exceptionalism and, later, Progressivism.

### 1.1 Historical conditions laying the groundwork for managers

Economic history refers to the period between the 1880s and the 1920s as 'the age of big business', 'the decline of *laissez-faire*', or 'the rise of the visible hand'. All three imply that small businesses and loosely related regional markets became consolidated, coordinated, or controlled by large industrial combinations. During this period, the factory system was established, capital was centralized, production standardized, organizations bureaucratized, and labor incorporated into large firms.

Management was ideologically formed during this period of unprecedented industrial growth.[8] By 1920, manufacturing firms employed 86 percent of all wage earners. By the late 1920s, the organization of production was characterized by multi-unit, large-scale, complex bureaucratic firms employing wage labor supervised by professional managers (Chandler 1977).[9] Some manufacturing establishments grew so large that they employed thousands or tens of thousands of workers (Nelson 1975; Guillen 1994). The fact that wage labor became a widespread institution had two consequences. First, there was a substantial increase in union membership around the turn of the century.[10] Second, wage labor generated the 'dark side' of industrial growth, which took the form of one of the bloodiest and most violent struggles in industrial history.[11] Despite the fact that the US labor movement has been among the least radical, its strike rate and intensity of violence have been very high compared with other countries (Taft and Ross 1969; Edwards 1981). While serial data on violence are unavailable, official records of strikes have been kept in the USA since 1880. A comparison of the annual frequency of strikes (standardized for the number of non-agricultural employees) suggests that the figure gradually rose during the

1880s, fell in the 1890s, and then grew to peak levels in the early 1900s. The strike frequency remained high throughout the Progressive era (until 1918/19), and then saw a dramatic decline in the 1920s, reaching its lowest level in 1929 (Peterson 1938). Industrial unrest, broadly defined for the early period as a struggle over the legitimacy of industrial capitalism, therefore lasted for almost five decades (until approximately the mid-1930s).

During the final twenty years of the nineteenth century, there was downward pressure on wages, owing to a continuous unemployment period (Kaufman 1993). The cut-throat competition for jobs resulted not only in lower wages but also in pressures to speed up the work pace—in the absence of elementary safety precautions in working conditions. The oversupply of workers during those years had consequences too. It resulted in the growing affluence of the upper classes and in increased inequality in income and wealth. Economists agree that the real income of most wage earners increased very little during the twenty years after 1897 (Faulkner 1951: 251). The number of millionaires, on the other hand, increased from 100 in 1880 to 40,000 in 1916 (Howe 1980).

Low wages and uncomfortable working conditions were only partial explanations for the outburst of industrial unrest. A significant impetus for the conflict was the structural changes in the industrial order. It was a period of unprecedented growth in establishment size, partly a result of the mergers movement in the capital-intensive industries (Chandler 1977, 1984; Aldrich 1979; Fligstein 1990). The rise of large-scale capital-intensive and bureaucratic forms of production resulted in the replacement of hand tools with machines and of skilled craftsmen with semi-skilled (or unskilled) operators, and the use of standardized parts in place of customized ones (Kaufman 1993). Employers tried to reorganize industry along the lines of these changes. Workers had to submit to the authority of foremen in issues such as hiring, firing, pay, promotion, and workload. Most foremen used a 'drive system', a method involving strict supervision and verbal abuse. Employees resisted management attempts to generate submissive obedience to arbitrary rule (Jacoby 1985).

Reorganization did not originate in technological changes only. It was also a result of a struggle over control, productivity, and profits. The replacement of so-called 'inside contracting' (which dominated the coal, steel, machining, and arms assembly industries in the mid-nineteenth century) with engineering-based management systems can serve as a typical example of the process.[12]

Under inside contracting, employers owned the means of production. They provided floor space and machinery, supplied raw material and working capital, and arranged for the sale of the final product. The gap between raw material and finished product was filled by contractors rather than by a descending hierarchy of paid employees. Contractors hired their own helpers, supervised the work process, and received a piece rate from the company for completed goods (Buttrick 1952). Employers, however, lacked control over the production process and faced a high level of uncertainty. For instance, there is evidence that supervisors in the Winchester Repeating Arms Company—where such a system was employed—knew very little about methods of production. They could not figure out the actual piece rates paid by the contractor to his workers, nor did they know precisely how much profit they made (Buttrick 1952). Furthermore, inventory control was virtually non-existent, and there was only a superficial check on the flow of raw material going to each contractor or on the amount of spoilage. A contractor could store up a private inventory, which he could sell back to the company in the future, while he spread his profits over time in a manner advantageous to himself.

The Singer Sewing Manufacturing Company provides a similar example (see Clawson 1980). Employers there, too, could be kept in almost total ignorance of the real course of affairs in any contractor's department. It was impossible for employers to specify in advance how long it might take for a worker to understand a particular blueprint or drawing, and it was pointless to hurry the worker since errors of understanding could prove extremely costly. Moreover, it was to the contractor's advantage to manipulate the outpayments made on his account so that the profit would appear small in any year in which a price cut was imminent. The monopolistic position of owners and managers was thus threatened by the power of the contractors. This power depended upon the contractor's private knowledge, not only of production methods, but also of employees' loyalty to him, and of his position within the factory's social system.[13]

Under these circumstances, many of the younger generation of employers sought to replace the contractor by a system which offered the company greater predictability and control over the workforce and the manufacturing process. The first move was for employers to take charge of the hiring and firing process. Contractors could not recruit their own helpers but rather were only able to select workers from among those whom the foreman had already hired. The next step was to create a hierarchical organizational structure and to design a single integrated production process. Firms introduced systems of monitoring and controlling such as production control, cost accounting, gain sharing, and incentive plans based on shop orders, a voucher system of accounts, and time studies. Ancillary personnel such as engineers and inspection clerks were also hired, enlarging the manager's administrative staff (Chandler 1977: 277). The number of administrative employees in the industry doubled from 348,000 in 1899 to 750,000 in 1909, and had almost doubled again by 1923 when it reached 1,280,000 employees. The increase in the number of administrative employees exceeded the growth in labor force. The ratio of administrative to production employees doubled from 7.7 percent in 1899 to 15.6 percent in 1923 (Bendix 1956/1974: 214).

These processes were often justified by the need to 'systematize', to 'increase efficiency', and to 'reduce uncertainty'. This terminology was used by practitioners, by management scholars, and by historians of organizations alike. For example, the canonical interpretation in organization theory suggests that the rising complexity, increasing uncertainty, and lack of control within such industrial firms made it necessary to make these changes (see Chandler 1962, 1977; Williamson 1975, 1985). Within this framework, the systematization of organizational order is conceptualized as having been a means to implement efficient, rational order. The improvement of safety in industry is likewise explained in this way. The railroad industry, the argument goes, experienced a series of collisions in the 1840s and 1850s, in reaction to which the industry was rationalized and bureaucratized (see Chandler 1977; Yates 1989). Such explanations, predominant in the literature, grew and developed in the context of already extant managerial practice and were imbued with its epistemology and ideology. The reality enacted in (and by) organizations was all too readily adopted as a mainstream perspective by historians and social scientists in order to explain the rise of management.[14]

Systematization, however, should also be seen as part of an attempt to control the labor force. Gordon, Edwards, and Reich (1982) identified three distinct periods in labor history: 'labor proletarianization' (1820–90), 'labor homogenization' (1890–1930), and 'labor segmentation'. They argued that, following a period of 'unpredictability' associated with the 'proletarianization of labor', employers attempted to 'homogenize' the workforce. This meant forging a homogeneous proletariat from a heterogeneous pre-industrial workforce in an attempt to achieve control, order, and stability. Organizational 'systems' were conducive to homogenization. They were expected to rationalize employment relationships, to standardize behavior, and to increase predictability of internal and external transactions (see Braverman 1974; Marglin 1974; Stone 1974; Edwards 1979).

There is no need to attempt to adjudicate between the 'efficiency' and 'labor control' explanations since they are neither competing nor mutually exclusive. For efficient production, both human and non-human means need to be controlled. Administrative rules, voucher systems, productivity reports, and incentive wages all produce stable, compliant, and 'rational' behavior. These explanations should therefore be seen as flip sides of the same coin. Each of the explanations has its shortcomings, however. The functional necessity argument is teleological, was originally used by the systematizers themselves, and should be regarded as having been a self-fulfilling rhetoric. In fact, the movement for standardization preceded the so-called 'industrial revolution' in the United States. This is not to say that systematization did not increase efficiency, but rather that it was not always the rationale behind the process. The labor control argument is even more problematic. First, the rise of industrial systems characterized socialist and communist economies, not only capitalist society (e.g. Bendix 1956/1974; Merkle 1980). Second, there were substantial variations in the political culture, labor strife, and economic ideologies in the USA during the period of homogenization (1880–1930). Lastly, it would be misleading to view industrial engineers as 'mere servants of power' (Jacoby 1985). Engineers and management consultants developed priorities that were often different from those of capitalists or government officials (see Layton 1971 for examples).

Both the 'efficiency' and 'labor control' arguments put a heavy burden on the role of employers and shop owners in facilitating the systematization process. They both view systematization as a natural extension of the capitalist order. The efficiency argument implies that employers saw the efficiency merit in systems and therefore enforced the introduction of accountancy models, production control techniques, and wage schemes. The labor control argument implies that employers foresaw the repression potential in systems and pushed for their adoption.

The literature on professions provides a different angle. Abbott (1988) and Larson (1977) attribute autonomous roles to professionals but fail to apply this to engineers. Krause (1996), who deals directly with engineers, represents a stream of literature which argues that engineers were basically 'employee categories rather than potent political entities' (Larson 1977: 190–207; Krause 1996: 60–7). I wish to complement this literature by focusing on industrial engineers as producers and promoters of the systematization movement. The managerial and technical responsibilities of engineers in industry were fundamental to industrialization. In his inaugural presidential address, American Society of Mechanical Engineering (ASME) president Robert H. Thurston exaggerated to make his point. He reminded the members of ASME that they directed the labor of 3,000,000 workers, that they employed $2,500,000,000 worth of capital, that they annually disbursed $1,000,000,000 in wages, consumed each year $3,000,000,000 worth of raw materials, brought into play motive energy equivalent to 3,000,000 horsepower, and that they used all these resources to create manufactured goods with a value of $5,000,000,000 each year (Sinclair 1980: 29). In this address, Thurston fostered the impression that mechanical engineers were part of a collective effort to give working men the opportunity to escape the restriction of social class and political subordination. The individuals he was addressing, however, belonged to the wealthiest segment of society. Mechanical engineers espoused the language and practice of systems and promoted it as an integral part of their industrial agenda. To be sure, the impulse towards standardization and systematization had been around in engineering circles at least since the 1860s, with the intent of coping with technical issues. Later on it found a fertile ground in industry, given increasing labor unrest and what seemed to them to be the chaotic nature of firms.

The participation of engineers in industry started in the construction of large public works, particularly during the period 1816–50.[15] The pioneers of modern management—mainly Daniel McCallum,[16] Henry Poor,[17] George Whistler, Benjamin Latrobe, Edgar Thomson, and George McClellan—were trained civil engineers experienced in road construction (ASCE 1972; Chandler 1977).[18] I trace this network of engineers who were early carriers of managerial ideas, and who were enamored of the idea that organizations can be conceptualized as mechanical systems. I follow their writings from 1879 up to 1932, the year Berle and Means published their classic book canonizing the discourse about the 'managerial revolution'.

## 1.2  Early historical background of mechanical engineering

Mechanical engineering was practiced in the United States as early as the 1830s, but it was only in 1910 that it became listed, for the first time, as a separate occupation in the United States Census.[19] The 1880s marked the beginning of a 'golden age' for the application of engineering techniques in American industry. During these years mechanical engineering, as a profession, grew by leaps and bounds. It has been estimated that in 1800 there were no more than two dozen engineers in the United States. In the fifty years from 1880 to 1930, the number of engineers rose more than 3000 percent, from 7,000 to 230,000.[20] By 1900 the United States had the highest number of engineers relative to industrial employment, and the gap with its main competitor, Germany, widened further during the years 1910–20 (Guillen 1994: 40). In the course of this incorporation of engineers into industry, engineering was transformed from a craft into a profession (Layton 1971; Larson 1977). Furthermore, the general rubric 'civil engineer' split into further specializations in mining, metallurgical, mechanical, electrical, and chemical engineers. During the years 1884–1924, roughly two-thirds of engineering graduates became managers within fifteen years of leaving college (Noble 1977). The rise and professionalization of engineering was the breeding ground for management.

By 1900 there were 10,000 individuals who practiced mechanical engineering, most from the upper middle class. Their elitist attitudes were retained and diffused through a network composed of technical publications and professional associations. There were three main contributors to the development of American mechanical engineering as a profession: the machine shop, the railroad shop, and naval engineering.[21]

Machine shops produced such innovations as steam engines used to power factories, for steamships, and later for locomotives. The shop, rather than the laboratory, was the locus of technological innovation in the telegraph industry in the nineteenth century.[22] Other innovations included the automatic lathe for making screws and small components, the twist drill, the universal milling machine, and the synthetic grinding wheels (see Burshall 1965: 294). Machine shops varied in size and type. A small shop usually had one room doing repair work and building small steam engines (or tools) on a special order. They had several lathes and a small planer. Many such shops had grown up along the Erie and other canals by the second half of the nineteenth century. A large-size machine shop included dozens of lathes of all types, complemented by several planers and other machines such as shapers, and milling and grinding machines. A separate assembling room contained locomotives or large machine tools. The foundry included a drafting room and an office where books were kept, and from where engineers directed the operation. By the 1870s, with the advent of larger factories producing machinery, machine shops became specialized factories which produced a single type of steam engine or one line of standardized tools.[23]

Throughout the nineteenth century, mechanical engineering positions were filled by a self-perpetuating elite. Most of the main figures in the field were white, Anglo-Saxon Protestants who were born and raised in the industrial north-east (Calvert 1967; Noble 1977). Since most of them held a shop (rather than college) orientation, apprenticeship in the machine shop was a respectable way for them to train their children to become mechanical engineers.[24]

The railroad shop was a second source for the development of mechanical engineering. As early as the 1840s, a number of operating railroads had engineering administrators who held titles such as 'superintendent of engines and machinery', 'superintendent of motive power', or 'master mechanic' (Calvert 1967: 14). It was in the early 1850s that the explicit title 'mechanical engineer' was used for the first time in the supervision of railroad machinery. In 1853 *American Railroad Journal* inaugurated a mechanical engineering department under the direction of Zerah Colburn.[25]

Naval engineering was a third source of professional mechanical engineers. In 1837 'assistant engineers' were appointed to serve on the *Fulton*, the first regularly commissioned steam vessel in the United States navy. The Naval Academy at Annapolis, Maryland, was created in 1845 but it was not until 1866 that a special course in the steam engine was offered. One of the more active figures in designing the curriculum for mechanical engineering in the Academy was Robert H. Thurston, who later became a central figure in the American Society of Mechanical Engineering. In 1871 Thurston left the Naval Academy to become a professor of engineering at the Stevens Institute of Technology (SIT), founded in New Jersey in 1870 (Calvert 1967). Several central figures in mechanical engineering during the next fifty years held degrees from SIT.[26]

Several additional institutions offered academic education in mechanical engineering. Yale created a professorship of industrial mechanics and physics in 1859. Rensselaer Polytechnic Institute, which became a major training school for civil engineers, inaugurated a course in mechanical engineering in 1862. The Morrill Land Grant Colleges Act of 1862 provided an important push for the development of mechanical engineering departments (or 'Agriculture and the Mechanic Arts' as they were known).[27] By 1900, college enrollment in mechanical engineering outnumbered that of civil engineering by three to two (Calvert 1967). A bill passed in 1879 allowed the President of the USA to nominate an officer from the Naval Engineer Corps as a professor in any desired school. Between 1879 and 1896, forty-eight such appointments were made in diverse institutions (Calvert 1967). These appointments fostered a close relationship between naval engineering and mechanical engineering education.

Prior to the 1870s, however, there were hardly any stable mechanical engineering publications. Most of those that had existed prior to the professionalization of the field disappeared by mid-century. By 1860 when *Engineer*, a short-lived magazine, was founded in Philadelphia by Colburn, there were hardly any competitors, and those that existed were specific to the railroad industry.[28]

*American Railroad Journal*, which carried much of the discussion about the professionalization of engineering during the 1930s and 1940s, became mainly a financial paper with little information about engineering (Calhoun 1960). Three other magazines that existed at the time, *American Engineer*, *Franklin Institute Journal*, and *Scientific American*, were too broad and they hardly approached the experience and knowledge of practicing mechanical engineers, let alone the shop milieu (Calvert 1967). Also, the *Franklin Institute Journal* was specific to the building industry in Philadelphia only. When *Engineer* disappeared, the mechanical engineering elite remained 'without a voice or a conscience in print' (Calvert 1967: 135). It was only in the 1870s that more long-lived, widely circulated technical journals were founded.[29]

### 1.3 Prophets of industrial management within engineering circles: *American Machinist* and *Engineering Magazine*

*American Machinist* was founded in 1877. In his study of mechanical engineering, Monte Calvert (1967: 136) stated that *American Machinist* was 'first in quality and scope among the post-1876 journals'. Calvin W. Rice, an activist in the mechanical engineering movement and a secretary of ASME, called *American Machinist* a 'clearinghouse' for ideas of the 'machine-minded man' and a 'spot where he might find mental contact with men who were meeting problems like his' (Colvin 1947: 72). *American Machinist* arguably provided the impetus for a snowballing process that eventually led to the professionalization of mechanical engineering. It was a weekly publication, contained on average eight to ten pages per issue, and included editorials (two or three), short articles (mainly about machine tools), regular columns, news from the industrial world, and letters to the editors. Over time there were variations in length and structure of the publication. It is probably safe to say that at least until 1905 ASME and the mechanical engineering profession were oriented toward the shop culture. *American Machinist* was at that time a major voice of this community.

In 1888, when *American Machinist* was fairly well established, its owners and managers (Horace Miller and Lycurgus B. Moore) branched out into the field of locomotive operation with the establishment of a more specialized magazine, *Locomotive Engineer*. Whereas *American Machinist* served the general machine-shop owners and workers, *Locomotive Engineer* was to serve the railroad mechanical community (see Colvin 1947). In 1891 *Engineering Magazine*, another engineering periodical, was founded.

*Engineering Magazine* was a monthly periodical. It included an editorial, several relatively longer articles, and a section reviewing articles from newspapers, magazines, and books in such diverse areas as engineering, economics, sociology, and political science. This review section became a data base from which the famous *Engineering Index* was later compiled.

The formation of the magazine indicated the emergence of a new field, an offspring of mechanical engineering known as industrial engineering, or efficiency engineering. The first editor and publisher, John Dunlap, was one of the most active journalistic leaders of the management movement. In 1916 he shifted the magazine's attention to management issues and changed its title to *Industrial Management*. One of the magazine's subsequent editors was Leon P. Alford, previously an editor of *American Machinist* and an active member of ASME. He served twice on committees to examine the state of management in industrial affairs.

In the Appendix, I provide detailed description of the two magazines: their editors, their networks, and the content of their writings. There are three issues to bear in mind in evaluating the selection of these two publications. First, both *American Machinist* and *Engineering Magazine* expressed firm interest in the management movement, its nuances, and various participants.[30] They were pioneers in publishing articles on production management and organizational systems during the nineteenth century, and they provided generous outlets for the formation of theories about industrial administration. Mott, who studied *The History of American Magazines*, as well as Jenks (1961), Nelson (1975), and other scholars (see Jelinek 1980; Jacoby 1985; Montgomery 1987),[31] ranked them as the most active and important vehicles for discussions about management.[32] The advent of these publications marked a historical event in the history of management. It was the birth of a textual project and the formation of institutional settings for authors and readers about organizations.[33] Furthermore, despite the fact that both periodicals were active in forming the professional aspects of modern management, they both provided room for a wide range of opinions including a strong and enduring criticism of management fads.

Another issue in the selection of these two publications is that *American Machinist* and *Engineering Magazine* had a broader role than just serving as sources for empirical data. Both were significant players in the evolving world of mechanical engineering in the last two decades of the nineteenth century, providing initial impulse to the rise of engineering as a legitimate independent profession. *American Machinist* was important in providing legitimacy for mechanical engineering,[34] and had a pivotal function in the formation of ASME in 1880. The editors of *American Machinist* assumed numerous positions within the society in the years to come. *Engineering Magazine* helped Harrington Emerson and Henry Gantt to establish the Taylor Society and the Efficiency Society, and both were connected with the Scientific Management movement. *Engineering Magazine* became an outlet within which industrial engineering was crystallized as a profession. Furthermore, several pioneers of modern management acknowledged the 'excellent service' and the efforts of the journals in the dissemination and diffusion of organizational ideas (*American Machinist*, 8 July 1915: 62).

While both publications were different in age, orientation, frequency of publication, and structure, they shared the same network of individuals. Several editors of *American Machinist* served as presidents of ASME and a number of individuals wrote simultaneously for both periodicals. Two prominent individuals, Leon Alford and John Van Deventer, served as editors for both *American Machinist* and *Engineering Magazine* and fulfilled several roles in ASME.[35]

Despite the acknowledged salience of these publications, and despite the widespread reference to them, there are hardly any systematic, primary empirical analyses of the two periodicals. Probably the single most important contribution was made by Litterer.[36] He studied both magazines from their inception until 1900, and provided rich textual materials to document management practices. Litterer's contribution lies in his demonstration that Taylorism was a product of a movement that started in the 1870s, a 'pre-history' which is often ignored. Furthermore, he pointed out that there was substantial variation within the management movement prior to the beginning of the century. Without ignoring Litterer's significant contribution, I attempt to establish a different epistemological approach to the understanding of the rise of management theory. First, Litterer mainly understood the content of management from the point of view of the actors themselves. That is, he (albeit elegantly) restated their ideological claims as valid historical explanations.[37] Second, rather than studying the engineering publications merely as sources of information, as Litterer did, I situate them within their own milieu as active agents of change. These publications took sides in the debates and promoted their own agenda. Thus, their position in the social matrix should be juxtaposed with their ideas. By so doing, I treat the magazines not as isolated bodies of literature but as an integral part of their histories. Third, whereas Litterer studied nineteenth-century practices, I extend the period under study beyond the year 1900, up until 1932. I therefore also link the intellectual products of these publications with the cultural, economic, and political trends of the Progressive era, which represented a departure from nineteenth-century industrial ideologies. Fourth, in addition to textual analysis, I provide a novel qualitative content analysis, for example regarding the use of the term 'system' in the two magazines, as well as additional external sources, such as the Department of Labor or ASME.

*American Machinist* played a pivotal role in forming a network of professional mechanical engineers. The first editor of *American Machinist*, Jackson Bailey, started in 1879 a correspondence with John Edson Sweet—a professor at Cornell University who was known for his precision tests of roll-grinding machines—concerning the establishment of a national society for the advancement of mechanical engineering. Sweet was interested, but lacked organizational skills and was reluctant to carry the burden. Bailey visited Sweet in Syracuse and persuaded him to prepare a list of persons to whom invitations could be sent. Sweet contacted two of the well-known figures of the mechanical engineering elite: Alexander Lyman Holley and Robert H. Thurston.[38] The three of them jointly issued a letter calling for a meeting at the *American Machinist* office at 96 Fulton Street in New York City.[39] Upon a successful ending of the evening, the group decided to have the first official meeting of ASME on 7 April of the same year.[40] They also suggested a policy on membership rights and elected Alexander Lyman Holley as chairman of the new society.[41] *American Machinist* described the results of the first meeting, and suggested that the prime movers in the society should be 'men who were not absolutely manufacturers' (*American Machinist*, 6 March 1880). This was an understatement predicting the conflicting interests of engineers and manufacturers in the proximate future.

Once established, ASME was dominated by a self-perpetuating oligarchy of elite engineers and manufacturers (Calvert 1967). It had a particularly strong base in the machine-production, automobile, and electricity utilities industries (Sinclair 1980). Over half of the society's members (54 per cent) were manufacturers, managers, and shop executives. Furthermore, the great majority of the early presidents of the society were either owners or managers of large firms. During the period 1880–1915, the nominating committee elected as presidents three marine engineers, four educators, six consulting engineers, and twenty-three manufacturers and managers of shops (Calvert 1967). Several, such as Eckley B. Coxe, were individuals of considerable inherited wealth and prestige (Sinclair 1980).

Shop culture and school culture clashed over the best way to educate and socialize the mechanical engineer. F. Hemenway, later an editor for *American Machinist*, wrote in 1880 that the mechanical engineer needs to be an entrepreneur (*American Machinist*, 12 June 1880: 5). He perceived the core of the profession to be composed of those people who practiced technical work more than those who came out of technical schools. *American Engineer*, on the other hand, assumed the opposite orientation. According to *American Engineer*, the virtue of the shop elite was no more than 'old and time-worn shop kinks and wrinkles'. The magazine criticized *American Machinist* for 'catering to men who gloried in titles but had not earned them' (Calvert 1967: 137). At least until 1905 ASME was dominated by representatives of shop culture.[42] The domination of the 'shop-culture' orientation partly explains the historical nexus between American mechanical engineering and American management.[43] It was only from about 1905 that the society was opened to younger, scientifically trained members.[44] The leaders of this trend were Frederick Taylor, Frederick Halsey, and ASME secretary Calvin Rice. Sinclair refers to this trend, which posed a threat to the old authoritarian power structure, as the 'Junior movement' within ASME (Sinclair 1980: 66). They attacked the inefficiency of the society's administration and condemned its financial mismanagement. In this spirit, Harrington Emerson suggested the application of Scientific Management to the society's own administration by solving financial problems via cutting waste rather than increasing membership rates (Sinclair 1980: 69). Emerson later made a remarkably similar argument in his testimony in the Eastern Rate Case in 1910.

By 1907, after the new generation of mechanical engineers took over, Frederick R. Hutton, secretary of the society, formulated its orientation toward issues of management. The engineer was no longer an old fashioned machine-shop craftsman who drew diagrams and designed boilers, but he was 'more and more a manager of men' (Layton 1971: 36). This statement revived an older proposal from 1886, when Henry Towne suggested in an ASME meeting that the society should establish an 'economic section' to deal with issues of management and organizations (see *American Machinist*, 19 June 1886: 8). At this meeting in Chicago, Towne presided, since Coleman Sellers, the president, was ill. Towne's paper was considered 'the first proposition that industrial management should be recognized as a distinct science' (*Engineering Magazine*, April 1916).

From 1905 on, membership of the society grew eventually to include more than half of the mechanical engineers in the country. Whereas in 1880 there were only 191 members in the society, the number rose to more than 15,000 in 1921 (see Fig. 1 and Table 1). Many of the newcomers were college graduates.[45] From its first day until 1906, all ASME professional and administrative matters were handled from the *American Machinist*'s office, which served as the society's headquarters.[46]

Following ASME, *American Machinist*, *Locomotive Engineer*, *Engineering Magazine*, and the few other technical magazines, the National Machine Tool Builders' Association became the next most significant organization of the mechanical engineering elite. It was founded in 1902 when seventeen lathe builders were called together at the invitation of William Lodge, president of the Lodge & Shipley Machine Tool Company of Cincinnati. Its main goal was to coordinate and organize the machine-tool industry. The first agenda presented before the association in 1902 by Fred Halsey (who five years later became an editor of *American Machinist*) dealt with the metric system controversy. The association adopted Halsey's view that such a system would require enormous cost for new equipment, the cost of maintaining a double standard for repairs, and hence an increase in the cost of the product.[47] In 1908 ASME began publishing its own magazine, *Mechanical Engineering*, and *American Machinist* lost some of its centrality in the profession.[48]

Whereas the individual writers, editors, and their relative standing in the community are all of interest to my study, I am ultimately concerned with the emergent properties of the textual materials. I do not follow each column, letter, or editorial as they pertain specifically to individual writers. Rather, I trace the ideological overtones surfacing out of these pages to complete a cumulative picture. In the following chapters I trace the contours of the ideological picture by focusing on the central issues of standardization and systematization. But first a word of methodological caution.

## 1.4 A word of (methodological) caution

Generalizations should be made circumspectly. When one reads through the two magazines discussed here from one issue to another, it becomes clear that the

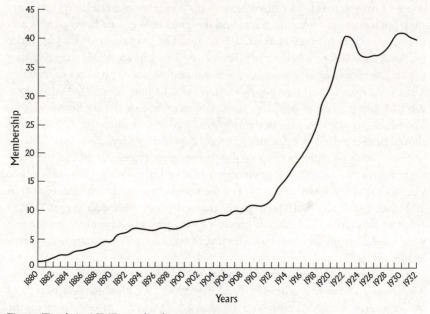

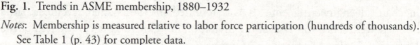

**Fig. 1.** Trends in ASME membership, 1880–1932

*Notes*: Membership is measured relative to labor force participation (hundreds of thousands). See Table 1 (p. 43) for complete data.

history of ideas does not unfold in a coherent, unilinear manner, nor are ideational categories neatly packed and presented. Many engineers were interested in managerial issues, but they encountered opposition as well. Many promoted the idea of standardization and systematization, while others criticized it. Furthermore, the reading of these publications often offers a conflictual reality. Examples of conflicts and divergent interests are ample. Even though *American Machinist* represented in general the 'shop-culture' approach to mechanical engineering, its editorials were not always consistent with this orientation. During his editorship, Fred Miller, for instance, expressed strong support for the 'metric bill', even though it was incongruent with the interests of shop owners. On the other hand, Fred Halsey, Miller's associate editor, wrote a series of articles offering negative assessments of the bill. His arguments, which appeared in *American Machinist* and in his polemical book *The Metric Fallacy*, were used in the campaign to defeat the congressional measure in 1905–6. There were other cases in which *American Machinist* supported the heterodoxy rather than the orthodoxy of ASME.[49]

In his article regarding technical journals and the history of technology, Ferguson cautioned against using deductions about a concrete historical period based on knowledge derived only from a contemporary journal, as he has painfully learned from his own study of *Scientific American*. He warned his readers that 'technical editors used their journals to formulate opinion and mold thought' and therefore should not be treated as an objective representation of their surrounding reality (Ferguson 1989: 53). This became the guideline of my analysis, too. If, for example, the editors argued that systems put an end to labor unrest, I did not evaluate the validity of such a claim. Rather, I inferred that they sold systems as a solution to unrest (see Chapter 6). Finally, in cases where I wanted to learn about practices outside the domains of each magazine, I made a point of cross-referencing information with secondary materials or corroborating the information in *American Machinist* and *Engineering Magazine*. The simultaneous study of both magazines and secondary materials therefore ensures variations within the texts and conclusions that are not magazine-specific.

My historical analysis of the engineers-cum-managers is based on a simple, yet crucial, heuristic periodization: engineering prior to and following the year 1900. This periodization also reflects a paradigm shift in American society at large. Prior to 1900, the ideology of American Exceptionalism was very strong in American culture, and its footprint was apparent in the engineering discourse as well. After 1900, the Progressive period provided the major legitimization for the professionalization of mechanical engineering and its claim for systematization. The next chapters will focus on the engineering discourse; in the balance of this chapter I briefly sketch the essentials of these two perspectives.

## 1.5 American Exceptionalism

American Exceptionalism is a statement about American nationalism. According to this ideology of American Exceptionalism, the USA occupies a unique place in the history of the Western world, and has a distinctive mission to perform which marks it off from the rest of the world.[50] In this vein, 'inherent' political principles of rationality, liberalism, and democracy—together with affluence and a broad opportunity structure—provided a basis for a society that could escape the miseries of class struggle. America was perceived as the only country in the world that was born perfect since it had no indigenous feudal institutions (Hamilton and Sutton 1989). Progress was perceived as a quantitative multiplication of its founding institutions, not a process of qualitative change (Ross 1993). As Hawthorn explains, the American Revolution was not a revolution against the ancient regime, as was the case in Europe, but rather an attempt to secure what began in a historical vacuum. In his own words, 'America seemed already to have reached perfection. The past had been consolidated in a future whose integrity lay in remaining as much like the present as possible' (Hawthorn 1987: 194). This rhetoric supported the belief that America, unlike Europe, was pursuing a utopian course of historical development. The French philosopher Jean Baudrillard comments, 'The tragedy of a utopian dream made reality . . . This is America's problem and, through America, it has become the whole world's problem' (Baudrillard 1989: 28–30).

The rhetoric of Exceptionalism abounded in popular culture, media, and the social sciences throughout the nineteenth century. In Ross's words, Exceptionalism was 'the discursive frame within which the social sciences worked, the language which set their core problem and shaped the logic of their solutions to it' (Ross 1993: 104). For example, American economists believed that Malthus's ideas might have held true for Britain but not for America, where free land guaranteed the production of food beyond population needs. The existing opportunity structure, mobility, and a liberal market (that distributes its benefits widely) made wage labor a temporary condition in the life cycle of American people and would eliminate class conflict. Commons's famous study of the history of shoemakers outlined the Wisconsin School version of the American Exceptionalist perspective. Commons believed that there was no revolutionary working class in the United States since universal manhood suffrage (which was achieved early in American history) mitigated against the development of a revolutionary working-class consciousness among laborers (Wunderlin 1992). In accordance with the Exceptionalist perspective, the engineering literature in the nineteenth century perceived American machinery and industry as superior to that of Europe in three regards: workers and their productivity, the use of machinery, and the general organization of business (Litterer 1986). The implications of this ideology will be discussed in subsequent chapters, particularly 2 and 5.

## 1.6  The Progressive period

The years 1900–17 are known as the Progressive period in the United States. Progressivism can be traced back to the Populist surge of the 1870s and 1880s and the writings of Henry George and Edward Bellamy (see Hofstadter 1955). However, while the Populist movement centered in rural America, the twentieth-century Progressive leadership was urban and had its base among the independent middle class, and among intellectuals and professionals. The movement received stimulation when giant industrial corporations gained incredible power and politics seemed to be corrupted.

Progressive leaders called for reforms to revitalize the democratic spirit and restore equality through the adoption of initiatives and the referendum. Progressivists attempted to promote the cause of women, elect senators by direct vote, aid lower-income groups, establish a minimum wage, or encourage trade unionism (Wren 1972). Perhaps the most familiar tenet of Progressivism centered around anti-monopoly legislation and its most influential spokesman, Woodrow Wilson. Progressivists demanded redistribution of wealth by means of welfare legislation and the rebalancing of economic power with antitrust legislation. They demanded government regulation of business and strove to 'clean up city hall', to make the 'business of government' more orderly, efficient, and honest, preferring city managers to city bosses (Noble 1977: 59). Progressivism's political culture did not present one coherent scheme but rather an amalgam of ideas and ideals that converged under a single label. For example, all three contenders at the 1912 presidential elections—Republican William Taft, Democrat Woodrow Wilson, and Republican breakaway Teddy Roosevelt—ran on 'progressive' tickets (Hofstadter 1955; Hays 1957; Kolko 1963; Haber 1964; Kloppenberg 1986; Kaufman, Zacharias, and Karson 1995).

The Progressive period is also known as the golden age of professionalism in America (Larson 1977; Abbott 1988). During this period, 'only the professional administrator, the doctor, the social worker, the architect, the economist, could show the way' (Wiebe 1967: 174). In turn, professional control became more elaborate. It involved measurement and prediction and the development of professional techniques for guiding events to predictable outcomes (Hays 1959). The experts 'devised rudimentary government budgets, introduced central, audited purchasing, and rationalized the structure of offices' (Wiebe 1967: 168). This type of control was not only characteristic of professionals in large corporate systems. It characterized social movements, the management of schools, roads, towns, and political systems. Hays (1959), who examined the political culture of the Progressive era through the prism of the conservation movement, argued that loyalty to professional ideals, and not close association with the grass-roots public, set the tone for the movement. Furthermore, the Roosevelt administration maintained close relationships with all engineering societies, including ASME. In return, the societies supported Roosevelt's attempts to bring efficiency and rational management into government. Hays concluded that 'efficiency', 'expertise', and 'system' infused the entire social order of Progressivism. This was congruent with the general trend of 'anti-chaos' reforms, labeled by Wiebe as 'the search for order', and characterized by 'bureaucratic vision' and a desire for 'perfect systematization' (Wiebe 1967).

The professional tools developed by the Progressivists were perceived to be objective and rational, above the give-and-take of political conflict. The struggle of Progressivists to find a common ground for society as a whole generated a pragmatic culture in which conflicts were diffused and ideological differences resolved. Science and engineering provided the 'assurance that from the same set of facts men will come approximately to the same conclusion' (Kloppenberg 1986: 383). Progressive culture represented the triumph of scientific and engineering-based management (for a legal historical perspective see Kaufman, Zacharias, and Karson 1995). As Bendix and Guillen have suggested, at the turn of the century organizational ideas broke asunder from traditional entrepreneurial and religious ideologies. The typical nineteenth-century industrial thought was based on a Protestant ethic. It presented the frontiersman, the self-made man, as a role model for entrepreneurial spirit. It implicitly criticized wage labor and endorsed self-employment. This approach also coincided with the popularity of Social Darwinism, which theorized survival of the fittest in society (Bendix 1956/1974; Guillen 1994). Up until the Progressive era, Social Darwinist and religious ideas were prominent in American industrial culture. Herbert Spencer's ideas were adopted by G. Sumner, who said that the accumulation of wealth was an outcome of the struggle for survival and divine choice, while to people like Andrew Carnegie, 'business is religion' (Bendix 1956/1974: 257). The idea that businessmen fulfill the will of God gave room to use of religion as a legitimizing factor in industrial ideology. For example, in 1902 George F. Baer, president of the Reading Railroad, stated that most Christian men to whom God gave fortunes knew best what was good for workers and how to manage them (Baritz 1960: 3). Or as one minister argued, 'If God gives us the possibilities and power to get wealth, to acquire influence, to be forces in the world, what is the true conception of life but divine ownership and human administration?' (Bendix 1956/1974: 257).

At the end of the Progressive period, business philosophy was crystallized around secular engineering ideals rather than around religious, philanthropic, paternalistic, or Social Darwinist ones (Barley and Kunda 1992; Guillen 1994). The rise of the engineering profession was one historical corollary of this fundamental change. Under the aegis of engineering ideology, a resort to politics was no longer needed, since political conflicts could be redefined in technical terms. Social, political, and ideological problems were often cast in terms of efficiency. Engineering expertise seemed appropriate to solving them (Larson 1977). Standardization was congruent with the values of the Progressive era (1900–17)—'the true line of progress is the exhaustive study of machines', *American Machinist* stated (*American Machinist*, 16 January 1913: 109). It was widely believed that engineering-based expertise would take industry beyond "anarchy", which so characterized the robber baron era, and lead toward more progressive and prosperous times (Chandler 1977; Sinclair 1980).

In Chapter 2 I begin a genealogical journey in search of the origins of management ideology among the historical factors of industrial growth and labor unrest, as well as the political forces of Exceptionalism and Progressivism. I describe the movement for standardization in US industry, and how the leaders of the engineering literature were active figures in this process. However, they were never blind promoters of standardization. The editors of *American Machinist* suggested that engineers should 'establish standards with provisions for change', that 'no general rule should be applied with eyes closed', and that general rules can become a fetish (12 October 1922: 585). That is, there was argument and counter-argument, convergence and divergence, consensus and dissension. This heterogeneity and diversity of ideas is disadvantageous to us on the one hand, since it impairs our ability to make generalizations. On the other hand, it is particularly this problematization and non-linearity in the progress of rationality that explains best the history of management systems. This is a story of ideology as practice, of ideology through application, not only through the discourse of remote intellectuals.

Notes

1. On the history of the Wharton School see Sass 1982.

2. Schools of management and business administration were established at Berkeley and Chicago in 1898, at Dartmouth and New York University in 1900, and at Harvard in 1908. All the rest were established thereafter. See Chandler 1977; Lash and Urry 1987.

3. For some exceptions see Lash and Urry 1987; Fligstein 1990; Freeland 1994.

4. This is typical of management theory since Taylor. Successive theories—such as Human Relations, Open Systems, Management by Objectives, Quality Circles, Organizational Culture, among many others—are conceptualized as the outcome of evolutionary processes. Each stage of management theory and practice is considered a better approximation of organizational reality. See also Quigel 1992.

5. McKenna 1995 does not accept the contention that engineering was the breeding ground for management ideology. He argues that after 1932 there was a proliferation of consulting firms in the United States, but contrary to common understanding, Taylorism was not the predominant influence on their development. Rather, management engineers drew on the practices of accountants, engineers, and lawyers to offer CEO-level studies of organization, strategy, and operations (p. 57).

6. To be sure, there is an important stream of literature concerning the rise of managerial ideologies (for the most indicative of this line see Bendix 1956/1974; Barley and Kunda 1992; Guillen 1994; Abrahamson 1997). Barley and Kunda present successive surges in the development of managerial ideology over a period of 100 years: Industrial Betterment, Scientific Management, Human Relations, System Rationalism, and Organizational Culture. While admittedly useful and informative, their study has a major drawback. It presents managerial ideology, for each period of time, as a coherent philosophy which was represented in its entirety by the management community of the time. However, management activists were not cut of the same cloth. The description of one dominant ideology per period conceals variations and conflicts that took place within each period (see Chapter 4 for a description of such cleavages). Furthermore, some literature on managerial ideology performs a quantum leap from the owner-based type of management to Frederick Taylor's Scientific Management, considered the birth of managerial ideology. Peter Drucker (1986) went so far as to claim that Taylor had as much impact on the modern world as Karl Marx and Sigmund Freud. However, Taylor was only one actor—albeit important and critical—in the invention of management as a free enterprise. The sole focus on Taylor's work ignores much of the efforts made by engineers prior to his appearance, and the alternative efforts of management activists outside the scope of Scientific Management. Furthermore, it is only in relation to the other factions in the management movement that Taylorism can be understood in a contextual and historical perspective.

7. See Appendix for detailed description of the magazines.

8. To use some statistics, capital investment increased by 500 percent in the thirty-year period from 1880 to 1910. See *American Machinist*, 11 June 1914: 1033. Manufacturing output increased at a rate greater than population growth. The value of an establishment's average product rose from $13,429 in 1859 to $215,157 in 1919. A significant change took place in the non-agricultural workforce, which grew

from 6 million in 1870 to 18 million in 1900, contrasted with a rise from 6.8 million to 10.9 million in the agricultural workforce (see Litterer 1986: 29). The number of manufacturing establishments grew from 252,148 to 512,191 (Litterer 1986: 31). The average number of workers in an establishment increased more than 300 percent, from 9.34 in 1859 to 31.36 in 1919 (20.49 in 1899, 25.30 in 1904, 24.64 in 1909, and 25.51 in 1914) according to *The Statistical Abstract of the United States*, 1921; see also Faulkner 1951.

9. Additional changes such as the abandonment of inside contracting (Buttrick 1952), the evolution of accountancy, cost-keeping, and wage systems (Garner 1954; Johnson and Kaplan 1987; Oakes 1988; Miranti 1990; Hopwood 1994), the elaboration of formal communication (Yates 1989), and the emergence of MDFs (Chandler 1962) are all related phenomena.

10. Whereas in 1897 there were only 447,000 union members, the figure rose to 3,104,000 in 1917 and to over 5,111,000 in 1920.

11. Taft and Ross (1969) argued that the USA had the 'bloodiest and most violent labor history of any industrial nation of the world'. Goldstein disqualified their conclusion, arguing that they did not make a serious comparative study and therefore 'their comment should be read as indicating the high level of violence in American labor history rather than a definitive comparative statement'. It might be possible to argue, however, that with a 'minimum of ideologically motivated class conflict, the United States has somehow had a maximum of industrial violence' (Goldstein, 1978: 4). But the Taft and Ross statement was backed by Zieger (1986: 6), who argued that strikes in America were 'more savage and bloody' than anywhere else in the industrial world. See Guillen 1994: 39.

12. See Buttrick 1952; Clawson 1980; for further evidence of the inside-contracting system see 'Piece Work on Yearly Contract', *American Machinist*, 28 May 1881: 7; *American Machinist*, 9 August 1894: 8; and *American Machinist*, 30 November 1905: 747; see also Henry Roland, 'Six Examples of Successful Shop Management', *Engineering Magazine*, March 1897: 994–1000.

13. Sidney Pollard (1965) emphasized that in the early days of the newly established factories in the 18th century, British experiments with appointed managers were disastrous: disloyalty, bribery, alcoholism, and stealing were widespread. A predominant solution was the appointment of managers upon the basis of trust and loyalty, rather than proven managerial skills. Kanter (1977: 51) reported that in 1912, J. P. Morgan testified before the House Committee on Banking and Currency and insisted that what ruled the financial world was 'character' rather than money or property. Likewise, Buttrick (1952: 215) reported that during the prevalence of the 'inside-contracting' system, management scrutinized the accounts of the more important contractors and the company occasionally sent loyal employees to get jobs in some of the departments.

14. In fact, there is evidence that it was in the interest of the contractors to increase productivity as greatly as possible. Harold Williamson constructed an index in which he shows that contractors improved productivity dramatically and cut down their prices by half over a period of twenty years (Clawson 1980: 81). Even Henry Roland, who opposed the contracting system, admitted that it ensured constant reduction of cost (ibid.: 81). Clawson (1980: 119) concludes that

'neither consideration of efficiency nor dissatisfaction with inside contracting's technical capacity to perform the work were significant issues at the time'.

15. The rise of American engineering education (mainly civil engineering) in leading institutions such as Harvard, Yale, Columbia, and Pennsylvania and Virginia Universities in the 1850s and 1860s was also stimulated by the railroads (Chandler 1977).

16. McCallum developed a system of organizational specification in the Erie. He even developed a formal organizational chart that was distributed and sold to the general public. There is no doubt that this was one of the first organizational innovations in the United States. See Chandler 1977.

17. Poor was the editor of the *American Railroad Journal*, and a spokesman for the railroad industry. He made it the leading business magazine prior to the Civil War. Alfred Chandler, who was the great-grandson of Henry Poor, described his contributions in Chandler 1956.

18. Civil engineering had originally emerged from military engineering and many of the civil engineers in the first half of the 19th century were trained at the United States Military Academy at West Point (Calvert 1967).

19. See an editorial attack on the American Census in the *American Machinist*, 19 June 1890: 8.

20. 45,000 in 1900 and 136,000 in 1920. See also Table 1 for the growth in the distribution of professional membership among engineers. Despite its rapid growth, it should be emphasized that engineering was a tiny elite. By 1930 there were only 45 engineers for every 10,000 workers in the industry. See Layton 1971; Noble 1977; Stark 1980.

21. This description is based on Calvert 1967.

22. Hounshell (1984) argues that some of the shops were owned by mechanic-inventors who began their careers sometimes as telegraph operators and knew the industry very well. See also Israel 1992.

23. For a fuller description see Calvert 1967. Also, many industries emerged out of the traditional craft knowledge. The two main industries that emerged from the soil of scientific knowledge were the chemical and the electrical industries. See Noble 1977.

24. College and shop cultures were two competing orientations over the question of how to train mechanical engineers.

25. Colburn was never a practicing railway mechanical superintendent, but he had a devoted career in technical journalism. Colburn was probably the first to sign his editorials in the *American Railroad Journal* as 'Mechanical Engineer' (Calvert 1967: 17). In 1854 he started his own weekly *Railroad Advocate* which he sold to Alexander Holley, with whom he traveled to Europe in 1857 to gather information for a book on coal-burning boilers on European railroads. He then edited the *Engineer* in England, resigned, and started a magazine with the same title in Philadelphia in 1860. After five months, because of lack of support he returned to London and the magazine was closed. In 1866, Colburn published another weekly entitled *Engineering* (for a detailed description of Colburn see Ferguson 1989). During his years in London Colburn published books on steam-boiler explosions and locomotive engineering. He also joined the Institution of Civil Engineers, the Institution of Mechanical Engineers, and served as president of the London Society of Engineers. In 1866 Colburn started

in London another new weekly journal, *Engineering*. In his first editorial he wrote that he had started this journal 'because its conductor is convinced that there is no other magazine worthy to represent engineering' (Ferguson 1989: 60). He further revealed that engineering journals, to this date, were seldom conducted by engineers, and the editors took accounts of new bridges, blast furnaces, and railway stations from 'the Times', 'which really contains far more engineering news than all the technical papers taken together' (Ferguson 1989: 60).

26. Not only that, but faculty members—such as Alexander C. Humphreys, Harvey N. Davis, and David S. Jacobus—served as presidents of ASME (Sinclair 1980).

27. See Dexter S. Kimball, 'Engineering Education and Industry', *American Machinist*, 19 May 1927: 806. Under the Act, the federal government turned over to the states certain lands in order to finance the creation of agricultural and mechanical colleges. Typical of such programs that set up curricula in mechanics and industrial training were the departments in the University of Wisconsin (founded in 1870) and in Purdue University in Indiana (founded in 1874).

28. For example: *American Railroad Journal*, *American Railway Times*, and *American Railway Review*.

29. There were three reasons for this. First, it was a period of fascination with machines, particularly following the World's Centennial Exhibition of 1876, (Colvin 1947). Second, during this period there was widespread use of high-speed rotary printing presses that ran by steam power and of cheap wood-pulp paper. Third, the mail system was expanded through the development of the railroad network and facilitated the circulation of journals (Calvert 1967).

30. See Mott 1957, on the history of American magazines.

31. I also considered studying the magazine *System*. However, it was founded rather late (1900) for it to meet my research objectives, and was rather narrow since its emphasis was on office systematization (see Haber 1964: 20).

32. As a spin-off of this study I examined an additional journal: *Transactions of the ASME* (Shenhav 1995). *Transactions of the ASME* printed proceedings from the ASME meetings and contained mainly articles. It appeared twice a year and had no editorial, news columns, or letters to the editors. As such, *Transactions of the ASME* was less sensitive to 'current events', particularly given the rich coverage of strikes, politics, management concerns, and economic changes in the other two periodicals. Furthermore, *Transactions of the ASME* was ambivalent about its attitude to management. Admittedly, the first public awareness of management issues emerged in the ASME conference of 1886. But there were splits within the society regarding the extent to which engineers should be concerned with non-technical issues. Although this study is based on the systematic examination of the *American Machinist* and *Engineering Magazine*, I have occasionally used additional materials from *Transactions of the ASME*.

33. For advantages and disadvantages of using technical periodicals as historical sources, see Ferguson 1989.

34. See for example 'Editorial', *American Machinist*, 18 April 1889: 8; also *American Machinist*, 21 May 1881: 8.

35. Biographical notes in this chapter are based on ASME 1980, biographical descriptions in *Engineering* magazine, and additional materials, particularly Colvin 1947; Calvert 1967; and Jaffe 1957.

36. My first interest in these magazines was stimulated by reading Litterer's work. See Litterer 1961*a*, 1963, 1986.

37. For example, if the systematizers claimed that the rise of systems was a necessity dictated by the growing size of the industrial factory, Litterer used this rationale as a theoretical explanation.

38. The definition of what constituted a mechanical rather than another type of engineer was hazy at the time. In fact, both Holley and Thurston served as officers in the American Institute of Mining Engineers (AIME). Holey was its president in 1875 and Thurston was a vice-president from 1878 to 1879, the year before becoming ASME's first president. A few other individuals, such as Eckley B. Coxe, Robert W. Hunt, and William Metcalf, served both societies (see Sinclair 1980: 27).

39. The concluding line of the letter pleaded, 'please avoid allowing this to be made public' (*American Machinist*, 3 April 1930: 551). During the meeting on 16 February 1880, Horace B. Miller, the publisher of the *American Machinist*, who had foreseen the possibility of a clash of personalities and orientations, invited all the twenty-six participants to a fancy dinner at the old Astor House in New York to diffuse the tension (see Calvert 1967).

40. At the time, there were only a few other journalists involved in the process of forming the society. James C. Bayles, editor of *Iron Age*, served as secretary of the 7 April 1880 meeting at the Stevens Institute, and Matthias Forney, editor of *Railway Age*, served on the first committee of publication (Sinclair 1980).

41. Alexander Holley was a well-known figure in engineering circles. He was born into a well-to-do Connecticut family and his father, a successful cutlery manufacturer, was governor of the state. Holley graduated in the 1850s from Brown University as a civil engineer. He was a draftsman and a machinist, became a partner with Zerah Colburn in *Railroad Advocate* in 1855, published the *American Engineer*, and wrote articles on engineering issues for the *New York Times* (see Ferguson 1989).

42. The elitist shop-oriented views of ASME and of the *American Machinist* and its editors were evident in the debates surrounding membership in the society. A suggestion was made at the first ASME meeting that a candidate for membership should pass three of five qualifications involving experience as a designer of machinery, supervising machinery operation, being an apprentice in an engineering business, holding an engineering degree (or teaching in a school of engineering), and being either the author of a book on engineering or an inventor of a machine or a process. Bailey, the editor of the *American Machinist*, suggested simplifying the requirements to allow for the inclusion of practical people as well. According to his suggestion candidates could be proposed by at least three members to whom they must be personally known, together with a statement in writing including an account of their professional service (Colvin 1947: 66–7). His suggestion was accepted. Fred Colvin, a future editor of the *Machinist*, commented on this event in his autobiography, describing Bailey as instrumental in removing a rigid definition of membership heavily based on college education. One should realize, however, that what Colvin—an insider in the *American Machinist* office—defined as removing a 'rigid definition' was in fact a method of perpetuating the centrality of the 'old boys' network' in the society. Bailey did not only 'simplify' membership. He helped the old machine-shop elite to retain its stronghold within the society. Indeed, for about

twenty-five years ASME was an organization into which one mainly entered through personal recommendation.

43. This was not the case in Germany, for example. German engineering was initially dominated by a segment of engineering professors who sought to achieve scientific standards and viewed engineering as pure science (Gispen 1989: 9).

44. In fact, ASME was founded by three men whose careers illustrate the gradual transition of mechanical engineering from a craft-based art to a scientific and academically based profession. John E. Sweet represented the older generation. He was a pattern-maker, draftsman, contractor, inventor, and manufacturer and then a professor at Cornell University. Alexander L. Holley and Robert H. Thurston represented a newer generation of scientific engineers. See *American Machinist*, 3 April 1930, for a condensed history of ASME.

45. This did not go without argument. For example, there was a proposal in 1909 to raise the age of associate members from 26 to 30, a proposal that was eventually turned down (Calvert 1967).

46. For example, the magazine's treasurer, Lycurgus Moore, served the society as well. However, the affiliation between the *American Machinist* and ASME was so close that it drew criticism. The *Mechanical Engineer* complained that no other journals were given advance notice regarding the first ASME meeting so as to print the information for their readers. Bailey recognized the conflict of interests and suggested a rule that no editors of trade journals be appointed to the society committees or council. It was only after a few years that this rule was forgotten (Calvert 1967). In 1890 ASME bought the New York Academy of Medicine building on West 31st Street and stayed there until 1906, when it moved to a permanent address in the fifteen-story engineering building donated by Andrew Carnegie.

47. Nevertheless, down the line the association took a role in working out the classification of machine tools. See, for example: 'Editorial', *American Machinist*, 10 July 1924.

48. This does not mean that the *American Machinist* and *Mechanical Engineering* were rivals or competitors. Fred Miller, an editor-in-chief of the *American Machinist*, was an active member of the committee on publications that made decisions about the publication of *Mechanical Engineering*.

49. For example, in November 1901 the editors reported that Fred Hutton, the secretary of the society, spent little time at the society house, and indicated that the clerical staff (four individuals) should be reduced by half (*American Machinist*, 28 November 1901: 1301). With these statements, the *American Machinist* sided with the criticism of the younger generation in ASME against the inefficiency of Hutton and the extravagant operation of the older generation (Sinclair 1980: 69). The editorials expressed dissatisfaction with the fact that the membership dues were about to increase without expenses being cut down. At the same time, the *American Machinist* joined in another related controversy over geography. The founding generation of ASME consisted of people who owned and managed firms in New York and its immediate vicinity. The rapid increase in ASME membership brought a change in the society's demographic structure. The New York base of the society did not accurately represent the new geographic spread. The *American Machinist* was adamant in its call for separate and distinct monthly meetings of mechanical

engineers in various locations (Sinclair 1980: 78). The ASME council felt threatened by such a decentralized structure, and in 1905 smashed an attempt of the Milwaukee members to establish a separate section for themselves. The *American Machinist* criticized the society for its rigid policy, pointing to the detrimental consequences of their action. Eventually, the Milwaukee branch split from ASME and created a separate local engineering society (*American Machinist*, 14 December 1905: 813, quoted in Sinclair 1980: 80).

50. See Ross 1991, as well as Lipset 1996, for contemporary examples of adherence to this thesis. Voss (1993) argues that the debate over American Exceptionalism (at least in the era of the labor struggle) dates from the publication of Werner Sombart's *Why Is There No Socialism in the United States* (1906). See also Shafer 1991; Tyrrell 1991.

TABLE 1. *Annual ASME membership and ratio of ASME membership relative to industrial employment*[a]

| Year | Membership | Ratio |
|------|-----------|-------|
| 1880 | 191 | 0.011 |
| 1881 | 222 | 0.012 |
| 1882 | 311[b] | 0.016 |
| 1883 | 401 | 0.021 |
| 1884 | 440 | 0.022 |
| 1885 | 558 | 0.027 |
| 1886 | 621 | 0.029 |
| 1887 | 715 | 0.033 |
| 1888 | 813 | 0.036 |
| 1889 | 985 | 0.043 |
| 1890 | 1,049 | 0.045 |
| 1891 | 1,344 | 0.056 |
| 1892 | 1,500 | 0.061 |
| 1893 | 1,675 | 0.066 |
| 1894 | 1,699[b] | 0.066 |
| 1895 | 1,723[b] | 0.066 |
| 1896 | 1,748 | 0.065 |
| 1897 | 1,867 | 0.068 |
| 1898 | 1,898[b] | 0.068 |
| 1899 | 1,929 | 0.067 |
| 1900 | 2,129 | 0.073 |
| 1901 | 2,325 | 0.079 |
| 1902 | 2,419 | 0.080 |
| 1903 | 2,573 | 0.083 |
| 1904 | 2,740 | 0.086 |
| 1905 | 2,929 | 0.090 |
| 1906 | 3,040 | 0.091 |
| 1907 | 3,366 | 0.098 |
| 1908 | 3,455 | 0.098 |
| 1909 | 3,832 | 0.107 |
| 1910 | 3,978 | 0.108 |
| 1911 | 4,115 | 0.109 |
| 1912 | 4,542 | 0.119 |

| Year | Membership | Ratio |
| --- | --- | --- |
| 1913 | 5,394 | 0.139 |
| 1914 | 6,142 | 0.155 |
| 1915 | 6,931 | 0.174 |
| 1916 | 7,704 | 0.191 |
| 1917 | 8,720 | 0.214 |
| 1918 | 10,189 | 0.243 |
| 1919 | 11,882 | 0.288 |
| 1920 | 13,251 | 0.317 |
| 1921 | 15,227 | 0.359 |
| 1922 | 17,210 | 0.402 |
| 1923 | 17,452 | 0.399 |
| 1924 | 16,666 | 0.374 |
| 1925 | 16,749 | 0.368 |
| 1926 | 17,036 | 0.371 |
| 1927 | 17,489 | 0.375 |
| 1928 | 18,295 | 0.386 |
| 1929 | 19,437 | 0.404 |
| 1930 | 20,011 | 0.410 |
| 1931 | 20,009 | 0.403 |
| 1932 | 20,079 | 0.398 |

[a] Ratio is calculated relative to industrial employment. Industrial employment is divided by 1,000,000.

[b] Interpolated information.

# 2

# Engineering Rationality: 'System Shall Replace Chaos'

*The American Machinist* opposed the extremists in management just as it now opposes similar extreme proposals of standardization. But rational standardization should and will have the support of every level-headed engineer and business man.

('Editorial', *American Machinist*, 7 May 1924: 668)

The chief risk lies in the tendency to concentrate the fixing of standards in a planning department which to be perfect should have, but in practice never can have all the wisdom of the universe.

('Editorial', *Engineering Magazine*, September 1911: 977)

Ohms and farads, kilograms and degrees (Celsius or Fahrenheit) were not given by nature, but settled upon by scientists, industrialists, bureaucrats, citizens, kings, and presidents.

(Porter 1994: 200)

The rise of the 'systems' paradigm—and its various interpretations—in American industry was an outcome of several intertwined processes, not the least of which was the growth of an engineering-based ideology of 'systematization'. Systematization was an ideology that crystallized within technical circles and was promoted by engineering magazines. The ideology stood for both rhetoric and practice, empirical and metaphysical, deductive and inductive, a category of the mind and a formal aspect of organizations. It was a mélange of ideas and arrangements, technical and administrative, that were categorized under one crude rubric: systems.

The advent of management systems represents a relocation of power from the traditional capitalist order into the hands of technocrats who did not control means of production but rather invented practices of engineering rationality. These technocrats did not base their authority on ownership, nor did they employ brute power. They worked by means of a discourse that shaped their surrounding reality. Their authority did not appear as controlling. They offered a helpful, rational hand for the mutual interest of employers and employees. Their ideology of rationality appeared neutral, outside the realm of power, politics, and ideology.

The cultural image that was promoted by this ideology trespassed from the technical field of engineering into social and economic domains. Eventually it also became a persuasive and enduring generic paradigm in the literature on organizations (see Meyer 1988 for a similar argument about mechanical images in sociology). The ideology found natural support in the political culture of the Progressive era, and in the political economy of labor relations. It became a formative language for the constitution of the ideological phase of the managerial revolution. One might follow this language to discover how it migrated from the technical to the human and social worlds. This language migration provides an index to the current pervasiveness of managerial rationality in the public sphere. In the following I will focus on mechanical engineering as a field of knowledge. Based on insights from the so-called Constructivist perspective I will show how engineers 'translated' social and managerial ideas to be homologous with technical systems (in particular see Callon 1980; Latour 1987. For further elaboration see Chapter 3).

## 2.1 Mechanization and modernization in industrial America

In his history of the American Society of Mechanical Engineers (ASME), Bruce Sinclair recalls that in 1930 mechanical engineers came under siege (Sinclair 1980). As the stock market crashed and the country dove into depression, engineers were blamed for driving industry into a state of overproduction, resulting in massive unemployment. Engineers were criticized for having created a 'machine civilization': a hyper-mechanized society characterized by monotonous jobs, alienated workers, lack of spirit, lack of aesthetic, and dehumanization (e.g. Chase 1929). The general feeling was that mechanization and systematization had gone too far.

Recollection of the fifty years prior to 1930 reveals quite a different picture. In the early 1880s, with the rapid increase in the number of engineers, there was a growing public fascination with machines and industrial technology. It was the heady age of the steam engine, the automatic lathe, and the automobile. The editors of *American Machinist*, the magazine that best represented the machine-shop culture, declared that 'the proper punishment for critics of industrial society . . . was to place them on an island with no machinery' (Clavert 1967: 175). An editorial rejecting arguments about the negative effects of machinery on civilization concluded with a blessing, in decidedly biblical overtones, that 'the automatic machine prosper and multiply' (*American Machinist*, 12 July 1922: 77). During this time it was not uncommon to find in the magazine a six- or eight-page story devoted to some new automatic screw machine, a heavy planer, a boring mill, or a new lathe design, illustrated with working drawings and glowing descriptions (see Tichi 1987).

The pace of development was burgeoning, and the machine technology seemed to have a limitless trajectory. The pride of engineering work was demonstrated by machine tools, thermostats with automatic control, band brakes, friction clutches, typewriters, internal combustion engines, boilers, steam turbines, the bicycle, or the automobile. As American economist Thorstein Veblen said: the machine was an undeniable fact (Haber 1964: 143). Frederick Colvin, a person who spent more than fifty years with *American Machinist*, suggested '[we] accept machines and the machine age as sturdy facts' and 'look upon man as a tool-using animal' (Colvin 1947: 9). Colvin animated machine tools as a biological species, saying that they are 'the only class of machines that can reproduce themselves'. The parts of a lathe are made on a pre-existing lathe, and the lathe that is made is used to turn out parts for a third-generation lathe and so forth. Colvin argued, 'One can almost think of these machines as propagating their species in accordance with the Biblical injunction given to old man Adam and his children.' Furthermore, he said, machines do live since 'the power of reproduction, biologists tell us, is one of the distinguishing characteristics of life' (Colvin 1947: 6). An editorial in *American Machinist* personified the machine, viewing it as 'canned human intelligence' that transforms input into output (*American Machinist*, 12 October 1922: 584).

Two myths of modernity accompanied machine development: the myth of equality and liberation on the one hand, and the myth of progress and reason on the other. Machine civilization was part of a universal struggle, a leading edge of the historical movement between the old agrarian elite and the emerging industrial order. As Sinclair put it, it was as if all of mankind's history could be divided into two periods: before and after the invention of the steam engine. The achievements of civilization were now being measured according to speed, size, and energy. Indeed, during this period European intellectuals believed that they could discover the unconscious of America in its technology (Hughes 1989*a*: 109), and they equated modernization with the logic of the American machine (Gispen 1989; Hughes 1989*b*). The realism of the machine seemed to reflect the logic of reason, an internal truth, and a representation of reality. Mechanization became a meta-narrative for the economy, politics, society, morality, culture, and aesthetics.

This was the heyday of the mechanical engineer: 'The engineer pins nature down and forces her to answer his question. He alone of all professional men has an unvarying criterion by which he may decide the right and wrong, the correct and the false. Other professional men are subject only to varying human laws and human notions and so get along without ever having before them an absolute standard' (*American Machinist*, 9 May 1901: 521). The early mechanical engineer, employed by a factory, was an expert. His main concerns focused on the production processes, his chief desire was to maintain their smooth and regular functioning. As characterized by an editorial in *American Machinist* in the year Taylor first published his ideas on shop management, 'mechanics deal with things that are exact and certain' (*American Machinist*, 18 October 1895: 808). Another writer claimed that: 'Above all other employments of a secular character, the study of mechanical science, using the term in its largest meaning, operates to familiarize the mind with the reality and the controlling nature of unseen things' (*American Machinist*, 9 May 1886: 4). The editors of *American Machinist* reminded their readers, 'It is not so far in the past that some of our readers must remember when a railroad trip was looked upon as almost as fool-hardy as flying is today. Now we grumble if we lose half an hour's time between New York and Chicago' (*American Machinist*, 5 March 1914: 434).

Henry Gantt, a graduate of the mechanical engineering department at Stevens Institute of Technology and later a disciple of Frederick Taylor, romanticized the 'new hegemony of the engineer' and the 'credo of production' (Haber 1964: 43). The editors of *American Machinist* observed that 'no class of men in all the world' exert influence upon the human family as those engineers who 'invent, design and build machinery' (*American Machinist*, 8 November 1906: 618–19). Elsewhere the editors determined that among the factors that make a nation prosperous are 'fertile land', 'painstaking', and a 'capable body of professional engineers' (*American Machinist*, 12 April 1894: 4). In *Engineering Magazine*, Oberlin Smith, an expert on drawing presses and a person well connected with ASME, suggested that engineers dominated civilization and the progress of the world (*Engineering Magazine*, February 1892: 675). The strength of mechanical engineers was grounded in the success of the machine-production industry. The connection to steam power linked them to the electrical utilities industries, an emerging industrial giant at the beginning of the century (Sinclair 1980). Another editorial declared: 'The root-idea of engineering is form. The engineer's work is to form, to inform, to conform, to reform, to formulate, to perform' (*Engineering Magazine*, May 1908: 180).

The fascination with mechanization and mechanical engineering peaked during the 1910s, at the height of the Progressive period. Engineers' thinking often paralleled that of Progressive reformers. Engineers shared the Progressives' desire for reforms as long as they were in line with 'rationality', 'mechanization', 'efficiency', 'scientific method', and 'progress' (Kolko 1963; Haber 1964; Kloppenberg 1986). For example, in 1913 representatives of ASME made a trip to meet colleagues in the Verein Deutscher Ingenieure (VDI), the German Engineering Society. Reflecting on the German experience—one of the world's most advanced theoretical research centers prior to the First World War—*American Machinist* concluded that 'public administration should be put in charge of competent engineers'. The editorial, probably written by editor-in-chief Leon Alford, extended the territory of engineers: 'Why should not an engineer be elected President of the United States?' (*American Machinist*, 7 August 1913: 247). Indeed, years later the editors of *American Machinist* promoted the candidacy of Herbert Hoover, who was described as 'engineering method personified'. In an article entitled 'An Engineer in the White House', Condit and Colvin stated that owing to Hoover's 'sterling Americanism', his outstanding ability as an 'economic thinker' and a 'constructive organizer of human endeavor . . . *American Machinist* stands in support of Herbert Hoover for President of the United States' (*American Machinist*, 8 March 1928: 436. See also *American Machinist*, 28 June 1928: 1060).

The First World War proved an opportunity for engineers to enhance their professional self-esteem. They criticized the lack of American preparedness, using it as an opportunity to expand the boundaries of engineering and its social role.[1] Richard L. Humphrey, the chair of the Joint Conference Committee of four engineering societies, concluded in the organizing conference that the war displayed 'the brilliant work' of engineers and brought 'a universal recognition of [their] importance'.[2] He further argued that the war 'awakened the public to a keener realization of the service of the engineer' (*American Machinist*, 17 June 1920: 1320).

## 2.2 The origin of systems ideology

Systems ideology had two identifiable historical sources. First, the term 'system' was originally applied to the tangible and physical aspects of manufacturing, and was used in relation to the 'American system' of production, notorious in Europe for its uniform, interchangeable parts (Hounshell 1984). As Litterer observed, the skill and knowledge of Europeans was equal and sometimes superior to that of Americans. 'The difference was in how this technical knowledge and skill was used. The European manufacturer used it to make a product. The American manufacturer used it to make a process for making a product'; hence 'the American system' (Litterer 1961*a*: 467). The entry 'system' first appeared in the index of *American Machinist* in 1882. The concept was commonly used in the mechanical engineering literature to refer to any method of ordering engineering ideas and practices.

The second source of systems ideology emerged from the movement for standardization in American industry. The general claim of the movement was that the adoption of universal standards would result in technical predictability, and would provide greater control over irregularities, anomalies, and uncertainties. This movement, which focused initially on technical matters, spilled over eventually to human affairs, social institutions, and the design of government bureaucracies. These two sources fed the collective consciousness of mechanical engineers and eventually translated into an image of organizations as mechanical systems.

### 2.2.1 The 'American system'

The term 'American system' was known to the European industrial community at least from the early 1850s.[3] In nineteenth-century American technology it referred to the 'means of manufacturing involving "the sequential series of operations carried out on successive special-purpose machines that produce interchangeable parts" ' (Hounshell 1984: 15). Unlike the current interpretation of the term 'system', early usage of the term denoted a 'method', 'principle', 'arrangement', 'mode'. As one engineer stated, the term system 'is neither more nor less than method' (*Engineering Magazine*, November 1904: 211). Hounshell explains that early users 'did not consciously endow "system" with great significance or with transcendent qualities' (Hounshell 1984: 16). It was only during the twentieth century that 'system' developed into a dynamic construct with abstract and deductive qualities.

Historians tend to agree that the concept—or more accurately, the expression—'system' originated in 1851 at the Crystal Palace Exhibition in London. The official catalogue of the exhibition did not use the term system, but an American manufacturer of revolvers, Samuel Colt, was the center of attention and was invited to deliver an address before the Institution of Civil Engineers. Colt never referred to his method of manufacture as 'system', but during the discussions one engineer referred to 'Colonel Colt's system of manufacturing'. Subsequently, the editor of *Civil Engineer* and *Architect's Journal* summarized the event and evoked the terms 'system' and the 'American system' (Hounshell 1984: 331). In 1853 Charles Tomlinson published an edition of his *Rudimentary Treatise on the Construction of Locks*, contrasting the 'handicraft system' with the 'factory system', and observing that the 'system of manufacturing on a large scale [was] more nearly universal in the United States than in England' (ibid.). Subsequently, the British commissioners to the New York Crystal Palace Exhibition reused in their 1854 report the expression 'American system of manufactures'. Following this report the British Parliament appointed a committee to study the 'existing system' of arms, referring again to the 'American plan', the 'Springfield principle', the 'Springfield system', and the 'almost perfect system of Samuel Colt' (Hounshell 1984: 332). By 'system' they basically referred to the uniformity and interchangeability of parts.[4] The publication of the autobiography of James Nasmyth, an inventor in the toolmaking industry, edited by Samuel Smiles in New York (1883), 'solidified the term American system, at least for later-day historians' (Hounshell 1984: 334).

Twelve years prior to Taylor's first public appearance, James See, a central figure in ASME and a correspondent for *American Machinist*, referred to the sewing machine industry as a 'scientific system of production' (*American Machinist*, 16 June 1883: 2–3). In 1890, B. F. Spalding linked the American system to interchangeable manufacture. In an article in *American Machinist* he said, 'It was for such doings as these that the term "American" was bestowed upon the system, and it was a title earned, won, and granted in the open field' (*American Machinist*, 6 November 1890: 2–4; See also *American Machinist*, 13 November 1890: 2–3; *American Machinist*, 20 November 1890: 11–12). Spalding further clarified the term 'system':

The American system is based upon the perfection of the units that are combined in the total which the complete machine represents. It considers the whole as a combination of integers, rather than as the sum of added fractions. It individualizes each piece and gives it importance, with special attention to its peculiarities. Each operation is the work of a specialist. The excellence of the whole is assured by the attention which the system secures to every part. (*American Machinist*, 6 November 1890: 2–4)

The features of 'system' that are enacted in this statement are 'wholeness'—a property which cannot be summarized by added fractions—and 'interdependence' of the different parts.

As far as the historiography of systems is concerned, Hounshell argues that J. W. Roe, a Yale professor of mechanical engineering, provided modern historians with their understanding of the origin of the expression 'American system'. In his 1914 article in *American Machinist*, Roe suggested that the 'system' of interchangeable manufacture is of American origin (*American Machinist*, 17 December 1914: 1079–84). This statement was reproduced in books and periodicals and was cited by subsequent historians of technology and engineering (*American Machinist*, 16 August 1923: 239; *American Machinist*, 27 September 1923: 463–7; and many others).

The glorification of the 'American system' occurred at a time when the spirit of Exceptionalism dominated American thought, prior to the Progressive era. In the context of industry, manufacturers and engineers conceptualized the development of machines and technology as unique. They argued that the USA had the best industry, the best workmen, and the best system of production. James W. See (who used the pseudonym Chordal) wrote in 1883 that 'Our American systems of labor-saving machinery and devices are probably, in a general way, the most marvelous and perfect in the world' (*American Machinist*, 5 May 1883: 4). In this vein, Horace Arnold (also known as Henry Roland) claimed in *American Machinist* in 1903, 'the United States has the best toolmakers' (10 October 1903: 1367–69).

Fordism was the ultimate symbol of a perfect and unique American system of manufacturing. Engineers at Ford were proud of their designs and invited technical journalists to tour around the shops and describe the methods of 'mass production' (Hounshell 1984). 'System, system, system!' wrote an enthusiastic visitor to Ford to the *Detroit Journal*, describing its production process (quoted in Hounshell 1984: 229). During 1913–15, Frederick Colvin and Horace Arnold published articles on Ford Motors in *American Machinist* and in *Engineering Magazine*.[5] Through personal contacts with Harold Wills, Colvin received an invitation to visit the plant in Detroit to watch Ford's revolutionary system of mass production. With more than 100 photographs of the various installations and operations, Colvin disseminated the news that created a stir in journalistic circles. Colvin documented carefully how 'every critical part of the Model T was machined in standard fixtures and checked by standard gauges both during and after the operation sequence' (Hounshell 1984: 229). According to Hounshell, Colvin's understanding of the concept of system evolved during his visits to Ford Motors. Colvin was impressed with the order of machine tools and their sequencing:

So thoroughly is the sequence of operation followed that we not only find drilling machines sandwiched in between heavy millers and even punch presses, but also carbonizing furnaces and babbitting equipment in the midst of the machines. This reduces the handling of work to the minimum; for, when a piece has reached the carbonizing stage, it has also arrived at the furnace which carbonizes it, and, in case of work to be finished by grinding, the grinders are within easy reach when it comes from the carbonizing treatment. (Quoted in Hounshell 1984: 229)

The order with which Colvin was so fascinated was described by a Ford's machine-tool expert in the following way: ' "The machines are arranged very much like the tin-can machines"—one right after the other' (ibid.: 229). To both the local expert and to the visitor, the American system was equated with sequential order.

Hounshell claims that the glorified belief in the uniqueness of American technology still affects the work of historians to this date. Although contemporary historians have acknowledged that technology can be easily transferred across boundaries and recognize its universal nature, 'they have nevertheless continued to celebrate Yankee ingenuity while suggesting implicitly that new technology in the United States after the Civil War was largely homegrown, democratic, and superior' (Hounshell 1989: 216). Such a tone, Hounshell argues, is still part of 'nationalistic contemporary work'. He believes that the contemporary exhibition at the Smithsonian National Museum of American History continues to reinforce the image that the United States had established an independent technical tradition and was thus ready to assume a position of world leadership. To refute the uniqueness hypothesis, Hounshell notes the European origin of engineering theory in thermodynamics, mechanics, hydrodynamics, aerodynamics, electrodynamics, statics, and other important areas. Hounshell's critique of American Exceptionalism alludes to an interesting epistemological circularity according to which social scientists tend to examine the world using nineteenth- century analytic categories and explanations—in this case the Exceptionalist thesis—in order to explain the nineteenth-century social world (Meyer 1988).

Regarding the evolution of nineteenth-century 'systems' ideology, Hounshell argues that the notion of systems referred not only to order, but also to uniformity and standardization of machine tools. The production engineers at Ford placed accuracy at the top of the list in machine-tool design since they were 'excited by the rationality of absolute interchangeability of parts and painfully aware of the problems created by non-interchangeability' (Hounshell 1984: 230). The fact that engineers assigned a premium to rationality through uniformity was manifested in the movement for standardization that emerged in US industry in the early 1880s.

## 2.2.2 The engineering ideology of standardization

With factories growing more widespread, and with the appearance, in the 1880s, of the first integrated corporations, the 'need' for standardized production processes became paramount. Mechanical engineers became more concerned with the problem of systematizing and standardizing the materials with which they worked and with rationalizing the manufacture of machinery. The movement to standardization received glowing evaluations from G. K. Burgess, a director of the National Bureau of Standards. In a 1927 reflection on fifty years (1877–1927) of standardization activity he wrote:

The phenomenal development of the standardization movement has been accomplished almost wholly within the past half century . . . The progress from year to year is marked with substantial contribution and extension of scope, affecting international as well as national relations, securing economies of production and distribution, improving standard of living and influencing in many ways advantageously our whole modern civilization. (*American Machinist*, 19 May 1927: 808)

According to Burgess, American society had started to realize the profits yielded by 'sane standardization'. This quest for 'sane standardization' in industry emerged as a property of engineering work at the beginning of the nineteenth century, and turned into a full-fledged movement of 'engineering rationality'.

The first clear awareness of standardization appeared among Philadelphia machine builders as early as the 1830s. A group of engineers and machine builders in the Franklin Institute investigated the most effective use of waterpower, the strength of materials, and the causes of steam-boiler explosions. Many individuals who were later involved with the formation and the operation of ASME had ties with the Franklin Institute and subscribed to its publication, *Journal of the Franklin Institute*. In addition to furnishing technical designs, the journal reprinted information on studies conducted in Europe and elsewhere (e.g. 'Animal Strength', *Journal of the Franklin Institute* 5, 1828: 109). Philadelphia thus grew to become the center of American machine builders prior to the Civil War (Sinclair 1980: 46). One Philadelphia entrepreneur, William Sellers, was the first to propose an American standard screw thread system in 1864. In 1876, Charles B. Dudley was hired to establish a chemical laboratory at the Pennsylvania Railroad Company, perhaps the first corporate laboratory in the United States. His laboratory focused on standardization, and on the testing of supplies that were used by the railroad. Hounshell explains that Dudley devoted his professional life to the establishment of standards for industrial materials. His work at Pennsylvania Railroad developed into a national movement and led to the establishment of the American Society for Testing Materials, of which Dudley served as president (Hounshell 1996).[6]

During the rapid growth of industry in the 1880s, different industrial competitors sought to promote their own unique methods of production. Technological operations thus became diversified, which in turn led to confusion in production and to a duplication of efforts, particularly in machine shops and in the heavy industries. As Harold B. Maynard, a manager from the Westinghouse Electric and Manufacturing Co. in Pittsburgh, cautioned, 'standardization is so vital to efficient production that methods and machine parts should be kept as standard as possible'. Maynard explained that the standardization of materials minimizes stocks of raw materials, shortens time taken to complete a task, and avoids the danger of running out of material at an important time (*American Machinist*, 6 May 1926: 729). Not only was lack of standardization considered costly, it was also thought to retard efforts to develop regularity in production. When Henry Towne attempted to gather information on procedures used in the United States to test the strength of iron and steel, he discovered that there was not even a common language for analysis or comparison (Sinclair 1980: 145). From an engineering standpoint this was untenable. Planning production, and design and performance of equipment, it was thought, required uniform industrial specifications and interchangeable parts. For example, burner threads in the gaslight industry should be standardized since fixtures and burners needed to be interchangeable. Standardization and progress were thus equated. As Oberlin Smith, an engineer, inventor, and writer, argued in 1889, standards were 'powerful tools for the advancement of civilization' (Sinclair 1980: 145).

During the first twenty years of its existence, ASME encouraged the government to support the standardization of experimental activities in industry. Robert Thurston, president of ASME, envisioned in his inaugural address, 'We are to endeavor to hasten the approach of that great day when we shall have acquired a complete and symmetrical system of mechanical and scientific philosophy' (Calvert 1967: 169). In the first annual meeting of ASME, George Stetson, of the Morse Twist Drill Company, read a paper entitled 'Standard Sizes of Screw Threads', and Coleman Sellers, a partner in William Sellers and Company, presented a paper analyzing the metric system of standardization (Sinclair 1980: 47). Subsequently, one of the society's prominent figures, Oberlin Smith, made a comprehensive statement in which he demanded order and system in experiments and the elimination of duplicated efforts. Experiments had to be recorded and made accessible to the mechanical engineering community in a properly indexed form. Smith told the society in 1881 that only the steam engine was 'rationalized' and the problem of 'ascertaining by tentative methods the fitness, strengths and qualities of different materials' had never been systematically attempted because industry was only concerned with profits (Calvert 1967: 171). Hence, systematization and profit-making were not always congruent. Standards for screw threads and steam engines were only the beginning of the systematization impulse, according to Smith. In a series of articles, Smith pleaded for the adoption of systematic nomenclature of machine details in order to achieve systematic manufacturing (*American Machinist*, 17 November 1888: 2; *American Machinist*, 31 October 1885: 1). He thought that the society should standardize shop drawing symbols, wire gauge, pulleys and line shafting, machine screws, nut bevels, key-seats, drawing boards, and mechanical dictionaries (Sinclair 1980: 50). Smith hoped for the establishment of a central council for the systematic direction of these activities and envisioned a day when 'system shall replace chaos'.[7] As Sinclair suggested, Smith's model was something halfway between *Engineering Index* and the National Bureau of Standards, neither of which existed at the time (Sinclair 1980: 42).

Likewise, Thomas Egleston of the Columbia University School of Mines pushed for the formulation and enforcement of a uniform code of methods for testing. According to Egleston, the systematization of practices and the creation of standards were expected to yield predictability and regularity in production, and greater control over anomalies. William Kent was the chairman of the committee which reported to ASME in 1885 on standard methods of conducting steam-boiler tests. Kent demonstrated to a room full of mechanical engineers that each of them used a different method of testing steam boilers (Sinclair 1980: 145). He explained that in the absence of standards, 'every engineer who makes a boiler test makes a rule for himself, which may be varied from time to time to suit the convenience or interests of the party for whom the test is made' (Sinclair 1980: 51). According to Kent, standard codes granted that tests transcend testers and circumstances, and yield objective judgements.

Contemporary engineering magazines contributed to this view. Judging by the content of the *Transactions of the ASME*, discussions of codes and standards took up 10 percent more of the agenda of mechanical engineering at the end of the 1880s than at the beginning of the decade (Shenhav 1995: 559). An examination of *American Machinist* shows an increasing rate of discussions on standardization. Whereas in 1880 references to standardization were few and far between, they intensified at the end of the decade to include discussions about the standard taper of gas and steam pipe taps; editorials advocating the establishment of the United States Board of Tests; or criticism of the Master Car Builders' Association, which had hesitated to adopt one standard from 3,000 car coupler patents (*American Machinist*, 19 May 1927: 808–9). Letters from mechanical engineers to *American Machinist* called for an end to 'mechanical provincialisms', and encouraged the introduction of standard terms for machine parts (*American Machinist*, 9 April 1881: 6). Rather than using designations such as a 'lower-left-hand-cutting-blade-set-screw-lock nut', it was proposed that a comprehensive system of letters, numbers, and symbols should be introduced to rationalize the description of machine parts. In 1893 *American Machinist* encouraged a movement in favor of a standard size for trade catalogues (*American Machinist*, 2 March 1893: 8). The great need for uniformity in the size of catalogues was perceived as a matter of efficiency. Lack of uniformity would result in imperfect filing and in the loss of a great amount of valuable information. The editors stated that they had decided to practice what they preached by adopting an ASME standard for catalogues. In 1897, *American Machinist* told its readers that standardized machinery produces more in a given time than can be done otherwise (*American Machinist*, 28 October 1897: 820; quoted in Litterer 1986: 48). In 1898, the year the American Section of the International Association for Testing Materials was established, John Dunlap told his readers in *Engineering Magazine*, 'It is most gratifying to friends of the movement [of standard specifications in testing materials] . . . to find how appreciative a reception is given to the fruits of their work' ('The Progress of the International Association for

Testing Materials', January 1900: 603). Dunlap demonstrated in a series of articles on the Topeka shops of the Topeka & Santa Fe Railway that standardization
was vital for efficient production (*Engineering Magazine*, January 1907:
609–20). He also reviewed a paper by Harrington Emerson published in
*American Engineer* and *Railroad Journal* which offered concrete examples of the
economic benefits derived from standardization (*Engineering Magazine*, August
1907: 783).

However, the origin of the movement for standardization was not entirely
economic or efficiency based. An important impetus to the movement was the
concern engineers had regarding safety issues in technology. Several events raised
public interest in the safety-standardization equation during the last quarter of
the nineteenth century. Particularly acute was the issue of steam boilers, which
had a tendency to explode, causing injuries and loss of life, despite precautions
and stronger construction. Under the leadership of F. R. Stevens, Congress was
convinced in 1872 to appropriate $100,000 for an investigation to determine
the exact causes of boiler explosions (Calvert 1967). One of the study's major
conclusions was the urgent need to standardize the production of boilers and
their parts. By that time only ten states and nineteen municipalities had laws in
force to regulate the construction, inspection, and operation of boilers. This
meant a variation in compatibility and certification. As Sinclair argues, if one
thinks of the steam-boiler industry as a single community—of manufacturers,
consumers, inspectors, and insurers—then standardization was necessary
(Sinclair 1980: 147). Members were convinced that the formal adoption of standards would increase control, and would help a great deal in resolving the legal
disputes surrounding tests in materials and machines. A bill embodying the
suggestions was introduced in Congress, and in 1884 ASME established a
committee to formulate a uniform code of methods for testing boilers
(*Transactions of the ASME*, 6, 1884–5: 16–17).

In the same year, *American Machinist* analyzed different versions of boiler tests
and encouraged ASME to get involved. ASME, the magazine suggested, could
form a committee to examine standard parts of machine tools better to eliminate
disasters and to facilitate the compatibility of products in the market. In 1892
the society held a special session in Philadelphia to discuss the need for standard
tests for the strength of materials. For all practical purposes, the question of
ASME policy regarding standards was settled in 1895. The resolution came out
of a reconsideration of uniform boiler-testing methods (Sinclair 1980: 56). In
1914 the society published the first edition of the ASME's Boiler and Pressure
Vessel Code.[8] The committee report justified the code, citing safety considerations. Its primary concern was 'to put an end to the killing of so many men'
(Sinclair 1980: 146). By then (1914) there were literally hundreds of organizations publishing standards, most formulated without systematic methods of
cooperation or exchange of information. To unify these efforts, the American
Engineering Standards Committee was formed as a coordinating body.

Despite the fact that standardization was stimulated by 'external' needs of efficiency and industrial safety, the creation of standards was also rooted in the work of physical scientists who laid the groundwork for engineering standardization.[9] Scientists developed measurement devices and dictated their own imperative standard of precision. James Watt, back in the early nineteenth century, for example, had encountered considerable difficulty trying to secure the right tools to bore engine cylinders with the uniformity demanded by his own designs (Noble 1977). America's first Nobel laureate, A. A. Michelson, invented and perfected an apparatus for the measurement of physical length. The attainment of perfect measures initialized a dynamic in which further improvements were generated that corroborated the need to standardize.

As an outcome of their scientific work, two university professors, H. A. Rowland and M. B. Snyder, presented to the National Conference of Electricians a report outlining a proposed National Bureau of Physical Standards. This was in 1884, three years prior to the establishment of the first national technical institute for standards in Germany (*American Machinist*, 19 May 1927: 809). Another scientist, Henry S. Pritchett, developed an instrument used to standardize time in the central time zone when it was inaugurated in 1883 (Noble 1977: 72). In 1900 Pritchett became the president of MIT. When Fred Halsey delivered his paper expressing objections to the adoption of the metric system in the machine-tool industry (described below), Pritchett denounced him and supported governmental standardization for industrial and scientific matters. At that time, the Office of Weights and Measures, headed by Charles Sanders Pierce—the philosopher of pragmatism—was barely functioning.[10] Pritchett convinced Samuel Stratton, a physicist from the University of Chicago, to help him reorganize the office. Later he prepared a report on the necessity of a Bureau of Standards. Lyman Gage, Secretary of the Treasury, who was one of the promoters of Chicago's World Colombian Exposition of 1893, helped pass a bill endorsing the creation of the bureau in 1902. Its establishment was in part an outgrowth of small units in the Coast and Geodetic Survey, the oldest government bureau. Testifying before the Senate committee, Gage spelled out the role of standards in 'the search for a new social order' (Noble 1977: 74). He pleaded 'recognition by the government of an absolute standard, to which fidelity in all relations of life affected by that standard is required'. Gage justified the need for standards, saying, 'We are the victims of looseness in our methods; of too much looseness in our ideas; of too much of that sort of spirit, born out of our rapid development, perhaps, of a disregard or a lack of comprehension of the binding sanction of accuracy in every relation of life' (Noble 1977: 75).

These efforts in favor of standardization and the elimination of technical uncertainties placed the mechanical engineer at the epicenter of industrial conduct. By the 1920s, the standardization of industrial products and the role of the mechanical engineer as an expert in making production predictable and rational were widely accepted, but not without objections and conflicts, as we see in the next section.

### 2.3 Opposition to standardization

Despite its sweeping influence, not everyone in mechanical engineering circles was in concordance with the ideology of standardization. For example, Louis Bell, a university professor and editor of the *Electrical World*, believed, 'Standardization, however desirable from a pecuniary standpoint, means the cessation of active improvement.' Bell explained that the 'goods of types standardized for domestic trade do not always or often meet the requirements of, for instance, the South American markets, and the increasing demands of those countries'. It also led toward inflexibility which 'extends to the methods of distribution as well' (*Engineering Magazine*, September 1906: 801–8).

In what follows, I attempt to problematize the impression that standardization was inevitable. I do so by evidencing the struggle of various interest groups against this ideology. If standardization is considered an instance of industrial rationalization, my describing it thus also carries an important implication for the study of rationality. While most economic and organizational writings have viewed rationality as naturally unfolding, I hope to demonstrate that its development was conflictual, debated, and circular. In the mid-1880s there was, in fact, considerable opposition within ASME about whether to adopt, or to try to enforce, standards arbitrarily.

In 1889 James W. See, a correspondent for *American Machinist*, gave a speech before ASME in which he attacked the lack of standards for such various items as carriage clips, washers, bricks, picture frames, needles, and files. See pointed out that 'the arts are full of reckless things that had better be standardized' (Sinclair 1980: 145). Naming over a hundred items, he called for the creation of a division in the Patent Office, and of a government bureau, which would record all standards. See maintained that government oversight would guard against confusion.

Paradoxically, the individuals who represented the so-called 'shop culture' in ASME—Oberlin Smith, Coleman Sellers, and Henry Towne—supported this position. Robert Thurston, and other leaders of the 'school group', opposed it. Sinclair argued that one would have expected the opposite, i.e. that the adoption of standards would be costly to the shop and therefore would generate opposition from this camp. This alignment between shop-oriented engineers behind See's proposal makes sense only when one realizes that See's proposal suggested only recording (mainly with some sort of industrial census) and not establishing standards. Recording was insufficient for the educators and was beneficial for the shop representatives.[11] Most school-oriented engineers perceived themselves as arbiters of standards, and they preferred a centralized establishment of standards by governmental and engineering bodies.

Liberal shop-oriented engineers reasoned that the free market should regulate standardization. They argued that standardization constrains free trade, is costly, and interferes with the freedom of industrial producers and their entrepreneurial spirit. They argued that few individuals possessed the competence to judge a standard anyway, that the adoption of a standard implied business partnership with those engaged in making and selling articles affected by the standard, that a standard would be difficult to change once adopted, and that ASME would be held legally responsible for pecuniary damage done to those forced by its action to adopt a standard (Calvert 1967: 177). The opposition succeeded and the society did not adopt the recommendations.[12]

*American Machinist* reported, during the debate, on the various positions, and it particularly emphasized the 'objection of manufacturers to making the things they manufacture interchange with those made by other manufacturers' (*American Machinist*, 4 July 1889: 8). Despite their ambivalent position—being associated with both shop owners and ASME—the editors supported James See and assumed the task of convincing manufacturers that their objection was erroneous. They argued that lack of standardization 'holds the trade'. Without standardization, they said, producers who go out of business will hurt other producers who will not be able to find alternative parts. Standardization, they continued, is a method of integration and progress since 'the establishment of one standard is a help towards the establishment of others'. The editors concluded, 'Standardizing articles of manufacture is something that should be done with due deliberation, or more harm than good may be done.' The consequences of this debate were evident in another one over the metric system, which was supposed to allow convenient standardization and simple calculation. In the 1890s there was a new push for the metric system among the new and big industries and among professional engineers and scientists. Industrial figures such as Andrew Carnegie, Thomas Edison, George Westinghouse, Alexander Graham Bell, and Henry Ford favored the system. Small-scale machine owners who had already invested capital and could not afford the consequences of the change stood against it. Being in the same camp, leaders of the shop-oriented engineers in ASME—mainly Coleman Sellers, Fred Halsey, and Henry R. Worthingon— led the majority of ASME to vote against 'any legislation tending to make obligatory the introduction of the metric system of measurement into our industrial establishments' (Noble 1977: 77). A committee was established in ASME in 1896, 'in opposition to legislation to make the metric system and its use compulsory' (Noble 1977: 77). The opposition succeeded, and the debate was not revived again until the First World War.

In 1916, at the National Conference on Weights and Measures (held in Washington under the auspices of the National Bureau of Standards), the conferees endorsed the metric system and appointed a committee to advocate its adoption. It was argued that manufacturers who export their products must use redundant systems, resulting in confusion and extra costs. However,

representatives of manufacturing interests at the conference opposed the resolution on the grounds that several large manufacturers had tried the metric system
and found it unsatisfactory (*Engineering Magazine*, August 1916: 749). In a
1919 editorial, *American Machinist* attacked the proposal to adopt the metric
system: 'The baccalaureate Bolsheviki who believe that the sun, moon and stars
operate exclusively on the metric system, are making another attempt to upset
America's industrial digestion by forcing us to take a dose of their dangerous
concoction' (*American Machinist*, 8 May 1919: 909–10). The editorial ridiculed
attempts made by various organizations to submit a petition to President
Wilson. These organizations, the editors said, ask President Woodrow Wilson
and his administration:

that they pause a moment from their trivial duties of rearranging world boundaries and
national relations, to take up the really important work of abolishing the yard and the
inch. . . . What a pathetic picture! Think of the poor fishermen who are now deprived of
their catches because they have no metric worms, of the canners and growers who see
golden opportunities withheld them because this Government does not compel by law
the asparagus and tomato plants to grow to metric measure. . . . We strongly advise you
as a precaution against a paralyzing industrial calamity which would follow the abandonment of our standard tools, gages, jigs and fixtures, and more serious than that, the
abandonment of our instinctive familiarity with our own measures—to tell your
congressman what the loss of the inch and the foot would mean to your business.
(*American Machinist*, 8 May 1919: 909–10)

Frederick Halsey, who led the campaign against the metric system in the late
nineteenth century, expressed his opinions again in 1921 when two bills were
presented before the committees of both the House and the Senate (Bills HR
15,240 and S. 4,675). The bills demanded that within four years after the
passage and approval of the Act, no one should manufacture or purchase any
weight or measure 'or weighing or measuring device designed, constructed,
marked, or graduated to determine, indicate or deliver weights or measures in
any other system than the metric system of weights and measures' (*American
Machinist*, 28 April 1921: 735). Halsey attacked this proposition. In an article in
*American Machinist*, he came out 'against the claim that the system is universal
nearly everywhere, we now have proof that it is universal nowhere. And against
the repeated assertion that the change is easy, we have proof that it is of such
difficulty that no country has completed while few have made much progress
toward it' (*American Machinist*, 12 May 1921: 815). The editors of *American
Machinist* made a point of publishing reports estimating the costs of these
changes to manufacturers, including evidence received from L. W. Wallace, executive secretary of the Federated American Engineering Societies (FAES), regarding the financial estimates of these industrial transformations. A letter received
by the American Institute of Weights and Measures from a Cincinnati firm
provided a comprehensive report with cost estimates covering such changes. The
estimate of $341,000 was accompanied with a covering letter: 'This report was

made up very carefully, and the result is simply astounding. The cost would amount to confiscation of profits for many years to come, if they were years of normal profits' (*American Machinist*, 24 March 1921: 513–741). *American Machinist* elaborated:

While the cost is a great burden and will undoubtedly be resented, a far greater burden is laid on the machinists by the metric legislator. By compelling the workman to use unfamiliar and unhandy tools, by insisting that he think in a strange language alien to his experience, he is deprived of value, of his capital, of his possession. (*American Machinist*, 28 April 1921: 735)

It is interesting to note that this exact rationale was used by the workers' associations against the introduction of the Taylor system and the codes issued by the planning room ten years earlier (Clawson 1980; Shenhav 1994). In 1926, the editors renewed their opposition to a compulsory metric bill (known as HR 10): 'If you can devise one [method] better calculated to confuse and hamper business transactions, you deserve a leather medal' (*American Machinist*, 28 January 1926: 174).

Manufacturers' opposition to the standardization movement was not exclusively in relation to the metric bill but to a variety of suggestions to impose outside standards. In a controversial article entitled 'Wake up America!', Louis Bell warned the engineering community that there are dangers 'lurking in overconfidence in system' and that workmen became 'mere belts, wheels, and oilcans' where 'one can hardly find an artisan' (*Engineering Magazine*, September 1906: 801–8). An editorial in *Engineering Magazine* in 1911 specified the dangers associated with standardization, acknowledging the limits of human reason: 'The chief risk lies in the tendency to concentrate the fixing of standards in a planning department which to be perfect should have, but in practice never can have all the wisdom of the universe.' The editors further announced the perils associated with standardization: 'The policy of close task regulation which discountenances initiative, at least until the worker has fully mastered the standard way, may silence and dismiss the innovator who has genius of invention but not manual skill to learn the standard way.' Nevertheless, the editors took a pragmatic approach:

Granting the expediency, indeed the necessity, of standardization . . . We must not lose sight of its attendant and inherent danger—crystallization . . . The problem is to suppress the folly of individualism which prefers sliding down a rope to using the standardized staircase, and yet not suppress the benefactor of standards who can evolve the escalator. (*Engineering Magazine*, September 1911: 977)

Even as late as 1923 we find evidence that manufacturers were reluctant to accept the logic of standardization. An article in *American Machinist* attempted to convince reluctant manufacturers that a 'conservative policy of manufacturers regarding changes in methods of production' is a hindrance to standardization (*American Machinist*, 28 June 1923: 937–9). After listing the fears of manufacturers, the writer concludes: 'While some of these hindrances are purely imaginary, nevertheless they are present; and, if the movement for standardization is to continue to gain adherents, find a place in a growing number of manufacturing plants and become the means of improving the general industrial efficiency of the nation, provisions must be made for their removal.'

The systematization movement proved stronger than its opponents. The support by engineers was weighty. 'Most engineers believed that it was desirable to have rationalized standards of measurement, nomenclature, fittings, screws, nuts, bolts, and everything else with which they came in daily contact' (Calvert 1967: 178). In addition to the strong influence of engineers there were at least three additional social forces that supported systematization's victory. First, there was the matter of the frequent accidents that were attributed to the lack of standards. These were not exclusive to the steam-boiler industry, which I described, but occurred in other industries as well. In 1904, for example, Baltimore's entire business district was destroyed by fire, despite their having an ample water supply with which to fight the blaze, because the screw threads on the fire hydrants did not fit couplings on the hoses of fire engines that arrived from other towns (Sinclair 1980). Such incidents reinforced the claim for the urgent need to standardize.

Second, standardization was supported by large firms as a response to the antitrust movement. As Haber (1964) and Hounshell (1996) explain, Progressive activists (such as Louis Brandeis) demanded that monopolistic firms increase their efficiency. Standardization seemed to eliminate duplication, to lower costs, and to be congruent with the demand for efficiency. This logic is partly corroborated by Noble when he observes that standardization was a more straightforward affair in industries that were dominated by large firms (Noble 1977). The standardization program at Westinghouse, for example, was adopted throughout the electrical industry. Likewise, standards for the telephone industry were developed by AT&T and adopted by the Federal Communication Commission. This led to institutional justifications for the need to adopt standards, given that dominant firms had already done so (see *American Machinist*, 3 July 1913: 15); this logic is in line with the mimetic isomorphism argument of institutional theorists (e.g. DiMaggio and Powell 1983). Standardization in the chemical industry, a more diverse industry, had to await the consolidation of the industry in the post-war era.

Finally, the First World War stimulated some governmental activity in standardization. During 1915–16, *American Machinist* was filled with information about the grinders for shell bodies, millers for shell bases, drilling machines, and special machinery for rifle manufacturing. Editor Leon Alford mobilized the war to legitimize standardization activities. Alford's efforts resulted in the book *Manufacture of Artillery Ammunition*, published in 1917 by McGraw-Hill, with contributions from Colvin, Suverkrop, Mawson, and Van Deventer (Jaffe 1957: 78). Alford aimed to codify 'principles of standardization and procurement of machine tools in organizing for American industrial preparedness'. His idea was that engineers could apply what they already knew in one field to what they were studying in another (Jaffe 1957: 77). Consequently, the National Screw Thread Commission was established in 1918 (and was made permanent in 1926); and the Federal Specifications Board was created in 1921, unifying the multiple purchase requirements of the federal government. It promulgated nearly 500 specifications which were mandatory for government purchases. In the same year, President Hoover organized the Division of Simplified Practice, which developed procedures to cut down the number of sizes, varieties, and grades of numerous commodities. The Bureau of Standards published a Standard Year Book describing the standardizing activities in the country and issued a Directory of Specifications which gave a picture of a 'needless multiplicity of specifications'.

During the 1920s, texts on standardization, tolerance, and systematization of machine tools were plentiful. An editorial in *American Machinist* said: 'Standardization is in the air. Let us all work for rational standards for such parts as do not hamper future development of design' (*American Machinist*, 25 May 25 1922: 789). Condit and Colvin said that people who argue that standardization is against individualism forget that 'the only man who can freely express his individuality is a Crusoe on a desert island'. They explained that the minute a second individual appears,

Some of the first settler's individuality must be restricted. And restriction increases as towns, cities and countries grow larger. You might prefer a 20-ft. sidewalk in front of your house but if all the neighbors felt that one 10 ft. wide was sufficient, your individuality would go a-glimmering . . . If anyone wishes to express his individuality by buying odd-sized tires, machines, bolts or windows for his house, he can always be accommodated—at a price. (*American Machinist*, 25 May 1922: 789)

A few years later Condit and Colvin explained that 'standardization and simplification continue to be misunderstood' since 'adopting standard sizes of grinding wheels does not mean that other sizes cannot be obtained when really needed'. The editors warned that standardization should not be extreme, and that standards should not be seen as 'infallible or fixed for all time' (*American Machinist*, 28 January 1926: 174). In one of the subsequent issues the editors examined the report submitted by the Plain Gage Committee of ASME. Considering the issue of tolerances they concluded that one should not go with precision to the $n$th degree, and create 'unnecessary accuracy' as scientists and engineers often do (*American Machinist*, 4 February 1926: 216).

The editors of *American Machinist* qualified their support of standardization, saying, 'A few fanatics standardize everything to its illogical conclusion.' Thus, as far as the editorial policy was concerned, it opposed extreme proposals of standardization. Nevertheless, 'Rational standardization should and will have the support of every level-headed engineer and business man.' The editors denied that standardization implied that all builders had the same production lines and the same general characteristics. Such fears were groundless, they argued, noting the wide variation in automobile design despite the fact that this industry was standardized to a greater extent than any other. To the editors, standardization meant 'the elimination of useless sizes and shapes and the use of such parts as having proved satisfactory, in as many machines as possible' (*American Machinist*, 13 October 1927: 596). On a different occasion, they encouraged the American Engineering Standards Committee to study standardization practices in the automobile industry (*American Machinist*, 30 December 1926: 1078). In another editorial, the editors referred to the automobile industry as the shining example of standardization: 'The Society of Automotive Engineers has adopted many standards and these have helped to make possible the improved quality and lower prices of automobiles. Yet these standards are constantly under exam-ination, and revisions are made whenever it seems advisable' (*American Machinist*, 17 July 1926: 958). From this example they deduced that—contrary to the policy of this industry—'the worst enemy of standardization is the man who considers any standard in any line as the last word and uses it as an alibi for not investigating the desirability of new and better methods'. The editors agreed that some limits to standardization are called for in order to encourage engi-neering innovation and creativity in design (*American Machinist*, 13 July 1922: 77). The editors also gave voice to the opposition that the movement for stan-dardization generated. For example, in 1920 they published a long letter from 'a well-known engineer' who concluded, 'I do not think there is any sense in attempting to standardize machine tools' (*American Machinist*, 10 April 1920: 286).

## 2.4 Standardization and the state

*American Machinist* dedicated a series of editorials in 1927 to a proposal to trans-form the American Engineering Standards Committee from a clearing house for standards into a standards-making body (*American Machinist*, 25 August 1927: 328. See also *American Machinist*, 6 October 1927: 552). The proposal reflected the complex forces behind standardization in America. Unlike the governments of other countries, such as Germany and France, the US government was not an active agent in the diffusion of industrial models (McCraw 1984; Hamilton and Sutton 1989; Dobbin 1994; Guillen 1994; Hounshell 1996). Despite pleas to the government throughout the years, the administration was a weak catalyst in the process of standardization and systematization, leaving initiatives to the private sector and the engineering societies.

An example of the weak contribution of the US government is the work of the Federal Trade Commission (FTC), which was founded in 1914 to establish standardized methods of market competition for corporations (see for example Kaufman, Zacharias, and Karson 1995). The editor of *Engineering Magazine* used a report issued by the FTC to support the claim that the introduction of a standard cost system is functionally necessary (*Engineering Magazine*, June 1916: 432). The editorial quoted statistics reported by the vice-chairman of the commission, revealing that only 10 percent of the manufacturers and merchants know what their costs are, and 40 percent rely on rough estimates. The remaining 50 percent use no method at all for estimating costs. The editor argued, 'these percentages may fairly be taken as indicative of our industrial efficiency'. Contrary to expectation, the introduction of cost systems was not promoted by manufacturers. It was principally engineers and accountants who pushed the systems agenda, and attempted to convince government officials to facilitate the introduction of cost systems into business. President Wilson 'warmly endorsed' the efforts of the FTC to introduce such systems. In a letter to Edward N. Hurley, the vice-chairman of the FTC, Wilson wrote (ibid.): 'I wish to commend your efforts generally, and in particular your endeavour to assist the small manufacturer and merchant to better his condition by helping him to improve the cost accounting methods.' President Wilson further endorsed the application of standardized methods to the management of business firms:

If we are to be an important factor in a world's market, we must be more thorough and efficient in production. The encouragement of trade associations and standardization and the installing of better cost accounting methods in our business concerns will go a long way toward accomplishing this end. (ibid.)

In August 1916 Dunlap acknowledged that 'the importance of right cost-keeping methods has been emphasized anew to the manufacturers of the country through the activities of the Federal Trade Commission, and particularly the efforts of Commissioner Hurley' (*Engineering Magazine*, August 1916: 747). But this was mainly lip service. The government was hardly active. Colvin and Condit explained this point: 'The technical men of the country have been doing a very difficult series of pioneer tasks for industry, but those responsible for industrial management are not yet generally awake to the fact that they as executives are alone responsible for bringing order out of the existing chaos in the field of standardization' (*American Machinist*, 19 May 1927: 809). That is, for all practical purposes, standardization emerged essentially as a professional project. This is in accordance with what comparative studies of economic practices have concluded. Frank Dobbin notes that while the French government, for example, took an active role in organizing national monopolies and in nationalizing the railroad industry, the US government's ICC (Interstate Commerce Commission) was paralyzed for years (Dobbin 1994). Or as Mauro Guillen observed, in Germany the government was instrumental in the rationalization process through the National Board of Efficiency (RKW), but in the USA the state was rather weak and had no role in the process (Guillen 1994). If anything, it retarded the process by banning the adoption of scientific-managerial techniques in the navy (see Chapter 3).

The editors of *American Machinist* often alluded to the German experience as a desired model of cooperation for standardization. In an editorial entitled 'The Amazing Progress of German Standardization', they observed that standardization was a never-ending process in that country: 'Each month sees a respectable volume of new standards printed and distributed' (*American Machinist*, 24 January 1924: 150). *American Machinist* referred to the strategic economic advantage associated with standardization, and reiterated that the administration provides only weak support to standardization, in comparison with the German government's efforts to facilitate one of the most complex and advanced research systems in the world prior to the war (Hounshell 1996).

The comparison between Germany and the USA highlights the reluctance of the federal state to impose standards in a firm way, partly since the government had no tradition of active involvement in the economy.[13] Even after the creation of the National Bureau of Standards in 1901, the formulation and promulgation of standards was left to the private sector (Noble 1977; Guillen 1994). Checks and balances, it was felt, would be achieved by the interplay between consumers and producers, and enhanced by various codes designed by professionals, who represented the public at large. By 1917 there were literally hundreds of organizations publishing all sorts of standards for industrial life, with little governmental orchestration.

In 1929, with growing signs that the economy had entered a severe economic depression, several European countries displayed orchestrated efforts 'to rationalize' the market and impose standardization in manufacturing. The deliberate 'rationalization' of the economy became a major project linking politics and economics.[14] As the report of the National Industrial Conference Board in Germany titled 'Rationalization of German Industry' explained,

Rationalisation, in its broadest sense, aims to eliminate errors of judgement due to faulty knowledge of market conditions by vesting the power to regulate production, fix prices and allocate territories in a central authority. Rationalisation represents the idea of enlightened leadership embracing an entire industry in its relation to other industries and to the national economy. (Mason 1931: 640)

These consolidated efforts in Europe left American professionals feeling some ambivalence. In an editorial in *American Machinist* that announced that 'there is a new word in the air . . . Rationalization', the editors told their readers that the entire German nation works toward this one objective (11 August 1927: 248). The editors were apprehensive about the possibility of establishing such a movement in the United States, but suggested that the USA should follow and examine the European experience. This position, which emphasized the universal nature of these processes, collided with the concept of American Exceptionalism. Indeed, a few years later, it was argued that the term 'rationalization' was originally American and had merely become a European name for Scientific Management (*American Machinist*, 30 October 1930: 690). This was in fact partly true since most developments of industrial efficiency in Europe were modeled after the US experience (Nolan 1994).

To be sure, rationalization was a problematic concept not only in the USA but in Germany as well. Urwick himself noted that the Germans had a strong prejudice against trusts and combines. It was clear that the concentration of power was possible only if necessary precaution—*die Rationalisierung*—was taken. A dubious psychological distinction was made between amalgamation of resources motivated by personal ambition or capitalist development, and integration with a deliberate unification of markets as part of a national economic and political scheme. Under such conditions, it is clear that the term rationalization assumed substantial national, political, and cultural variation. As Dobbin put it in a comparative analysis of railroad policy in the USA, Britain, and France: 'Political culture had an unmistakable effect on how these notions came to understand, and institutionalize, economic rationality' (Dobbin 1994: 214). In the United States, the closest explicit strategy to what Europeans meant by 'rationalization' was the post-First World War economic macro-management employed by the Department of Commerce under Herbert Hoover. This policy advanced the rapid spread of standardization and simplification and aimed to eliminate economic waste (Alchon 1985).

While in several European countries economic action was conceptualized and understood to be within the realm of politics, in the USA the economy was largely understood in either professional or market-based terms. This cross-national difference is essential to the argument advanced in this book. American actors conceptualized economic and organizational action in apolitical, decontextualized, terms. In the next chapters I describe how this process of depoliticization was developed in industrial America. I demonstrate the manner by which 'systems perspective'—originally political in nature—was stripped of its political associations and how subsequently American social sciences bought into these parameters.

### 2.5 Standardization and organization systems: the final frontier

The introduction of organization systems was stimulated both by the achievements of production engineers at the shop (or the plant) level (i.e. 'the American system') on the one hand, and by the activities of the standardization movement at the professional level on the other. Hounshell attempts to determine to what extent the reverse was true, namely, to what extent the discourse on systems stimulated production practices. Examining the experience in the Ford Motor Company, Hounshell suggests that such stimulation was likely to take place, since Fordism arose when Taylorism was at its peak during the period of Brandeis's testimony in the Eastern Rate case and the publication of *Principles of Scientific Management* in 1911. During this period, 'motion study' had been carefully examined in engineering periodicals and within engineering circles

(Hounshell 1984: 236). Ford engineers standardized work routines at Highland Park after they had analyzed jobs and workflow patterns according to the rules of Scientific Management. As early as 1912–13 they had a time-study department, known as the 'work standard department'. On the other hand, Hounshell cautions against facile conclusions in this regard. Ford himself claimed that the Ford Motor Company had not relied on Taylorism. As Horace Arnold acknowledged in 1914, 'In reply to a direct question he [Ford] disclaimed any systematic theory of organization and administration, or any dependence upon Scientific Management' (Hounshell 1984: 236). One should also, Hounshell says, not misjudge the difference between Taylorism and Fordism. Taylorism took a given production process and improved the efficiency of the workers through time and motion analyses and a differential piece-rate system of payment. Fordism sought to accomplish the same through mechanical means, by changing the machinery and the production process. It is probably safe to argue that the work of the systematizers and scientific managers, and the perfection of production processes, co-evolved. It is therefore impossible (and unnecessary) to decide which process determined the other.

Organization systems originated both in the practice and ideology of production processes. Indeed, there is evidence that the systematizers saw the system as a physical as well as abstract expression of the logic of production. For example, in an article entitled 'Organization versus System', the editor of *American Machinist* observed, ' "System" may be defined as the physical expression of the workings of the organization. The system is the tool of managers' (*American Machinist*, 29 April 1915: 750). The 'organization', on the other hand, was defined as 'a network of intangible ties that holds the executive together, defining their functions, responsibilities, authorities and requirements for cooperation'. This quote demarcates the physical origin from the abstract entity of system, to be described in the next chapters. At any rate, concurrent with the debates and struggles around standardization, this notion spilled over to organizations. This was expressed clearly in an editorial in *American Machinist*:

To the engineer one interesting phase of the matter is the movement toward standardization in business methods. The advantages of standards are so vital in connection with material things, and are so well recognized by manufacturers that we wonder that so little standardization has crept into the mechanism of business. We believe that in this field, at least, business can learn from the engineering profession. (*American Machinist*, 22 August 1908: 212)

As the standardization movement thrived with the expansion of technology and the increase in the number of engineers, the engineering domain expanded to include human and social elements.

The assembly line at Ford Motors, the American system of manufacturing, and the movement for standardization were the first steps in the development of organization systems. Even Adam Smith, who strongly objected to the idea that corporations can function efficiently, acknowledged the relevance of standardization and systematization to their performance. Smith argued, 'The only trades which seem possible for a joint stock company to carry on successfully, without an exclusive privilege, are those . . . Capable of being reduced to what is called a routine, or to such a uniformity of method as admits of little or no variation' (Smith 1937: 713). Smith's prophecy proved to be a self-fulfilling one. The engineers, who pioneered the standardization of instruments, gradually extended their expertise to the standardization of workers. The following chapter examines in detail the extension of systematization and standardization into the management of organizations. Within the Constructivist framework this is termed 'translation': elements distinct from one another—technical and organizational systems—are made homologous. I posit that mechanical engineers 'translated' elements from the distinct realm of the technical to the uniquely different sphere of the social and organizational (see Callon 1980; Latour 1987).

### Notes

1. A similar argument was made regarding scientists. See Hounshell 1996.
2. The four societies—American Society of Civil Engineers (ASCE), American Society of Mechanical Engineers (ASME), American Institute of Electrical Engineers (AIEE), and American Institute of Mining and Metallurgical Engineers (AIMM)—established an organizing conference to which 110 engineering and allied technical organizations and societies were invited. Humphrey reported that 60 percent of those invited attended and they represented an aggregate membership of over 100,000 individuals, or 83 percent of the membership of all organizations and societies invited. See *American Machinist*, 17 June 1920: 1320.
3. See Hounshell 1984: Appendix 1 for the evolution of the expression 'The American System of Manufactures'. See also Mayr and Post 1982; Hughes 1989*a*.
4. Charles F. Scribner observed in 1913 that 'the first application of the principles of interchangeable manufacturing can be traced to the making of firearms by Eli Whitney, at the beginning of the Civil War' (*American Machinist*, 4 September 1913: 399). Whatever version we take for the origin of production based on interchangeable parts, it belonged to the armament industry in the United States.
5. This series resulted in a book by Horace Lucien Arnold and Fay Leone Faurote, *Ford Methods and the Ford Shops* (1915). See Hounshell 1984: 228, 260; See also the editorial in *Engineering Magazine*, March 1913: 961.
6. Hounshell based his account on Steven Walter Usselman's Ph.D. dissertation 'Running the Machine: The Management of Technological Innovation on American Railroads, 1860–1910' (1985).
7. The full statement was 'when one well done calculation or experiment shall replace a thousand half done, and system shall replace chaos' (Calvert 1967: 171).
8. Again, there was opposition to the publication of the code. For example, John Clinton Parker protested against 'further backing of the propaganda for state control of boiler design'. See Sinclair 1980: 177.

9. For a review of the appearance of industrial R&D laboratories see Hounshell 1996.

10. The Office of Weights and Measures was established in 1836 to promote regulation and uniformity.

11. We should qualify this statement too. Sinclair argues that industrialists recognized a demand for systematization of production processes (1980). One of the first efforts to extend the rationalization of manufacturing was made by William Sellers, in Philadelphia in 1863. He proposed a standardized American screw thread and suggested a range of activities for a national engineering society.

12. Such a split did not take place among electrical and chemical engineers, whose field was more closely attached to the physical sciences. The American Institute of Electrical Engineers (AIEE) and the American Chemical Society established standards committees in the 1890s to coordinate standardization in the electrical and the chemical industries. The development of these industries was dependent on reliable instruments calibrated by standards for the measurement not only of length, weight, and volume but also pressure, heat, light, and magnetism to determine the rating, efficiency, and durability of machines, devices, and processes (see Noble 1977: 72).

13. For contradictory arguments see Kolko (1963) and Roy (1997). Kolko believes that the Progressive movement was, first and foremost, used by industrialists to encourage the government to consolidate market control, an outcome which capitalists could not have achieved without the participation of governmental bodies. Roy argues that the industrial corporation is a social and historical creation that evolved from the public corporation used by the state to accomplish public purposes and was given special privileges (e.g. monopoly, limited liability).

14. L. Urwick documented in this context a turning point in the development of the term 'rationalization' as an explicit 'visible hand' ideology. Urwick—one of the earliest management scholars—published in 1929 an article titled 'Rationalization: Europe's New Industrial Philosophy', in *Factory and Industrial Management* (an offspring of *Engineering Magazine*), January 1929: 38–40. He argued there that the term 'rationalization' first came into worldwide dominance as a result of a conference that took place in Geneva in 1927. The conference hosted economists, employers, and labor organizations from all over the world and was prompted by the depression and increasing unemployment rate. Among other resolutions that were made there, the conference announced that governments, public institutions, and professional and industrial organizations should encourage and promote the 'ascertainment' and comparison of the 'most efficient methods' to achieve rationalization. In the conference's view, 'rationalization' referred to a deliberate attempt to exercise rational control and the measure used to determine rational from non-rational was scientific. The conference participants juxtaposed a number of developments from various countries to be included under the term 'rationalization'.

# 3

# Colonizing the Mind: The Translation of Systematization to the Management of Organizations

'America,' said a witty foreigner, 'is God's own country—for any man who has a new system.'

(*Engineering Magazine*, August 1916: 678)

The previous chapter examined the technical project of systematization, advanced by engineers in the world of industry. In this chapter I add another layer to the meaning of 'system' as it was originally propagated by mechanical engineers.[1] I describe how engineers took this project one step forward, creating a grand vision of society, promoting it as a remedy for 'social problems', and inventing a new language. This new language became the backbone of American managerial ideology. I explore how it emerged out of this technical project to become a symbolic configuration for a political campaign in the public sphere. The icons of systems and efficiency—central to mechanical standardization—were now translated to social, political, and moral domains. Engineers disseminated their newly emerging vision through magazines and professional associations. In essence, engineers universalized their particularistic and peculiar agenda to claim it was of interest to humanity. By the 1920s, the power and legitimization of this newly emerging language was undeniable.

Theoretically, the analysis rests on the sociological-Constructivist stance that the human mind is a social one. I therefore assume that knowledge, science, and professional constructs are produced and shaped by human communities in institutionalized fields of knowledge.[2] Sociologists of knowledge argue that the very definition of a situation is the outcome of social negotiations within a particular field.[3] To define a condition as a 'social problem' it is first necessary to show that the situation is undesirable and that there are solutions available to remedy it, that the outcomes may be bettered. This approach to the development of knowledge emphasizes the diversity of choices inherent in any sphere of action and the socially constructed nature of empirical objects. Hence the question the Constructivist approach deals with is the selection of the course of action actually chosen and institutionalized. Accordingly, the authority of professionals, respected practitioners, and examples from neighboring fields can become part of a network that supports a particular claim to reality (Callon 1980; Latour 1987). It neither dismisses functional-instrumental arguments (usually accepted by organizational actors) nor does it argue that people's objective reality is unreal. Rather, it attempts to describe the manner in which such objective reality is constituted and constructed. In this, the Constructivist and the functional-instrumental logic provide two differing, not necessarily negating, theoretical stands.

The analysis which follows leans on the notion of 'translation'. Translation affirms the underlying unity between elements distinct from one another and involves creating convergences and homologies by relating things that were previously unrelated (Callon 1980; Latour 1986; Czarniawska and Sevon 1996). This notion postulates the existence of a single field of significations, concerns, and interests, the expression of a shared desire to arrive at the same result. The notion of 'system' was used by a network of engineer-managers, or more specifically practitioners in the field of mechanical engineering, as a rhetorical and practical device to promote their professional agenda and to justify their trespassing into the realm of management.[4] These engineers 'translated' the concept of system to be applicable to social and organizational problems, rendering them homologous with technical ones. Thus, the process of translation embodies the social construction of organizations and labor as 'engineerable'. The influence of this network, against the backdrop of the cultural and political forces existing at the time of the formation of management as a distinct discipline, best explains the reason and the manner in which the concept of 'system' was translated to become central in organization theory and management studies. In the following I show how this 'translation' was achieved.

### 3.1 Molding an engineering-based social thought

> It is beginning to be recognized that the human as well as the non-human machine must be standardized . . . By human machines is meant the industrial workers themselves. As physical entities such workers are complexes of body and mind. They are human organisms, and may be regarded with reference to standards of industrial efficiency as human mechanisms. (*American Machinist*, 28 June 1923: 939)

In the 1850s, the first practicing managers were civil engineers,[5] but it was mechanical engineering that spawned and nurtured the management movement until it was 'ready and strong enough' to attempt to reform and reorganize American industry (Calvert 1967: 236). At first, mechanical engineers were professionally concerned with the formulation of uniform codes and standards, and with achieving predictability and regularity in production. With the rapid growth of the large corporate firm, and upon successfully dealing with technical uncertainties, mechanical engineers expanded their professional engagement to include the reduction of organizational uncertainty through the introduction of administrative systems. Engineers were well equipped to provide solutions and systems, such as the one perfected in Ford Motors, which seemingly provided order and certainty. They brought in professional road maps, tools, and the (predominant) metaphor that the organization is analogous to a machine composed of interchangeable parts. As Dunlap, editor of *Engineering Magazine*, summarized, 'The cold logic of a mechanical demonstration may be more effective in industrial reform than any sympathetic appeal of the humanitarian' (*Engineering Magazine*, November 1902: 223–30). Dexter S. Kimball, dean of engineering at Cornell University, advocated 'the extension of the principles of standardization to the human element in production' (Noble 1977: 83). The *American Machinist* asked, 'Should engineers interest themselves in sociology?' (*American Machinist*, 16 March 1905: 369). The editors reply in the affirmative, explaining: 'We think that the engineer is perhaps more bound by considerations of humanity to consider such things than is any other member of society, because his work produces such a profound result upon the manner of life of the majority of people living under modern conditions.'[6]

Engineering rationality of systematization and standardization started to expand, setting out to colonize human, social, political, moral, and economic issues in the management of the firm (e.g. *American Machinist*, 8 November 1906: 618–19). In other words, entities previously distinct became related, 'translated' into a single unified field (see Callon 1980; Latour 1987). *American Machinist* explicitly promoted 'the application of the methods of investigation adopted in physical researches' to social issues (*American Machinist*, 8 November 1906: 618–19). Elsewhere, a writer in *American Machinist* redefined the range of materials with which the mechanical engineer was and should be engaged: 'One of the most important, if not the most important, and at the same time most elusive, difficult to handle and fickle materials the mechanical engineer has to deal with is the human material, the man behind the lathe, miller or planer' (*American Machinist*, 21 January 1909: 90). An editorial in *Industrial Management* (previously *Engineering Magazine*) quoted Thomas Edison predicting that problems in human engineering will receive 'the same genius and attention which the nineteenth century gave to the more material forms of engineering' (*Industrial Management* (previously *Engineering Magazine*), October 1920: 4. Cited in Noble 1977: 257). After all, engineering was perceived not only as a technical endeavor but also as 'the noblest study of man' (*Engineering Magazine*, April 1892: 1).

The distinction between the worker and the machine was becoming blurred in mechanical engineering discourse. The following quotations from engineering periodicals of the time illustrate this well. 'There seems to be an ever increasing desire to make the worker more and more part of the machine he is manipulating, until even his understanding is mechanical' (*American Machinist*, 4 July 1891: 27). 'Mechanics and workmen are in a certain sense engines whose energies are directed toward a certain end' (*American Machinist*, 14 April 1884:

8). 'It is a difficult question, perhaps, to decide just to what extent a man employed in a manufacturing establishment should be considered as a mere machine, or a sentient being' (*American Machinist*, April 17 1894: 8). 'Hiring a man and buying a machine are very much alike' (*American Machinist*, 23 March 1900: 208). One writer put it most bluntly: 'There is no engine like the engine which pumps the blood through the human system. There are no pipe lines for the transportation of liquids that are comparable to the arteries and veins' (*American Machinist*, 11 August 1921: 226). The same author summarized this ideology:

Machines of iron and steel, however, are not the only machines which are essential to industry. They are not the only mechanisms which are subject to scientific analysis, and which are worthy of the closest scrutiny with regard to the speed at which they should be run, the care which they should receive, and the output which they should produce. To them must be added human machines. By human machines is meant the industrial workers themselves. As physical entities such workers are complexes of body and mind. They are human organisms, and may be regarded with reference to standards of industrial efficiency as human mechanisms. (*American Machinist*, 11 August 1921: 226)

Espousers of this unbounded engineering ideology argued that with the aid of standardization, 'parts are constructed with such accuracy that they may be assembled without hindrance, and each individual may be substituted for another of its kind' (*American Machinist*, 10 January 1901: 39).

Since the difference between the physical, social, and human realms was blurred by acts of translation, society itself was conceptualized and treated as a technical system. As such, society and organizations could, and should, be engineered as machines that are constantly being perfected. Hence, the management of organizations (and society at large) was seen to fall within the province of engineers. Social, cultural, and political issues (such as the 'labor problem' discussed in later chapters) could be framed and analyzed as 'systems' and 'subsystems' to be solved by technical means. The editor of the *Engineering Magazine* provided an excellent account of how these domains are molded together. Dunlap said:

the development and refinement of systematic, organized manufacturing [lies largely] within the domain of mechanical practice [and includes] much that is drawn from economics and much that is taken from commercial principles. But in turn, the genius of the engineer has remodeled economic and commercial methods by scientific study and adaptation, and given them back to the business world better than he received them. (*Engineering Magazine*, December 1907: 479)

This is in essence a process of co-optation of non-engineering domains in order to reproduce them within the scheme and territory of engineering.[7]

In the following section I describe empirically how engineers started to differentiate management, through practice and discourse, to make it an autonomous professional terrain.

## 3.2 Management branches out of engineering literature

In the early 1880s, editors and writers in the field of engineering strived to establish the role of the engineer as an expert in the management of organizations. For
example, the editors of *American Machinist* stressed the value of the professional
expert in manufacturing firms: 'In every other business than the establishment
of manufactures, men appreciate readily enough the value of expert opinion as a
guide. If a man is sick, the doctor is visited or called in to advise upon the case.'
But in the establishment of a manufacturing firm, a person 'often acts upon his
own unaided judgment' (*American Machinist*, 7 May 1881: 8). The editor of
*American Machinist* made a firm distinction between ownership and professional
management, where the latter should be viewed as a profession, 'as much as
medicine or law' (*American Machinist*, 25 January 1894: 8). It was clear to them
that engineers were in a position to manage and that they should legitimately do
so. W. B. Parsons explained:

the engineer of today, and more especially of the future, will, if he is to obtain the full
measure of success that is rightly his, be concerned not only with his calculations, but will
also have to study men and their needs; questions of industrial demand; the laws of
finance, and much in regard in general legislation. His it will be to conceive, to plan, to
design, to execute and then to manage. (*American Machinist*, 27 July 1905: 117)

By viewing organizations as technical systems, and the management of organization as an integral branch of mechanical engineering, engineers worked to extend
the boundaries of their profession. They sought to enhance their centrality
within industrial firms and to convince the public at large that their project was
socially responsible.

It was probably Henry Towne's paper 'The Engineer as an Economist',
presented at the ASME meeting in Chicago in 1885,[8] that for the first time
singled out management as a legitimate professional area for mechanical engineers.[9] It was the first formal attempt to integrate the new wave of engineering—
the engineering of social and human endeavors—into business ideology. In his
paper Towne recognized the 'executive duties of organizing and superintending
the operations of the industrial establishments' (*Transactions of the ASME*, 7,
1885–6: 428). He claimed that shop management is of equal importance to
technical engineering problems. While mechanical engineering was by then 'a
well-defined science, with a distinct literature, with numerous journals and with
many associations for the interchange of experience', the management of firms
was at a disadvantage (repr. in *Engineering Magazine*, April 1916: 12–16). It was
'unorganized, almost without literature, with no organ or medium for interchange of experience, and without associations or organizations of any kind'.
Towne was positive that the remedy 'should originate from engineers', mechanical rather than civil: 'We have in our membership much more than have the
Civil Engineers or Mining Engineers, men who are managers of labor, who are

either owners or representative of owners, and who therefore control capital. There are fewer purely professional men and men having no direct responsibility for the management of others in this Society than in either of the other engineering societies' (quoted in Noble 1977: 267). Towne recommended establishing an 'Economic Section' within ASME with two main divisions, one for 'Shop Management' and another for 'Shop Accounting'. The first would deal with issues of 'organization, responsibility, reports, systems of contract and piece work, and all that relates to the executive management of works, mills and factories'; and the second would deal with 'Time and wage systems, determination of costs . . . and all that enters into the system of accounting which relates to the manufacturing departments of a business'.

The expansion of the engineer's province, as Noble put it, to the management and economics of firms received more legitimization when individuals such as Oberlin Smith and Henry Metcalfe annexed additional territories such as inventory evaluation (*Transactions of the ASME*, 7, 1885: 433)[10] and shop orders (*Transactions of the ASME*, 7, 1885: 440)[11] as integral parts of mechanical engineering. To be sure, Towne, Metcalfe, and Smith did not present a unified concept of management, and the idea of establishing a specialized section was not immediately adopted. Nevertheless, these efforts represented a departure from the standard presentation of technical papers in ASME and the beginning of a managerial collective consciousness within ASME circles.[12] Furthermore, the expansion of engineering to management did not start with the 1885 ASME meeting. These presentations legitimized and formalized a movement that already existed in industry.

The question of how to trace the institutionalization of management often puzzles business historians. The systematic examination of the two magazines—*American Machinist* and *Engineering Magazine*—provides an opportunity, both quantitative and qualitative, to determine the historical time-frame in which management differentiated itself from engineering.[13] In order to quantify this evolution, I counted the volume of text concerned with management issues for each year during the period 1879–1932.[14] Over time there was an increasing managerial overtone in both publications.

In *American Machinist*, the average number of entries on management increased from 49 per year before 1895 to 112 items per year after 1905.[15] The number of entries related to management in *Engineering Magazine* approximated an average of 30 items per year.[16] After 1905, the average grew to 43 entries per year.[17] Fig. 2 and Table 2 present the steady growth of the literature on management from 1879 onward. The first time that the compiled index of *American Machinist* had a formal entry for 'management' was in 1896, but articles and editorials about management had existed since the establishment of *American Machinist* in 1877.

Most early entries on management addressed small fragments of managerial issues. For example, one writer discussed the spread of the 'industrial betterment

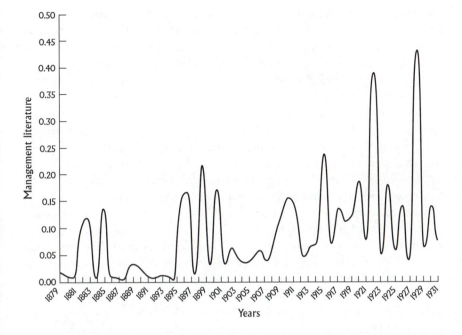

**Fig. 2.** Trends in literature on management relative to the annual volume of engineering literature, 1879–1932

*Note*: See Table 2 (p. 100) for complete data.

movement', arguing that it 'has improved employees' condition and increased the prosperity of many firms' (*American Machinist*, 23 November 1907: 716–18). Another discussed the legal problems associated with consolidation of two firms in which one had a contract with its employees and the other did not (*American Machinist*, 30 November 1905: 747). There were articles on 'Scientific versus Intuitive administration' (*Engineering Magazine*, September 1916: 849–54), the success of 'modern management methods', 'the liability of corporate directors' (*American Machinist*, 8 December 1904: 1652), personnel issues (for example 'Promoting the Training of Workmen', *American Machinist*, 14 February 1885: 3; 'Nepotism in Machine Shops', *American Machinist*, 12 January 1899: 36), authority and organization of responsibilities (for example 'The Duties of a Superintendent', *American Machinist*, 7 April 1883: 8; 'Control Should Equal Responsibility', *American Machinist*, 6 June 1895: 448; 'Responsibility and Control', *American Machinist*, 29 April 1897: 332), the role of the manager *vis-à-vis* other functions in the firm (for example, 'Skilled Workmen as Foremen', *American Machinist*, 1 November 1884: 8; 'Fine Management', *American Machinist*, 25 June 1896: 628; 'The Working Hustling Foreman', *American Machinist*, 9 February 1899: 110), the adequacy of engineers as managers (for example 'Executive Ability among Mechanics', *American Machinist*, 17 March 1892: 8), employer–employee relations (for example, 'Management of Workmen', *American Machinist*, 25 February 1882: 4), the training of managers (for example 'A Neglected Study', *American Machinist*, 8 January 1891: 8)—and there were invitations to visit shops which implemented novel management techniques (for example 'The Taylor System at Work', *American Machinist*, 16 April 1914: 703). There were efforts to disseminate the ideology of rational conduct, based on the reason of the manager: 'It is nature's fixed decree that mind shall be the master and muscle the servant. In this, manager intellect would assert its supremacy' (*Engineering Magazine*, February 1894: 626–32). Likewise, the editors of the *Engineering Magazine* were concerned with the training of engineers as managers, and led a campaign to introduce management and economics into schools of engineering (*Engineering Magazine*, April 1906: 99–100).

The concept of management as a unified whole was probably first articulated by a British engineer, Slater Lewis, in the late 1890s. Lewis served as general manager for several British companies, and became the director of the British Electrical Engineering Company. He also published a book on a systems approach to managing firms, entitled *The Commercial Organization of Factories* (Litterer 1986). In a series of articles in the *Engineering Magazine*, Lewis complained that the attention of engineers was traditionally focused on the design of products while 'the internal routine and administration of shops' have been left in the hand of 'practical' men with whom 'rule of thumb is supreme'. He offered a programmatic view, suggesting the adoption of 'a well directed theoretical plan, coupled with a system of record that enables . . . Weak points to be detected and the results of modification instantly to be seen' (J. Slater Lewis, 'Works Management for the Maximum of Production: Organization as a Factor of Output', *Engineering Magazine*, October 1899: 59). Lewis used the concept of 'organization' to designate the overall arrangement of the parts of management (Litterer 1986: 79). To him, the 'organization' of the firm was an entity that needed special research and care. A year later, Alexander Hamilton Church continued to develop this notion of unified organizations—entities that regulate actors and could be understood in abstract forms—and focused on the problems associated with controlling large organizations (*Engineering Magazine*, December 1900: 391). The writings of Lewis and Church crystallized an early awareness of organization and management theories.

The developing management discourse in mechanical engineering circles focused on two major themes: systems and efficiency (Abbott 1988). Both were pioneering in the translation of engineering into management. Below I discuss these themes in detail, describing how science became a unifying concept and a legitimizing framework for both. I have two objectives: the first is to reassert the underlying argument of this book about the autonomous role of engineers as carriers of the early managerial discourse. Second, I wish to draw attention to internal differences and conflicts within engineering circles. It should be noted, however, that most writers in the area of economic and management history argue that interest in systems was stimulated and justified by rapid industrial growth during these years and emergent problems of cost–price ratios, wages, the coordination of production, and the integration of firms (see, for example, Chandler 1977; Litterer 1986). The argument advanced in this book does not necessarily negate these claims. These phenomena were part of the reality of industrial firms, and they were indeed becoming problematic. I argue, however, that this rationale is insufficient in and of itself to explain the rising interest in systems, efficiency, and management. The discourse on management systems would not have been cultivated and would not have flourished if not for additional contextual forces that made management practice and discourse desired and legitimate. First among these forces was the ideological work of mechanical engineers whose enthusiasm about management issues cannot be overemphasized. The following discussion should therefore be read as an illustration of the professional project of constructing and legitimizing the two concepts by translating them from one realm to another.

### 3.3 Organizations objectified as systems

The terms 'system' and 'systematizing' were already in frequent use by engineers from the 1870s. Individuals such as Alexander Hamilton Church, John Dunlap, Horace Arnold, and Harrington Emerson, who were labeled 'expert systematizers' (see for example *Industrial Management*, January 1918: 14), praised the value of 'systematic organizations', promoted methods to advance 'systematization' (for example 'Overcapitalization Not Inconsistent with Good Methods', *American Machinist*, 24 July 1902: 1060), and even criticized 'over-systematization' for red tape or lack of concern with human interest (see for example 'Red Tape', *American Machinist*, 22 May 1902: 726–7; 'Over-Systematizing', *American Machinist*, 10 November 1904: 1499; 'Obsolete Methods and Current Practice in Shop Administration', *Engineering Magazine*, November 1904: 211–19). The work of the systematizers—which amounted less to a coherent theory than to a series of maxims—was recorded in various magazine articles and books.[18] They conceptualized the enterprise as a unified whole, controlled and coordinated in a systematic fashion.

However, complicated systems were hard to adopt instantly, and it was not before the 1900s that real interest in the systematization of organizations became widespread, mainly in the machine industry and in large chemical and electrical firms such as Du Pont, AT&T, and Standard Oil of New Jersey.[19] There were two main vehicles for the dissemination of systems discourse within industry: consulting firms and technical magazines. These institutional carriers pushed, mainly when the new field of industrial engineering started to be recognized in the beginning of the twentieth century, toward the adoption of recipes that made organization systems look alike (DiMaggio and Powell 1983; Meyer and Scott 1983). One manufacturer recounted: 'It was six years ago that I was first inoculated with the cost-system microbe' and 'I began to get interested.' However, 'about that time we received a letter from a New York firm of efficiency engineers, who made a specialty of putting in cost systems'. Not only cost systems, but they also offered to 'systematize our entire plant' (*American Machinist*, 3 July 1913: 15). In the following I use the engineering periodicals to provide a bird's-eye view on the institutionalization of systems.

As early as the 1870s, the number of articles concerning organizational systems was negligible, but during the 1880s and 1890s the subject became increasingly popular.[20] The concept of 'system' first entered the index of the *American Machinist* as a separate formal entry in 1882. Following this, the *American Machinist* and the *Engineering Magazine* published articles about systems of all kinds, specifying routes, delivery between offices, records of work and workers, correcting plans, methods for material requisition, weekly meetings of department heads with foremen, instructions regarding the planning department, and methods for ordering machine tools.

The following random list of titles exemplifies the kind of issues with which the literature on organizational systems was preoccupied:

'System' (*American Machinist*, 1 January 1891: 7);

'Shop Rules' (*American Machinist*, 21 May 1891: 8);

'A Cost Keeping System' (*American Machinist*, 8 February 1894: 1–3);

'A System for Keeping Records of Applicants for Work, Employees and Ex-employees' (*American Machinist*, 1 December 1898: 894–5);

'Trying to Fit the System to the Shop' (*American Machinist*, 3 March 1904: 294–6);

'Obsolete Methods and Current Practice in Shop Administration' (*Engineering Magazine*, November 1904: 211–19);

'Cost and Time Keeping Outfit of the Taylor System' (*American Machinist*, 13 December 1906: 761–3);

'Use your System or Kill it' (*American Machinist*, 21 May 1908: 812);

'A Time Keeping and Cost Record System' (*American Machinist*, 12 November 1908: 699–700);

'Practical Principles of Rational Management' (*Engineering Magazine*, June 1913: 405–11);

'Routing, Dispatching, Steering and Scheduling' (*American Machinist*, 7 January 1915: 35);

'System in a Factory Stock Department' (*Engineering Magazine*, May 1915: 174–83);

'Task Setting' (*Engineering Magazine*, September 1915: 894–900);

'Standardizing the Characteristics of Men' (*Engineering Magazine*, December 1916: 308–23);

'Factory Purchasing System, Methods, and Records' (*Engineering Magazine*, August 1917: 689–701);

'Employment Bureau for Classifying Workmen' (*American Machinist*, 11 January 1917: 64);

'Organizing a Time-Study Department' (*American Machinist*, 8 March 1917: 407–10);

'Routing from a Central Department' (*American Machinist*, 17 May 1917: 858–9);

'The Importance of Organization Laws in the World Crisis' (*Engineering Magazine*, January 1918: 14–15);

'Reorganization of the Labor Department' (*Engineering Magazine*, April 1918: 326);

'Rational Standardization' (*American Machinist*, 1 May 1924: 668);

'Advantages of Decentralization' (*American Machinist*, 9 December 1926: 953–4);

'Knowing Where Work is in the Shop' (*American Machinist*, 20 February 1930: 325–7);

'Who Should Control Routing?' (*American Machinist*, 6 March 1930: 402).

Fig. 3 quantifies the changes in the discourse about systems between 1879 and 1932. To operationalize the interest in systems thinking, I used the yearly cumulative volume of items published on systems as a percentage of the volume devoted to other management issues.[21] The percentage of the text on systems (out of the literature on management) is presented in the figure, showing an average figure of 26 percent per year (s.d. = 0.16).

The figure reveals two surges, one in 1882–3 and another in 1890–1, and a steady increase through the Progressive era. These two peaks can be interpreted as standing for the first and second stages of systematization, previously described as the move from technical tools standards to organizational systems. The figure clearly shows that the first decade of the Progressive era was the 'golden age' of systems. The discourse remained fairly strong until 1916, when it started to decline, showing an additional peak around 1924. This decline, in relative proportion, does not indicate a decay of the paradigm but rather its institutionalization under the general umbrella of management.[22] This is apparent from the relationship between 'system' and 'management'. While 'system' first entered the magazines in 1882, 'management' entered in 1904. In 1911, 'system' became a subcategory under 'management'. The references to 'system' as a separate domain started to decline in 1913, while references to 'systems' within 'management' started to increase. This link was widely accepted at the time. As one engineer wrote in 1913, 'We organize to manage. We manage through system' (*American Machinist*, 27 March 1913: 507). Or, 'The system is the tool of the managers' (*American Machinist*, 29 April 1915: 750). As Fig. 3 shows, the notion of system and its institutionalization as a dominant legitimizing idea

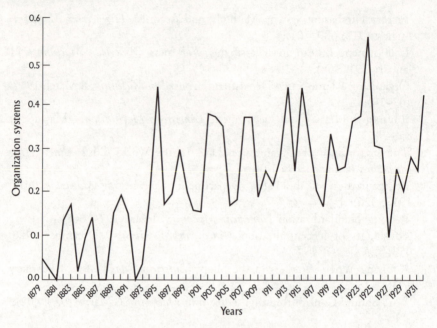

**Fig. 3.** Trends in literature on organization systems relative to the annual volume of literature on management, 1879–1932

*Note*: See Table 2 (p. 100) for complete data.

found fertile ground in the Progressive era. The discourse on management systems did not constitute a single coherent theory, but mostly a series of maxims. Early maxims were brief and unconditional (*American Machinist*, 1 January 1891: 7). Later, these maxims became more elaborate (*American Machinist*, 16 April 1908: 611).

Systems discourse emerged triumphantly from engineering literature, supporting the ideological phase of the managerial revolution early in the twentieth century. It ultimately became the master blueprint for the management and organization theories that were formalized in the 1940s–1960s (see Capra 1982). The work of translation done by engineers from the beginning of the century generated several rationalizations for the implementation of systems. These justifications addressed different constituencies and were based on standards accepted in American society particularly during the Progressive era (see also Litterer 1986). The relevance of this rhetoric to the struggle of establishing the legitimacy of systems ideology becomes clearer in the next chapters, which describe the political context within which engineers operated.

*Systems are efficient.* The main justification for the introduction of systems was anchored in a functionalist logic, necessitated by industry and the economy. As stated by Walter Snow: 'The shop where true system rules is always the one where the work is economically and expeditiously carried on. System and economy are interdependent and inseparable' (*American Machinist*, 1 January 1891: 7). Alexander Hamilton Church said: 'The evolution of this body of principles was bound to take place because it was called for by the necessities of modern industry' (*Engineering Magazine*, April 1911: 97–101).

'Systems have come into existence in response to an urgent demand, and the efficacy of their work in meeting it is evident wherever it is performed', it was argued at the New York meeting of ASME in 1905 (*American Machinist*, 7 December 1905: 760). System and order are 'of course' necessary, and 'as necessary and important in a small shop as in a big one' (*American Machinist*, 7 January 1904: 35). Albert W. Thompson, a noted engineer, described a large textile manufacturing firm employing 12,000 loom operatives which advocated the introduction of administrative systems since 'in a large shop a good clerical force does not add a relatively large amount to the general expense' (*Engineering Magazine*, September 1906: 873–83). Organizations, bringing together the latent intelligence of their workers and systems that left nothing to chance, were presented as the reasons behind American Exceptionalism:

In seeking the reason for the lasting and commanding success of American business organizations of today, two facts will stand out prominently. One is that the organizations are founded upon principles that are in accord with modern progressive ideas and tend to bring out the latent intelligence of all its members. The other is that the important details of factory work are cared for by systems which are homogeneous, flexible and efficient; systems which leave nothing to chance, but which care for the smallest and the most important details of factory work alike. (*Engineering Magazine*, April 1902: 15–18)

*Systems are universal.*   Some writers anchored their justifications in the universality of their efforts, arguing that 'all progressive nations have adopted some form of merit system for filling most of their positions' (*American Machinist*, 8 January 1914: 51). Others found legitimization in history. Systematizers introduced systems as a natural phenomenon known for ages:

The art of administration is as old as the human race. Organization is older than history, for the earliest documents, such as the code of Hammurabi, show the evidences of many generations of systematized social life. The real pioneers are the unknown promoters of the stone age, and the system-makers of the bronze age. (*Engineering Magazine*, October 1912: 1–6; see also October 1912: 185–90; December 1912: 321–6)

One writer argued that all great men of history who were considered charismatic leaders—Alexander, Caesar, Attila, Genghis Khan, or Napoleon—achieved their success through durable, though unconsciously practiced, standardized principles (*Engineering Magazine*, August 1911: 810–904). In the same vein, 'standardized operations' make great history possible:

The man who, blindfolded, plays twelve games of chess and wins them all, who plays without notes, in perfect sequence, time and expression a symphony of a hundred-thousand notes, who walks the chasm of Niagara on a tight-rope, who wins a presidential nomination and six-million votes by the magic of his voice; the men who made modern Italy, modern Germany, modern Japan; the camera that finds and shows the approaching comet, the spectroscope that reads the motion and materials of the distant stars—these show the possibilities and reach of standardized operations. (*Engineering Magazine*, April 1911: 23–32)

Systems were presented as transcendental, making them a corollary of the universal story of organizations. Systems were a necessary constituent of the universal realm of organizations since they transcended idiosyncrasies of operation in terms of time and place. Idiosyncrasies, it was said, interfere with the universal and efficient functioning of the system. The rule of transcendentality suggested that the system cannot be reduced to individual participants or to its elementary parts (*American Machinist*, 27 March 1924: 482). It marked the system as a durable structure that could survive people, locations, and history. Harrington Emerson stressed the ahistorical nature of the system: 'The object . . . is to annihilate time, to bring back the past, to look into the future, to annihilate space, to condense a whole railroad system into a single line' (*Engineering Magazine*, January 1911: 496).

*Systems ensure harmony of action.* As a corollary of its wholeness, the system was presented as ensuring harmony. The following description in *Engineering Magazine* put it in technical language: 'An example of perfect harmony of action is found in an automatic system, say for producing wood screws, or pins. The material goes in at one end and comes out of the other, commercially perfect; the process is wholly mechanical' (*Engineering Magazine*, November 1904: 211–19).

Such a harmony and clockwork precision interconnects machines, and human behavior was the focus of many systematizers. Admirers of technology suggested that the repeated pace of technological development led to the mechanization of human beings. Thorstein Veblen, for example, argued that the machine and its discipline shaped the human mind to be more rational and scientific. The systematization of management facilitated the view that organizational order should be machine-like (see Merkle 1980: 81).[23] In describing a system at the Tiffany Motor Co. of New Jersey, W. E. Thompson suggested that 'a system should keep the bearings oiled and the machine running smoothly'. He labeled the system as 'semi-automatic' (*American Machinist*, 15 January 1920: 127–31). John Dunlap, editor of *Engineering Magazine*, envisioned 'a completely automatic factory at the end of the industrial revolution' (*Engineering Magazine* January 1900: 616. Cited in Jenks 1961: 439). The definition of 'harmony' as an ideal technical relation of input and output was later echoed in the notion of 'dynamic equilibrium', promulgated in the 'open systems' perspective in organization theory.

*Systems transcend bounded rationality.* Frequently mentioned in the engineering literature as a reason for the introduction of systems were the limitations of individual actors in maintaining rational organization behavior. For example, Horace Arnold (known also as Henry Roland) stated in 1899:

Even if entire honesty and sincerity prevailed at all times in all business transactions, the mere differences due to variations in individual understandings of orders, would render it impossible to conduct any business of magnitude on verbal specifications . . . [Only if] all men had absolutely infallible memories, and were incapable of making any statement at variance with those memories, it would be possible, perhaps, to carry on a successful and prosperous manufacturing business without the use of shop books or factory accounts.[24]

Thus, organization systems were conceptualized in sharp contrast to the individual. As Taylor once said: 'in the past man has been first. In the future the system will be first' (Kanigel 1997). To the systematizers, general rules and laws had to be discerned and formalized, while individuals had to become invisible. Administrative systems—such as cost accounting, production control, and wage schemes—transcended the capriciousness of individual actors and reduced dependence upon them (Jelinek 1980). The editors of the *American Machinist* addressed this contrast on numerous occasions: 'In considering the methods of factory management . . . They fall naturally into two main classes. On the one hand is that class of the factory which depends on the individual capacity of its employees and on the other the one depending on the perfection of its system for its results' (*American Machinist*, 14 April 1904: 479).

Alexander Hamilton Church expressed his understanding of systems in the following way:

Under rational management the accumulation of experience, and its systematic use and application, form the first fighting line. But as life is too short for one man, or even one plant, to know everything of all that could be possibly known even about their own work, we must confine our efforts as far as possible to knowledge that can be coordinated—that is, worked up into useful working rules and guidance—instead of remaining forever in the condition of an immense unwieldy accumulation of unrelated facts. (*Engineering Magazine*, February 1913: 673–80)

Church and other writers seem to suggest that dependence on particular individuals should be eliminated since it results in highly variable actions that interfere with coordination and control (*American Machinist*, 17 April 1913: 639). The glorification of systems was accompanied by a strong attack on the philosophy of individualism: 'Just suppose each man in your bookkeeping department kept his books his own way; suppose each clerk in your ordering department had his own individual kind of order blank, and each man in the stock room had his own system of storing, handling and accounting. And suppose these men told you they had as much right to be individual' (*American Machinist*, 27 March 1924: 482).

Likewise, the establishment of an employment department in Westinghouse was justified by principles of efficiency and rationality independent of individual actors: 'It is a well-known fact that where the hiring of factory help is left to the foremen the selection is apt to be influenced by personal reasons, often resulting in the selection of relatives and general favoritism' (*American Machinist*, 23 June 1904: 832–3). Eventually, the system will make it possible for mediocre men to administer the shop more successfully than the most gifted individual could who did not use the system (Calvert 1967). This was described as follows: 'If a man has not the ability to select subordinates with certainty, his only chance is to so arrange matters that practically anyone can carry on the business by the routine he originates' (*American Machinist*, 14 April 1904: 479).

It should be noted that the importance of systems was extended to legitimize the succession of managerial positions too. As Horace Arnold acknowledged as early as 1898:

The young and ambitious manager who takes the helm of a successful old firm finds at once that he is not to know the details of the factory of his own knowledge. He is to take his information second hand, or go without it . . . Between a new manager who wants to know, and a force of old heads of departments who do know and will not tell, the board of directors is often called to arbitrate. (*Engineering Magazine*, April 1898: 77. Cited in Litterer 1986: 115)

The limitation of individual actors is also due to the enormous amount of information they must consider. The systematizers spoke of the necessity to collect information in an orderly fashion and present it in an integrated way. Church, for example, stated: 'The necessity for coordination is an inevitable result of the evolution of the factory. No one mind can grasp and hold all the details' (*Engineering Magazine*, December 1900: 395). The similarity of these arguments to the 'bounded rationality' argument as developed in the mid-twentieth-century organizational literature is striking (see Simon 1957).

Engineers offered the wholeness and interdependence of systems as a remedy for the bounded rationality of human beings. Systems were perceived as a unifying totality, a matrix operating under the logic that all elements are commensurable, and the whole is deterministic (Lyotard 1984). As one engineer explained,

Its ultimate purpose is to resolve the various forces at work into their component parts—to arrange them so as to enable these forces to follow well defined channels, that the work may be guided along the most logical lines and responsibility placed where it properly belongs; and finally to combine these forces firmly into one harmonious effort, placing at the head a master mind to supervise and direct. (*Engineering Magazine*, April 1908: 82–91)

There was plenty of evidence supporting the idea that the locus of rationality resided within the system rather than in the hands of individual participants. Rationality was embedded within the properties of the system, such as 'authority', 'specialization', or 'centralization'. Indeed, rationality was a term used explicitly by the systematizers. For example, in late 1912 and early 1913 the *American Machinist* and the *Engineering Magazine* published a series of articles by Alexander Hamilton Church on the principles of 'rational management' (*Engineering Magazine*, January 1913). Church suggested that the object of the 'administrative organization scheme' should be 'to collect knowledge of what is going forward, not merely qualitatively, but quantitatively: It should also provide the means of regulating as well as the means of recording' (*Engineering Magazine*, December 1900: 391. Quoted in Yates 1989: 13). The system becomes the depository of 'a mass of unrecorded information not possessed by the owner, and which he is glad not to be obliged to know, as this ignorance leaves his mind free for things of more present importance'. This was clarified in a different article in the *Engineering Magazine*: 'The manager's desk should be the Alpha and Omega of every transaction. It should also be the information bureau of the establishment. No work should be done without the manager's authority and sanction' (*Engineering Magazine*, December 1898: 385). These aspects of systematizing resulted in the compilation of handbooks, files, procedures, records, inventories, reports, shop orders, and networks of people, routines, and orders which are intertwined and coordinated with one another.

*Systems are a measure against uncertainty.* 'Uncertainty', the hobgoblin of organizational order, was constructed by organizational theorists as an entity feeding on human limitations and the 'given' complexity of the market. Systems were offered as rational measures to confront uncertainty (see Shenhav 1994; Weitz 1997). Systematizers were convinced that mechanical 'system' signified an underlying reality in organizations; that, in light of 'the chaotic state of factory practices' (Jenks 1961: 425), there was a real need to 'eliminate confusion, oversight and neglect', to 'coordinate efforts', and to accomplish these things by the use of standardized procedures and routine managerial work through 'system' (Litterer 1961*a*). The following excerpt from the *Engineering Magazine* in 1902 clarifies that systems require formal explication: 'One rule in particular is necessary for any system. That is, all orders must be in writing. This must be adhered to strictly. Written orders reduce the liability of error; they fix absolutely the responsibility. They promote accuracy and care in the preparation of orders' (*Engineering Magazine*, April 1902: 15–18). As Carpenter put it: 'Verbal orders don't go!' (ibid.).

There were several rationales given for the need to formalize the system. One of them was the limitation of the human mind. As early as 1885, Metcalf also linked formalization to the reduction of ambiguity, not in planning but in oper-. ation: 'The trouble is not in foreseeing necessities, nor in starting the work to meet them; but in constantly running over the back track to see that nothing ordered has been overlooked, and in settling disputes as to whether such and such an order was or was not actually given and received' (*Transactions of the ASME*, 7, 1885: 441).

Formalization transforms an implicit procedure or intention into a 'collectively shared consciousness', and provides an instrument for control. It consists of the 'laying out of the scope and limits of action' of groups and individuals (*American Machinist*, 27 March 1913: 507–11). The systematizers' emphasis on formalization through systems was promoted as rational, but it was a particular type of rationality, labeled by economist Friedrich Hayek as 'constructive rationality' or 'plan rationality' (see Hayek 1967).[25] Formalization through systems became the ideological kernel of planning and construction, and therefore a means of minimizing uncertainty. The binary opposites of rationality and uncertainty later became a dominant habit of thought within organization and management theory (see Chapter 7, for a discussion). Constructive rationality was useful for systematizers and managers in general since it replaced the never-ending criticism of one's premises with a deductive reasoning based on explicit yet indubitable premises.[26]

Formalization was also to include the company rules. Some suggested that company rules and policy should be posted in industrial bulletins (*American Machinist*, 22 October 1914: 711–12). For example, 'All new employees must understand and speak the English language', or 'The rate of pay is a personal matter between the individual employee and employer, and must not become the business of other persons.' It was suggested that each bulletin 'established harmony at once'. Furthermore, 'everyone seemed to be infused with a desire to make a good record' and with 'loyalty'.

Systematizers were in unanimous agreement as to the paramount role of record keeping. Formalization was feasible only through the production of written records. Emerson conceptualized the object of records: 'The Ten Commandments were graven on stone. The books that the Sibyle gave to Tarquin were written instructions. Magna Carta, the Declaration of Independence, codes of laws, are written; and they constitute standard practice instructions . . . Thus detecting and eliminating much that is arbitrary and contradictory' (*Engineering Magazine*, April 1911: 23–6).

Formalization was held to be good for efficiency, but also good for workers 'as it releases the workmen from the tyranny of the foremen'. In the early writings of systematizers, as in modern-day organization theory, formalization was presented as an objective benefit: it is not dependent 'upon personal likes and dislikes of some petty official' but rather enables the worker to attain true independence (*American Machinist*, 26 October 1911: 784–5).

The availability of organizational records and the minimization of uncertainty are therefore interdependent: 'The object of records is to increase the scope and number of warnings, to give us more information than is usually received immediately through our senses' (*Engineering Magazine*, January 1911: 496–506).

*Systems ensure discipline and control.* The introduction of systems was expected to facilitate organizational control particularly during an era that was perceived to be chaotic. One writer suggested that when a machine tool is purchased and found slightly unfitted, one can usually make a change in its construction to correct the difficulty. The story with human behavior is different: 'If the human machine could be controlled by the set rules that govern machine tool operation, the world would be a much different place' (*Review*, October 1910: 35. Cited in Noble 1977: 263). The underlying assumption in applying systems was clear: 'Organization to be of strength must subject the individual to the communal wherever they conflict.' In order to ensure such a *modus operandi*, 'the limits of each individual must be clearly and exactly defined and his duties and responsibilities thoroughly fixed and understood' (*American Machinist*, 17 April 1913: 639).

'The exception system', a new managerial invention, was also discussed by the editors of the *American Machinist* (*American Machinist*, 26 March 1908: 472–3). They described a successful company whose output was increased, while its workforce shrank and the product quality improved. The president of the company remained puzzled about the manager's performance: 'He really seems to have very little to do, his desk is never littered with papers, and if you call his office you are more apt to find him with a cigar in his mouth and his feet on his desk than you are to find him doing any visible work.' The editors of the *American Machinist* interviewed the manager and discovered that after getting the works in a running shape he had made it a rule to devote his attention to unusual cases and, except in a general way, to no others. In other words, this manager created a relatively predictable organizational environment, by ordering that all exceptional cases should be brought to his attention. He isolated the source of uncertainty and produced a procedure to tame it. Control becomes a living reality through the introduction of systems: 'Everything should be the subject of forecast as to the financial results, and of pre-arrangements as to the actual carrying out. And when it is completed, the records of what actually did take place should be capable of comparison with what was intended to take place. Control then becomes a living reality' (*Engineering Magazine*, December 1900: 397).

If control were to become a 'living reality', further organizational recipes for control would be needed. Hugo Diemer suggested that 'control may be based on the principles of military authority as exemplified by the line officers, on specialization, on functionalization or on a combination of these principles' (*American Machinist*, 27 March 1913: 507). 'The task of management, therefore, is to minimize and prevent variations from the planned procedure' (*American Machinist*, 13 February 1930: 308–9). Four elementary procedures embedded in the core of these systems—routing, dispatching, steering, and scheduling— provide such control (*American Machinist*, 7 January 1915: 35). Emerson also emphasized the need to secure 'discipline' (*Engineering Magazine*, November 1910: 161–74)—namely 'the subordination of the individual to the more important common good'—through these procedures. The necessity of these principles, which attempt to minimize differences, produce conformity, and increase control, was justified by metaphors and examples borrowed from nature. For example, Emerson claimed: 'Nature is a relentless disciplinarian.

Because the success of the whole plant depends not on its wealth or its men, or its product, but on its spirit and rule, penalties for persistent infraction should be relentlessly severe' (*Engineering Magazine*, November 1910: 163). He emphasized:

There can be organization without discipline, as in all plant life; there can be discipline without organization, as in most animal life. Because man has supernal ideals; because the progress of centuries can be lost in a year, in a minute, even if organization is weakened—the devil indeed catching the hindmost; because our unstable human organizations, even the integrity of the family, depend on discipline, it becomes a fundamental efficiency principle which continuously, vigorously, never falteringly enforces a series of standards of high individual or combined conduct. (*Engineering Magazine*, November 1910: 165)

Discipline, in the world-view of systematizers, became an indispensable part of organizational reality. Through the everyday use of company records, rules, and indoctrination, systems were designed to permeate the private sphere and become internalized. Ideally, the worker was to be the supervisor of his or her own work. Michel Foucault's analysis of Bentham's Panopticon can be used as a striking metaphor of these features (Foucault 1979). Panopticon is an architectural design of a prison where a tower is positioned in its center and an annular building at the periphery. The building is divided into cells, each with two windows, one on the inside corresponding to the windows of the tower, the other on the outside, which allows the light to cross the cell from one end to the other. 'By the effect of backlighting, one can observe from the tower, standing out precisely against the light, the small captive shadows in the cells of the periphery. They are like so many cages, so many small theatres, in which each actor is alone, perfectly individualized and constantly visible' (Foucault 1979: 200). Thus, 'the heaviness of the old "houses of security", with their fortress-like architecture could be replaced by the simple, economic geometry of a "house of certainty" ' (ibid. 202). Ironically, the inception of Modernism—the very moment where men (or women) invented themselves—simultaneously launched new and more subtle mechanisms of control (ibid. 202). In their durability, transcendence, and depersonalized nature, organization systems constituted the panopticon of managerial capitalism. Individuals in organization systems are not left to their own faculties or devices, nor do they search for the best means to attain a certain end. Everybody's rationality is bounded and is prescribed in the abstract blueprint of the systems.

*Systems are state of the art.* Systematizers were also aware of the ritualistic aspects of organizational behavior, not only with regard to instrumental procedures but also as far as management fads were concerned. As one systematizer put it: 'You must have a cost system. You can't retain the respect of the manufacturing public if you don't have one' (*American Machinist*, 3 July 1913: 15). Furthermore: 'A cost system is as necessary to your industrial prestige as a pair of pants is to your personal dignity. Let it once be known among your business connections that you do not maintain, I should say support, a cost system, and your status is not worth a fig. And figs, this season, are of a particularly poor quality' (ibid.). Similarly, F. W. Shibley, a vice-president at the Bankers Trust Company, recalled, 'We in the banks have observed the growth and progress of these corporations. We have compared their systems of operation with the systems of former days and which are still adhered to by many enterprises whose management are complacent and inert' (*American Machinist*, 19 May 1927: 868). These arguments are in accordance with the mimetic isomorphism argument advanced by the institutional theory of organizations.[27] The theory argues that industrial practices, new processes, and public policies are adopted, transformed, and reproduced not necessarily because their technical superiority has been demonstrated, but rather because people believe in certain ways of doing things. Meyer and Rowan have termed these powerful institutional rules 'highly rationalized myths' (see Meyer and Rowan 1977: 343).

### 3.4 The image of systems in context

At first, the justifications for systems described above were used as ideological claims during engineers' struggle to promote the agenda of systems. Over time they became the elementary forms of the most persuasive and enduring paradigm in the literature on organizations. Sold as an analytic category, 'organizations as mechanical systems' was, in fact, a cultural image advocated by a group of professional engineers. This cultural image had political ramifications for the struggle of engineers with manufacturers (see Chapter 4) and for the reshaping of labor relations (see Chapters 5 and 6).

Systems had special appeal in the Progressive era because its political culture entailed a desire to find common ground for society as a whole. The legitimacy of organizational systems during the Progressive period was supported among the public by two ideals dominant at the time: progress and equality. Progress, often expressed in terms of efficiency and productivity, meant the use of technology, production, and machines in the face of growing demands in industry (e.g. *American Machinist*, 7 January 1904: 35). All these were represented by engineers, managers, scientists, pragmatists, and economists who identified industry as the proper arena for Progressive reforms. And these agreed that 'the discipline of science is the only one which gives any assurance that from the same set of facts men will come approximately to the same conclusion' (Kloppenberg 1986: 383). For Pierce, who headed the Office of Weights and Measures (which in 1901 was transformed by an Act of Congress into the Bureau of Standards), 'practice' meant the activities of scientists and engineers and their experimental work *vis-à-vis* nature (Smith 1986: 54). Likewise, John Dewey envisioned scientific theories to be the 'leading principles' that guide action in the world.

Equality, in the public eye, was about the redistribution of wealth by means of welfare legislation, and limiting economic power through antitrust laws and unionism (Jacoby 1993). Despite the fact that themes of progress and equality often clash (Meyer 1994), the development of rational and efficient management systems, in both industry and government, seemed to provide a perfect vehicle for reforms acceptable to both camps.

In organizational systems, progress and equality meshed. They were perceived as a safeguard for the morality of organizations, managers, and employees (Kloppenberg 1986). Together, they appeared to bind individuals into mutual relations of responsibility and accountability, to depersonalize these relationships, and thus eliminate favoritism, nepotism, and other unethical practices. In systems, the trajectory of progress could be charted both for individuals and for the organization as a whole. Authority was no longer derived from privileged social positions, but 'grounded in the facts and techniques needed to perform and coordinate interdependent tasks' (Miller and O'Leary 1989: 255). Systems, therefore, were perceived to be objective, coherent, democratic, and progressive. John Dewey suggested that rights and duties should become universalized, removed to 'the care of society as a whole rather than of any partial group organization' (quoted from British sociologist Leonard Hobhouse. See Kloppenberg 1986: 352). Or, as Wiebe argued, systems promised to bring 'opportunity, progress, order and community' through which 'all men would enjoy a fair chance for success' (Wiebe 1967: 170).

Conceptualizing society as a 'whole' generated a pragmatic culture. Such a culture was eclectic, and marked by a rapid growth and dissolution of coalitions around different and often contradictory causes. For example, Progressivists lumped together such different individuals as Louis Brandeis, Eugene Debs, Herbert Croly, and Walter Lippman to promote a *via media* philosophy. Here, distinctions between idealism and empiricism in epistemology, intuitionism and utilitarianism in ethics, as well as socialism and *laissez-faire* liberalism in politics were waived, or discarded (Kloppenberg 1986). Morris L. Cooke's crusade in ASME against the utility and gas companies was another example of the creation of common ground. Air pollution was an appealing subject to Progressivists. Cooke suggested that inefficient fuel consumption caused both pollution and a waste of natural and human resources. He declared that as engineers were professionals with a civic consciousness and objective minds, the control of industrial pollutants should be part of their responsibility (Sinclair 1980: 98–100). As the director of Philadelphia's public works, Cooke further expounded the centrality of engineers by suggesting that their skills were useful to the efficient management of America's cities.[28]

In the midst of the Progressive period, probably around 1910, an efficiency craze overtook the country. Haber likened it to 'a flash flood, at first covering almost the entire landscape but soon collecting in various places to be absorbed slowly and to enrich the immediate surroundings' (Haber 1964: 52). Efficiency appealed to a huge public: industrialists, engineers, educators, home economists, and Progressivists at large. In the 1920s, the term 'efficiency engineering' appeared in many newspapers, journals, and magazines. The efficiency movement provided an additional layer to the legitimization of managerial language.

## 3.5 Efficiency discourse

The two magazines, and particularly the *Engineering Magazine*, took an active role in the construction of efficiency as both ideology and industrial practice. On its twentieth anniversary, the editor of the *Engineering Magazine*, John Dunlap, recollected, 'The Engineering Magazine recognized the pursuit of industrial efficiency as a distinct branch of engineering long before it was so distinguished by even its most prominent practitioners.' Elsewhere Dunlap argued, 'Efficiency is attained by obedience to great laws of the universe which are always and everywhere the same . . . these laws are suzerain, inerrant, and eternal as the laws of gravity or chemical affinity' (*Engineering Magazine*, September 1911: 9). Frederick Taylor was a pivotal figure in mobilizing widespread legitimization of efficiency management. His 'Scientific Management'—which is said to have started in 1895 and to have peaked in the 1920s—focused on two concepts: efficiency and science.[29] Taylor envisioned handbooks of 'elementary operations' codifying the laws of work, as an analogy to the laws of machines (Haber 1964: 29). The vision of Scientific Management procedures was 'nothing more than the logical extension of the mechanical engineering practices that begun with screw threads in the 1860s' (Sinclair 1980: 51). As an editorial in the *American Machinist* stated, many machines are made so that 'unnecessary vibration or stresses may be removed from the machines during operation in order to save power'. Similarly, the workman can 'conserve much of his physical power if he tries to make every motion count for the most' (*American Machinist*, 10 July 1913: 78).

One of the earliest activists in the efficiency movement and a prototype of the new breed of 'efficiency engineers' was Harrington Emerson. Following his studies in Germany, Emerson admired the organizational efforts of General Von Moltke, who helped make the Prussian military efficient (Wren 1972: 170). Emerson began his practical work as a troubleshooter for the general manager of the Burlington Railroad, and was a professor of engineering at the State University of Nebraska in the 1870s. Between 1904 and 1907 he became a consultant for the Santa Fe Railroad, where he inaugurated his efficiency program (which was called 'betterment work') (see *Factory and Industrial Management*, June 1931: 999; Wren 1972: 169). Emerson helped found the Efficiency Society in 1912 and served on Herbert Hoover's committee on waste elimination in industry. In 1933 he formed the Association of Consulting Management Engineers. The *Engineering Magazine* was one of the earliest forums for his writings and in 1908–9 he published a series of articles which were later republished in a single volume (Emerson 1911). As Dunlap recollected in 1910, these articles 'were essentially the statement of a philosophy—a philosophy so fine and so hopeful as to merit the designation we then gave it of a gospel' (*Engineering Magazine*, June 1910: 408). Waste and inefficiency were the two issues that Emerson most often attacked. Emerson made contributions in cost accounting via use of the Hollerith punch card for tabulating machines in accounting records, and he helped set standards for judging worker and shop efficiency.

Efficiency was considered just, since it was correlated with character-building and high moral standards. As the editor of the *Engineering Magazine* put it,

only a pessimist could deny that we are making progress away from the inefficiencies of dishonesty . . . We must admit that the rapid and considerable change is taking place in American canons of business morality . . . The gospel of efficiency, like every other gospel that has ever been preached, condemns dishonesty; but it goes further than preaching, and shows that the penalty for the sin of inefficiency does not depend on any outer judgment that may be evaded, but follows as inevitably as burning follows the handling of fire. (*Engineering Magazine*, April 1909: 96)

In June 1910, the *Engineering Magazine* started publishing a new series of articles, entitled 'The Twelve Principles of Efficiency', with the explicit goal of transforming the philosophy of efficiency into common industrial practice. Dunlap envisioned an organized National Efficiency program. He said, 'The appearance of such a teaching is peculiarly opportune, for the toll laid upon the nation by extravagance and waste due to inefficiency is growing too heavy to be borne, and the resistance to it is causing a great awakening of inquiry and effort toward relief.' Dunlap had faith that 'the new philosophy' could change the whole industry, energizing it without the wasteful warfare accompanying competition. As Harrington Emerson has argued, 'not by individual striving, but solely by establishing, from all the accumulated and available wisdom of the world, staff-knowledge standards for each act—by carrying staff standards into effect through directing line organization through rewards for individual excellence, persuading the individual to accept staff standards, to accept line direction and control, and under this double guidance to do his own uttermost best' (*Engineering Magazine*, November 1910: 257).

Following Brandeis's testimony in the Eastern Rate Case in 1911, the terms 'efficiency' and 'Scientific Management' became equated one with the other and they came to be popular catchwords (Haber 1964). The *New Republic* recommended that the State Industrial Commission should hire efficiency experts to inspect factory efficiency, similar to the way in which agencies inspect safety or sanitary conditions (Haber 1964: 89). Emerson himself offered up an efficiency plan which was a blend of management mechanisms and moral exhortation; he made his living selling efficiency kits (Haber 1964: 56). He sold, for example, a twenty-four-lesson home study course in efficiency, and added to his staff a 'character analyst' who applied phrenology for the 'scientific' selection of workers.

Emerson and others called for the development of 'efficiency conscience' as an obligation to oneself and to society (Haber 1964: 58). In February 1911, Dunlap observed that 'Mr. Emerson's formulation of definite principles of efficiency, which began in our issue of June, 1910, is attracting a growing momentum of interest and appreciation. It is exercising a force upon industrial thought' (*Engineering Magazine*, February 1911: 761).

During the Eastern Rate Case and the hearings in Washington, the editors of the *American Machinist* argued that the event brought home the point that 'efficiency has taken rank as a National issue'. They explained why efficiency was important to the continuation and progress of national welfare, and why this was a felicitous development. They observed an 'awakening among manufacturers' and were certain that the trend would eventually convince manufacturers and 'old-line' managers who had become overwhelmed by the complexities in production (*Engineering Magazine*, January 1911: 605). Dunlap explained that the very genius of efficiency engineering is that it places functional betterment in the hands of a separate staff, leaving the line officials free for routine administration. He argued, '[It] lightened the burdens of the operating men, instead of adding something more to them' (*Engineering Magazine*, January 1911: 606).

The editors of the *Engineering Magazine* created an identity between efficiency, equality, and the interest of the public at large. In an editorial comment in March 1911, they argued that,

in refusing the advances in rates which the railroads of the United States have sought to impose, the Interstate Commerce Commission has taken a stand that may prove to be a turning point in the progressive exploitation of the public by 'The Interests'—an exploitation heretofore almost unchecked, because resistance to it, though growing in bitterness, has lacked organization and has lacked efficient mode of expression. (*Engineering Magazine*, March 1911: 951)

The editors made public protection the basic rationale of efficiency. In the early part of the hearings, Commissioner Lane questioned the president of the Baltimore and Ohio: 'Is there any reason to believe that these increases [of rates] would stop with the present increase if it should be allowed?' President Willard replied, 'No, I think not. I think that the tendency of rates will be to continue upward.' This testimony corroborated, according to the editorial, Brandeis's statement that the consumer should 'beware of this vicious cycle of ever-increasing freight rates and ever-increasing cost of living'. The editors concluded the editorial by saying that even though the principles and methods of efficiency were initially ridiculed and faced the railways' hostility, eventually they would prove their salvation (*Engineering Magazine*, March 1911: 952).[30]

During the debate around the appropriation bill, which included a prohibition of applying Scientific Management in governmental shops, the editors of the *Engineering Magazine* capitalized again on equality and progress, suggesting that with the application of the efficiency system there is 'a substantial increase in the earnings of the men. Surely, such being the case, would it not be consummate folly to turn back the wheels of progress at this critical time?' (*Engineering Magazine*, January 1916: 608). In the same vein, institutional economist John Commons argued that Scientific Management and collective bargaining 'could and should flourish together' (Haber 1964: 148). Indeed, both Progressivists and engineers were horrified at the possibility of 'class warfare', and saw themselves as mediators between capital and labor. For Progressive engineers efficiency meant social harmony, making each workman's interest the same as that of his employers.

Efficiency societies spread rapidly in most of the major cities of the United States. The three centres of the efficiency movement in New York before the First World War were the Taylor Society, the Efficiency Society, and *Efficiency Magazine* (Haber 1964: 72). In 1914, an efficiency exposition was held in the Grand Central Palace in New York, with 69,000 people in attendance (Haber 1964: 61).[31] The spread of the efficiency craze in America spilled over—by acts of translation—to seemingly unrelated domains, colonizing religious, moral, and political thought. Feminists began to apply the principle of efficiency to the home: 'Our hope is to bring the masculine and the feminine mind more closely together in the industry of home-making by raising housework to the plane of Scientific Engineering' (Haber 1964: 62). Housekeeping experiment stations were set up to discover the principles of 'domestic engineering'. Home was defined as 'part of a great factory for the production of citizens' (Haber 1964: 62). Protestant churches were receptive to the idea, and in New York a Church Efficiency Committee was established. Such occurrences opened the door to consider applying this perspective to a wide range of human endeavors. Frank Gilbert, for example, took moving pictures of his children washing dishes, so he could figure out how they could reduce unnecessary motions (Gilbreth and Carey 1949: 2). Gilbreth extended motion studies to the work of musicians, baseball players, fencers, and oyster-openers (Haber 1964; see also Gilbreth and Carey 1949). Dunlap suggested that 'better concepts of efficiency are indeed sorely needed everywhere', including in the law. In reference to the McNamara trial—which took place following the destruction of the *Los Angeles Times* building which resulted in the death of twenty persons—Dunlap argued that the trial was managed inefficiently. He accused the trial staff of taking too much time examining witnesses (*Engineering Magazine*, November 1911: 251–2). The totalization of the public sphere by the instrumental logic of efficiency was pervasive. Its logic absorbed every aspect of culture, and became the American culture.

Litterer used the 'automatic pilot' metaphor to describe the emergence of literature on management systems (Litterer 1986). Systems represented an attempt to 'establish automatic management for sections of the internal operation of the firm, designed both to insure that these operations would be adequately performed, and to free managers, especially higher managers, for other managerial tasks' (Litterer 1986: 122). The organizational system, as an automatic pilot, gradually expanded its territory during 1882–1932, covering and depoliticizing such separate fields as accountancy, production, and wages. Systems of all kinds, however, were not applied without struggle. The engineers had to steer the boat of management in stormy water. These struggles are described in the next chapter.

## Notes

1. I do not mean to argue that engineers invented the notion of 'mechanical system'. Metaphors of the world as a machine emerged in Europe as early as the 17th century, and brought revolutionary changes in physics and astronomy. During the 19th century scientists continued to elaborate the mechanistic model of the universe in physics, chemistry, biology, psychology, and the social sciences (Capra 1982; see also Mumford 1970). However, as I argued in the introductory chapter, I refrain from equating the term 'ideology' with a scheme of abstract ideas. Rather I define ideology as practice and trace the manner in which ideas are invoked in the everyday practical life of engineers. This methodological and theoretical strategy suggests that abstract systems theory itself did not lead to the creation of American management discourse; only the peculiar application and interpretation of mechanical engineers did.

2. See Latour and Woolgar 1979; Callon 1980; Knorr-Cetina 1983; Latour 1987 for the essentials of the Constructivist approach developed here. For useful applications see Breslau 1998; Yonay 1998.

3. To distinguish between individuals and social entities organizational theorists use concepts such as organizational fields (DiMaggio and Powell 1983), interorganizational fields (Benson 1975), sectors (Scott and Meyer 1994), industrial systems (Hirsch 1972), and business systems (Whitely 1992). The concept of 'field' is used here to mean a configuration of objective relations between positions (Bourdieu 1992) that 'delimit a socially constructed space in which agents struggle, depending on the position they occupy in that space, either to change or to preserve its boundaries and form' (Wacquant 1992: 17; quoted in Kjir 1998). The concept is useful as it situates social entities as part of a decentralized relational structure that shapes and gives meaning to them (Kjir 1998).

4. It is not denied that industrialists and professional engineers operated in environments rife with uncertainty and technical problems. This book, however, is concerned with understanding the parameters that cultivated the discourse regarding systems, which enabled it to grow and eventually become legitimized and pivotal in management and organization theory.

5. One of the reasons that the railroad staff were involved with systematization was the need to coordinate it in light of safety violations. As early as 1841, a series of collisions on the Western Railroad promoted the initiation of administrative rules and structural changes. Managers were required to keep records about operation and report to superiors periodically—see Yates 1989: 5. One of the very first conceptualizations of organizations in the USA can be traced back to Daniel McCallum's report to the president of the New York Railroad Company in 1856. McCallum referred to 'a system perfect in its details, properly adapted and vigilantly

enforced'—quoted in Yates 1989: 7; see also Chandler 1977. Furthermore, managers of the railroad invented many of the modern accounting techniques.

6. The status of sociology as an ally of management will be discussed in depth in the concluding chapter.

7. The extension of the technical field to the world of organizations can be demonstrated quantitatively with regard to the notion of 'uncertainty'. Weitz (1997) quantified the discourse on technical uncertainty and the discourse on organizational uncertainty in the *American Machinist* to determine their evolution over time and their relationship to each other. Two time-periods were compared: 1879–1917 and 1918–32. The term 'uncertainty' was used in conjunction with related terms such as 'ambiguity', 'chance', 'chaos', 'vagueness', 'unpredictability', 'haziness', and 'risk'. The examination of the ratio of the reference to technical uncertainty and organization uncertainty in the two time-periods reveals that the proportion of technical uncertainty to organizational uncertainty in the first period (3.77) is 1.5 times as large as in the later period (2.38). A $t$-test indicated that this difference is statistically different from zero.

8. Henry Robinson Towne had a degree from the University of Pennsylvania and worked after his studies at the Yale Lock Company. When he presented the paper to ASME he was already the president of the company. That year Coleman Sellers, the president of ASME, was sick and Towne presided over the meeting.

9. Earlier, Robert Thurston had pointed out the relationship between mechanical engineers and the management of the firm. See Robert Thurston, 'The Mechanical Engineer, his Work and his Policy' *Transactions of the ASME*, 4, 1882.

10. Smith was the founder of a metal firm which he managed until his death in 1926. He is known in the engineering literature for his work on standard means for the identification of parts and shop orders as integral parts of mechanical engineering.

11. Metcalf began a military career after graduating from West Point in the period after the Civil War. He was an engineer in the Ordnance Department and a superintendent in various army arsenals. He wrote a book on cost accounting titled *The Cost of Manufacturers and the Administration of Workshops, Public and Private*.

12. See 'Editorial Comment', *Engineering Magazine*, March 1899: 1001 for a reflexive comment that describes the 'awakening in everything relating to workshop administration'.

13. As an example of such perception, see also Charles Day, 'Management Principles and the Consulting Engineer', *Engineering Magazine*, April 1911: 133–40.

14. Management is defined here in its broadest sense. All items concerned with the supervision of workers, recruitment, payments, organization and administration, economic issues, production control, cost accounting, finance, inventory control, office control, labor relations, efficiency and productivity, labor market, selection, training, or time and motion studies were included in the analysis.

15. The yearly average volume devoted to management was 10 percent out of the entire text (s.d. = 0.05).

16. Before 1895 there was an average of ten items per year (the *Engineering Magazine* published fewer and longer articles compared with the *American Machinist*).

17. For the purpose of this study I examined all forty-two years between 1891 and 1932 (approximately 61,985 pages). Four volumes (each covers six months) were missing

and could not be examined: vol. 20 (1900), vol. 26 (1903), vol. 43 (1912), and vol. 61 (1921). Since the magazine gradually became a management magazine, it was useless to compile data on management after 1918.

18. For example Slater J. Lewis, *The Commercial Organization of Factories* (1896); Clinton E. Woods, *Woods' Reports on Industrial Organization, Systematization, and Accounting* (1908); and Russell Robb, *Lectures on Organization* (1910). See Haber 1964: 20.

19. Acknowledgements regarding the connection of the systematizers with the large corporations are numerous. See for example 'A Rational and Economical System for Controlling Factory Detail', *Engineering Magazine*, February 1902: 693–702. See also Jenks 1961; Litterer 1961.

20. Nelson (1975; cited in Barley and Kunda 1992) has described a similar trend. Referring to the increasing frequency of papers concerned with systematic management in the late 1800s, he argues that 'Only 15 articles appeared before 1880. After that . . . The number increased rapidly. From 1880 to 1885, 60 articles appeared, between 1885 and 1890, 93, in the next five years, 68 and in the last five years of the century, 185.'

21. The division by management (the proportion of pages devoted to the discussion of management) was introduced to capture the growth of systems net of the growth of management. This measure was repeated for each periodical and was averaged for each year. To be included, items had to address the term 'system' directly, either in the title or in the text. In coding 'organizational system', I collapsed all categories (cost-accountancy systems, production control systems, wage systems, and hierarchical systems) into one. Here I assumed that uses of 'system' can be aggregated across writers and over time. By so doing, I do not imply that all systems look alike or that systems do not change. I do suggest, however, that all systems have certain common properties, an assumption made by Nelson (1975), as well.

22. As will become apparent in later chapters, systems discourse was fairly institutionalized during the First World War when it was supplemented by increasing preoccupation with industrial psychology. In 1916 Walter Scott developed psychological tests for industrial workers in Cheney Brothers and Joseph & Feiss Company. In 1917–18 he used this experience to conduct testing programs for the US army. See Nelson 1975 and Bendix 1956/1974.

23. There are exceptions, however; see for example Church's article on 'Machine Design and the Design of Systems', *American Machinist*, 8 July 1915: 61–6. Church argues that it is not always parallel since machines that are improperly designed cease working. Improper systems keep working and bring damage.

24. Horace Lucian Arnold, *The Complete Cost-Keeper* (1901). Cited in Litterer 1986: 109.

25. The concept of 'constructive rationality' can be traced back to 17th- and 18th-century rationalist philosophers who were central to changing the meaning of 'reason' from the capacity to recognize truth to a capacity for deductive reasoning based on explicit, undoubted premises. The immediate implication of this philosophy was that all useful human institutions are deliberate creations of conscious human reason. Reason became a method. As Ernst Cassirer put it, '[reason] was no longer an essence of innate ideas . . . [It became] a mode of acquisition' (Cassirer 1951; quoted by Wilson 1957).

26. Constructive rationality may well lead to an increased hierarchy, as exemplified by Dahrendorf's (1968: 215–31) dichotomy between constructive or plan rationality, and critical or market rationality. The first gives way to the 'visible hand' economy, while the latter encourages *laissez-faire* and market economy. Plan rationality is skeptical of agency and liberalism, and sees them as non-rational market arrangements that, if left unattended, invariably lead to chaos. It therefore encourages an a-priori design of the economy and society. I will return to these philosophical aspects in my concluding discussion of the political side of American social sciences. See also Shenhav 1994.

27. I use the term 'Institutional Theory' despite the existence of several versions. For a detailed discussion see Scott 1987; Zucker 1987.

28. This crusade generated a strong and furious reaction from engineers who were connected to utilities. For example, Alexander C. Humphreys, president of Stevens Institute and a consultant to the gas industry, denounced Cooke's efforts. The utilities were one of the largest employers of mechanical engineers. They were strong supporters of ASME and their engineers were prominent members of the society. See Sinclair 1980: 103–4.

29. The phase probably started with the publication of Taylor's paper, 'A Piece Rate System: A Step toward Partial Solution to the Labor Problem', in 1895. However, it was not until 1910 that it was recognized as a movement. See Haber 1964; Kanigel 1997.

30. Dunlap also announced that the Brandeis testimony presenting the case for efficiency was being issued in book form by the *Engineering Magazine* under the title 'Scientific Management and Railroads'.

31. During the exposition, the *American Machinist* suggested that real efficiency knows neither nationality nor locality. As the editors omnipotently suggested, 'We are big enough and broad enough to look at a machine for what it can do instead of inquiring into details of the pedigree of its builders.' See *American Machinist*, 16 April 1914: 696.

TABLE 2. *Literature on management (relative to the annual volume of engineering literature) and systems (relative to the annual volume of literature on management), 1879–1932*

| Year | Systems | Management |
| --- | --- | --- |
| 1879 | 0.049 | 0.019 |
| 1880 | 0.024 | 0.012 |
| 1881 | 0.000 | 0.011 |
| 1882 | 0.135 | 0.106 |
| 1883 | 0.169 | 0.115 |
| 1884 | 0.023 | 0.009 |
| 1885 | 0.096 | 0.136 |
| 1886 | 0.138 | 0.014 |
| 1887 | 0.000 | 0.008 |
| 1888 | 0.000 | 0.008 |
| 1889 | 0.154 | 0.033 |

| Year | Systems | Management |
|------|---------|------------|
| 1890 | 0.194 | 0.029 |
| 1891 | 0.075 | 0.017 |
| 1892 | 0.000 | 0.009 |
| 1893 | 0.017 | 0.014 |
| 1894 | 0.091 | 0.012 |
| 1895 | 0.297 | 0.008 |
| 1896 | 0.086 | 0.148 |
| 1897 | 0.399 | 0.164 |
| 1898 | 0.603 | 0.017 |
| 1899 | 0.326 | 0.217 |
| 1900 | 0.416 | 0.036 |
| 1901 | 0.329 | 0.172 |
| 1902 | 0.488 | 0.039 |
| 1903 | 0.359 | 0.065 |
| 1904 | 0.466 | 0.046 |
| 1905 | 0.543 | 0.039 |
| 1906 | 0.315 | 0.047 |
| 1907 | 0.463 | 0.061 |
| 1908 | 0.551 | 0.043 |
| 1909 | 0.554 | 0.076 |
| 1910 | 0.452 | 0.130 |
| 1911 | 0.507 | 0.158 |
| 1912 | 0.416 | 0.134 |
| 1913 | 0.527 | 0.054 |
| 1914 | 0.452 | 0.065 |
| 1915 | 0.319 | 0.079 |
| 1916 | 0.328 | 0.240 |
| 1917 | 0.313 | 0.077 |
| 1918 | 0.173 | 0.137 |
| 1919 | 0.334 | 0.116 |
| 1920 | 0.254 | 0.130 |
| 1921 | 0.261 | 0.189 |
| 1922 | 0.368 | 0.087 |
| 1923 | 0.379 | 0.392 |
| 1924 | 0.561 | 0.062 |
| 1925 | 0.312 | 0.183 |
| 1926 | 0.305 | 0.064 |
| 1927 | 0.102 | 0.144 |
| 1928 | 0.259 | 0.056 |
| 1929 | 0.208 | 0.435 |
| 1930 | 0.284 | 0.077 |
| 1931 | 0.254 | 0.144 |
| 1932 | 0.428 | 0.081 |

# 4

# Contested Rationality: Disturbances, Controversies, and Opposition to Management Systems

A system solution transformed the relation between the parties from one of qualified antagonism to more complete cooperation.

(Williamson 1975: 99)

There has always been opposition to system, and a feeling that much of it is red-tape.

(*House Magazine*, Scovill Manufacturing Company, quoted in Yates 1989: 195)

They had every man in the place running around with a pencil over his ear, and we didn't get the work done.

(A foreman describing the work of the systematizers, *American Machinist*, 29 April 1915: 750)

The organizing concepts around which managerial rationality was engineered were systematization and standardization. The underlying assumption was that the machine-like manufacturing firm would generate predictability, stability, consistency, and certainty. Unpredictable human behavior—defined in organizational language as uncertainty and inefficiency—would be controlled and tamed through machine-like organizational arrangements. This assumption was based on a cognitive and cultural equation containing two binary poles: on the one hand the desired end of rationality and certainty, on the other, that of uncertainty and irrationality. Conflicts, emotions, politics, 'otherness', and additional non-organizational traits fall under the rubric of irrationality, likely to evoke unpredictability.

Mainstream organization theory subscribes to this cultural equation and views capitalists/managers, as well as industrial technology, as the major forces of the rationalization of industry (Landes 1969). The advancement of organizational rationality is taken for granted to be the result of capitalists' and managers' economic motives, a means of conducting efficient operations to achieve profitable ends. It posits an evolutionary, almost universal, path of development with unavoidable logic.

The views of the economic historian Alfred Chandler are typical of the approach arguing that capitalists came to realize that they needed a much more systematic control mechanism for efficiency purposes (Chandler 1962, 1977, 1990; for a critique see DuBoff and Herman 1980). The advent of the first integrated enterprises during the 1880s and 1890s 'brought about' new problems, such as an increase in the volume of output, that 'led' to the building of the first administrative systems (Chandler 1977: 24). Chandler explicated the functional necessity of so-called managerial capitalism in the following terms:

Technological innovation, the rapid growth and spread of population, and expanding per capita income made the processes of production and distribution more complex, and increased the speed and volume of the flow of materials through them. Existing market mechanisms were often no longer able to co-ordinate these flows effectively. The new technologies and expanding markets thus created for the first time a need for administrative co-ordination. To carry out this function, entrepreneurs built multi-unit business enterprises and hired the managers needed to administer them. (Chandler 1977: 484)

Chandler is explicit about the force behind this process: 'As technology became both more complex and more productive, and as markets continued to expand, these managers assumed command in the central sectors of the American economy.' To Chandler, 'the appearance of managerial capitalism has been, therefore, an economic phenomenon', and not a political one (Chandler 1977: 497). Administrative systems were adopted as rational responses to problems of economic reality confronting capitalists. In Chandler's analysis, the development of systems had no reference to power, politics, and interests. Although Chandler was vague about agency ('led', 'brought about'), he attributes the rise of business administration to employers' and managers' (alike) attempts to meet the strategic challenges facing them (Chandler 1962).

Oliver Williamson, similarly, analyzes the replacement of the inside-contracting method, prevalent in the USA in the 1880s and 1890s (see Chapter 1), with formal organizational systems. The underlying theory in his explanation is that of 'transaction costs'. He argues that

a system solution transformed the relation between the parties from one of qualified antagonism to more complete cooperation . . . The firm offered managers job security and an internal equity system, in return for which managers agreed to being evaluated in terms of their contribution to the system as a whole—as revealed in part by their attitude of cooperation. (Williamson 1975: 99)

Williamson claims that the new system 'won' since it reduced uncertainty and curtailed opportunistic behavior, ultimately pacifying the relationship within the firm.

Richard Edwards offered a Neo-Marxist perspective which is often considered an alternative to these two evolutionary perspectives (Edwards 1979). But his approach proposes a similar logic, albeit from a very different theoretical base, as to the relationship between capitalists and managers regarding the rationalization of industry. At the turn of the century, he says, large corporations

> began to move in systematic ways to reorganize work, [since] pressure built up for more regularized and structured management practices . . . Large firms developed methods of organization that are more formalized and more consciously contrived than simple control . . . Consciously contrived controls could be embedded in either the physical structure of the labor process (producing 'technical' control) or in its social structure (producing 'bureaucratic' control). The new systems made control more institutional and less visible to workers. (Edwards 1979: 20, 30)

Edwards assumes that employers and managers had a shared interest in the systematization and depersonalization of organizational management. Although he holds a conflictual perspective, he allows no room for the conflicting interests between managers and capitalists.

In sum, the historical narratives offered by Chandler, Edwards, and Williamson share two basic assumptions.[1] First, that organizational rationality 'evolved', and was received as a natural and logical extension of American industrial capitalism. Second, that systems were introduced by employers, and their managers and consultants (conceptualized as functionaries of capital), who understood the importance of these systems and applied them to the betterment of their firms or to the maximization of their interests. These observations—although representing different ideological positions—divest management history of its inherent conflicts and often bitter disputes and portray the development of management to be identical with the rational logic of American capitalism.[2]

I would like to offer a different historical view, one which emphasizes the contested nature of rationality. According to this approach, the installation of systems—and the introduction of experts such as efficiency engineers, bookkeepers, timekeepers, auditors, stores keepers, inspectors, and production planners—encountered several hubs of opposition: of reluctant employers, of practicing managers and engineers, and of frustrated workers. The opposition of employers/capitalists—those who arguably had most to gain by rationalization and systematization—is most compelling and is hardly mentioned in management historiography. Exceptional are Lash and Urry, who noted that the growth of rational management 'was not something that was simply inevitable, resulting either from the logic of capitalist accumulation or the imperatives of modern technology' (Lash and Urry 1987: 162). To the contrary: 'The rise of modern management involved a substantial break in the logic of capitalist development, and was by no means inevitable' (ibid.: 163).

As shown below, this opposition between the rise of management and the logic of traditional capitalism provides the necessary historical problematization which is missing in contemporary management historiography. It suggests that there is no simple organizing historical logic to the rise of management systems and that the historical relationship between industrial capitalism and industrial management needs to be reconceptualized. The emphasis on the conflictual dimension of the history of systems points to the fact that 'rationality' was a controversial concept.[3] Its logic was embedded within a political structure that shaped its parameters and endorsed its legitimacy. It is the relationship between the rationality of systems and its political embeddedness that I address empirically in the following chapters.

### 4.1 Objection of employers and manufacturers to management systems

Despite the general blossoming of 'organizations as systems' in the engineering literature and despite the fact that it emerged out of 'shop culture', in practice, many employers were apprehensive about adopting the new administrative systems. An in-house magazine of one of the leading manufacturing firms pointed out that 'there has always been opposition to system, and a feeling that much of it is red-tape'.[4] The initial resistance of employers to the introduction of engineering management techniques has scarcely been studied, a lack made more poignant by the fact that engineers/managers and employers later became symbiotically co-dependent. While management techniques were also used by employers as a source of power and control, employers' initial resistance demonstrates that engineers and managers were not simply obedient 'organs of capitalism'. They each had their own agenda to promote. Manufacturers, particularly the smaller ones, viewed systematization as a strategy employed by engineers to expand their professional territory.[5] To the capitalist mind, the idea of 'systems' did not appear natural. To many, systems appeared costly and superfluous, and seemed to generate red tape, unpredictability, lack of control, conflicts, and instability (see Pollard 1965: 288, for a similar argument in Britain). One foreman, in describing the work of the systematizers, explained: 'they had every man in the place running around with a pencil over his ear, and we didn't get the work done' (*American Machinist*, 29 April 1915: 750). As John Dunlap, editor of *Engineering Magazine*, observed, employers perceived systematization as 'fantastically theoretical and highly impractical' (*Engineering Magazine*, May 1916: 272).

These objections troubled and baffled mechanical engineers. In an editorial in 1891, the editors of the *American Machinist* complained that engineers wanted to increase efficiency but found that their efforts were impeded by the very men who had most to gain by this progress. They argued that mechanical engineers needed to learn 'how to manage employers' without their suspecting that they were being managed (*American Machinist*, 8 January 1891: 8). During the first decade of the twentieth century, in the midst of the 'systematization' craze, the tension between engineers and employers was frequently discussed in the engineering literature. In several articles during 1901–2, Charles U. Carpenter, a mechanical engineer, described the objection of manufacturers to the introduction of management systems (*Engineering Magazine*, April 1902: 15–18). He explained that to the mind of the old-time manufacturer, the word system is associated with the horror of 'extra clerks'. Carpenter depicted the stance of 'unprogressive manufacturers': 'Oh, that is too much red-tape for me. When I or my men want a thing we go get it in the quickest and easiest way we can. No red-tape, no records for me. Every one helps himself, and we get the work [done] somehow.'

Carpenter tried to convince the readers that this was an erroneous position:

His 'somehow' product is generally not good in quality, not delivered promptly, nor sufficiently low in cost to enable him to hold his own in the business world . . . He does not understand that the losses he is daily bearing are many times the amount that his extra clerks would cost him. In fact, his 'extra clerks' would probably prove the best investment he could ever make . . . It is the old question of the man holding the coin so close to the eye as to shut out entirely the greater and broader horizon of his commercial possibilities in both the expansion of his business and in factory economies. (*Engineering Magazine*, April 1902: 15–18)

Carpenter sought to demonstrate that elements of the system—such as stock tracing, tabulation of costs, quality inspection—are of great efficiency while at the same time comparatively inexpensive. He concluded his article with an exhortation in language that capitalists could understand: '[the manufacturer] ought to realize that he should be guided in his system of factory management by the same principles that he uses in checking up his bank account, seeing that he is credited with all deposits, and debited only with that which is properly chargeable to him, by the same common-sense that he uses in keeping the proper trace of his account'.

Five years later, in 1907, Carpenter published an additional series of articles in which he was still attempting to persuade reluctant capitalists to adopt systems (the first article was Charles U. Carpenter, 'Profit Making in Shop and Factory Management: The Reorganization of a Run-Down Concern', *Engineering Magazine*, January 1907: 481–92). He said, 'There are still many manufacturers who are not satisfied to give their unqualified approval to modern [management] methods . . . The number is growing less every day, but there are thousands to whom these remarks apply.' In much the same spirit, a columnist in *American Machinist* reassured shop owners and attempted to demystify the term 'system': 'Don't get scared as soon as you hear the word "system" . . . as it means hanging your coat in the same place everyday . . . If it were to be called "common sense" perhaps you were to feel more kindly to it' (*American Machinist*, 12 October 1908: 488).

To many manufacturers, according to Carpenter, 'the very word "organization" implies something mysterious—something big and certainly expensive'. To the reluctant employers, 'the idea of "system" is indissolubly linked with "red tape." "System" to them means additions to their clerical force, and additions to their clerical force mean additional dollars spent upon "non producers" '. Carpenter emphasized the necessity of systems in light of the state of 'uncertainty' within which firms operate: 'Many manufacturers today have an uncomfortable sensation of uncertainty concerning the progress and profits of the establishment under their management.' System is a step to remedy this situation: 'Once your competitor has built his tools for economical production, [your profits] decrease. And the longer you delay adopting similar methods, the more the difficulties increase.' Carpenter addresses the reluctant manufacturer who has 'his hands tied' and 'his eyes closed'. Those, Carpenter said, 'realize that something is wrong, seriously wrong, and would be glad to apply modern methods if they but knew what they were and how to apply them'. This manufacturer 'faces ignorance, prejudice, false pride and stubbornness'. Carpenter is very explicit in his address to employers: '[We] must bring to them an absolutely unbiased mind and a determination to analyze the situation thoroughly and mercilessly, and so to form an accurate judgment.'

In 1912, Leon Alford, the influential editor of *American Machinist* from 1910 to 1917, was asked by ASME officials James Dodge and Fred Halsey to write a report on the status of industrial management. Alford examined the status of systematization and brought empirical evidence to illustrate the problems associated with the adoption of systems by manufacturers (*American Machinist*, 7 November 1912: 757–62). Alford reported that there was an agreement among industrialists that the work of the systematizers did not necessarily lead to more efficient production. According to the report, shop owners blamed systematizers for failing 'to view the plant from the investor's standpoint' and for using the plant as 'a laboratory offering opportunities for interesting and expensive experiments'. Out of their own self-serving agenda, the systematizers 'waste time and money on problems that will yield to scientific treatment, but which do not recur often enough to justify such a solution'. Manufacturers blamed the systematizers for using and publishing 'statistics regarding gains made through the use of particular systems, without a frank statement of the degree of inefficiency of the plants before reorganization'. The report further argued that the introduction of systems led to 'nonresponsibility on the part of any person for that total result' and to 'the frequent assumption that the treatment of the problems of similar plants should be identical'. The empirical evidence, then, points to the fact that at the time when management systems were first introduced by mechanical engineers and other systematizers, many manufacturers constituted an opposition that needed to be persuaded, even manipulated, to get them to cooperate with the 'rationalization' process. Further, the link between these systems and efficiency was not at all clear. The evidence, then, challenges the assumption that the introduction of management systems was a self-evident 'higher stage' in the evolution of industrial capitalism.[6]

## 4.2 Objection to systems within engineering circles

When the concept of 'systems' was first conceived, manufacturers were not alone in their ambivalence; the engineering community was not at all unanimous in embracing the concept. Concerned over restricting the autonomy of machinists with the imposition of bureaucratic rules, the editors of *American Machinist* found it questionable that stringent rules would improve the 'value of product per man employed' (*American Machinist*, 21 May 1891: 8). They reported in 1891 that 'one of the best and most successful shop managers in this country', employing 1,200 workers, decided 'to take down all the framed rules, and have no shop "rules and regulations" whatever'. In an article from the same year, Walter Snow qualified the applicability of systems in industry, arguing that systems must be made for the shop rather than vice versa. He believed that 'it is utterly impossible to dictate a standard system that shall be applicable to all classes of manufactures' (*American Machinist*, 1 January 1891: 7). In a 1904 article in *American Machinist* entitled 'Over-Systemizing', another author conceded, 'systematic management is certainly a necessity', but fads are troublesome things and 'there are indications that this subject of "production engineering" and "systemizing" is rapidly developing into such a fad' (*American Machinist*, 10 November 1904: 1499). While the author believed that a 'proper amount of system' decreases the cost and improves the quality of a product, he felt that too much system increases the cost and decreases the output. The article was careful to underscore that its purpose was not 'to advocate a return to the conditions surrounding the early stages of manufacturing, when the whole office force was under the Old Man's hat and all records were carried in his vest pocket'. On the contrary, its conclusion was that the difficulties associated with too much systematization justified the introduction of an additional expert, a 'systematic simplifier', or a 'deduction engineer', whose role would be to eliminate red tape. As is often the case, too much red tape was remedied with additional red tape.

At the turn of the century, debates surrounding the notion of systems intensified. In 1904 Egbert Watson, an engineer and a frequent contributor to the technical press,[7] observed that 'it is scarcely possible to take up a technical journal, or even a trade paper, that has not an illustrated system of some kind for producing goods, all of which goes to show that in the making of systems there is no end' (*Engineering Magazine*, November 1904: 211–19). Watson believed that only a 'few systems are elastic enough to admit of changes of form without throwing everything out of gear'. He explained that, 'when the human element is introduced by systems, there is always the possibility of derangement through the fallibility of man'. Since 'no system is perfect', he recommended adopting modest ones. Watson described a large metal shop, employing 3,000 workers, which did not have more than four men in the drawing room, with 'a very good system'. The editors of the *Engineering Magazine* did not disagree: 'Mr. Watson's review sounds a note of conservatism which will be welcome to many who find themselves unable to follow the modern pursuit of "system" to the extremes occasionally advocated.' Adopting a historical perspective, they noted that 'new and important movements, in the first flush of their power, are apt to be carried to extremes, and the modern tendency toward "system and organization" is probably no exception'.

This editorial was, no doubt, a criticism of radical systematization. Indeed, on a different occasion the editors deplored the tendency to make much of laws that 'unnecessarily and unjustly restrict personal freedom and clog human progress'. They concluded that system and order are, 'of course, necessary', but 'it is possible to carry them too far' (*American Machinist*, 7 January 1904: 35).

In September 1906, Louis Bell, a university professor and a consulting engineer,[8] sought to alarm the technological and business community in his article 'Wake up America!' (*Engineering Magazine*, September 1906: 801–8). Invoking the 'disaster' that American manufactures were facing given the 'German peril', or the 'Belgian peril', Bell warned of the dangers 'lurking in over-confidence in system' (*Engineering Magazine*, September 1906: 873). He believed that the automatic and standardized machinery of the 'American system'—which suffers 'from too close adherence to the principle of averages upon which it is founded'—results in workmen who are merely 'belts, wheels, and oil-cans'. If skilled workers and artisans are still found in American shops, he implied, they are rarely 'native American' but rather German, Swedish, or English. Bell criticized extant industrial organization for aggravating even further the evils 'which follow in the train of standardized output'. Bell made an exceptional political argument, referring to the consequences of the standardization of organizations. He believed that standardization

leads directly to the labor troubles which steadily increase in number and severity . . . As machinery has been perfected and the works have become a huge machine tool, so the workman has become less an individual. [Workers know] that they are merely parts of a machine which stops and starts, accelerates and slows down, from causes absolutely beyond their control . . . Only the blind in spirit can fail to see the handwriting on the wall: In the day when there is greater stability in conditions and keener actual competition, natural selection will get to work and standardized mediocrity will not be among the fittest to survive. (Ibid.)

Given this prophecy, he suggested that 'the greatest industrial problem today is to maintain the supply of active, intelligent, resourceful American labor in spite of the American system'. Bell's article stirred up a heated discussion. The editors of *Engineering Magazine* exclaimed:

It is almost ten years since *The Engineering Magazine* laid down the first clear definitions of that system of manufacturing which has come to be known as distinctively American . . . We have numbered among our contributors most of the great specialists in the practice of 'Production Engineering'—the modern profession based upon this highly modern literature—and the fundamental principles of systematized, specialized, standardized, and repetitive manufacture have been set forth more fully and lucidly here than anywhere else. (*Engineering Magazine*, September 1906: 801–8)

In this context, the editors apologetically defended the inclusion of Bell's article, 'We should not be true to our course or our calling if we did not examine fully the bounds of these methods, and seek to show the limits of their power and range, as well as to exploit the regions in which they have undoubted sway.'

William O. Weber, a consulting engineer and a member of ASME,[9] argued in the subsequent issue of *Engineering Magazine* that Bell's assumptions were not justified by the facts. He argued, 'It has never been my experience that "standardization" means the cessation of active improvement.' He restated the American Exceptionalist position: 'The American manufacturer is the quickest in the world to adopt an improvement and to make it a standard . . . His willingness to copy European improvements and adopt them shows the progressiveness of the American manufacturer.' Despite his confidence in standardization, the writer expressed reservations regarding the flexibility of system: 'In my mind, the most serious danger which American manufacturing interests have to confront is the idea that a system will ever entirely supplant the ability of a good working superintendent. A complex system of red-tape methods and reports will eventually enmesh a factory in a set of hide-bound methods which are almost impossible of adaptation to new and changed conditions.' Another writer argued that system alone is useless, however perfect and 'well-ordered' it may be (*American Machinist*, 29 April 1915: 750). He said, 'a systematizer will introduce forms and procedures, and think he has done a fine job, [but] the system won't work' if it stands alone. The factory which puts in a 'system, builds a house on sand', said the writer. Likewise, W. R. Basset of Miller, Franklin, Basset & Co. argued that 'system and routine are essential' but insufficient to ensure profit (*American Machinist*, 23 March 1922: 443). An editorial warned, 'Beware of the danger of expecting a system to do all your work for you' (*American Machinist*, 23 March 1922: 458). The editorial suggested, 'get a good system and make it work, but don't let it get you'. The editors did not recommend the adoption of the same system in different plants: 'Beware of the universal system; it's loaded.'

In 1911, following the Eastern Rate Case (see Chapter 3), the editor of *Engineering Magazine* declared,

In the sudden awakening that has lately taken place, there seem to be two chief dangers. One, as we have heretofore suggested, is the upstarting of many unskillful and incompetent practitioners, over-eager for employment. The other is the confusion of understanding by some who identify a system with science, a ritual with religion, and by rigid formalism make industrial reform repellent in its austerity when it should be attractive by its benevolent charity. (*Engineering Magazine*, April 1911: 148)

The editor of *American Machinist* had his fair share of arguments against systems, too:

There are few of the systems advocated which do not contain some good points, the main objections being in most cases that they attempt too much. The great danger is in building up a system that collects data which are never used or not worth what they cost, which puts a barrier between the workers and the executives and which becomes so top heavy that it falls into disrepute and becomes an object of contempt. A system, like a law, must either be enforced or it is worse than useless and should be taken out of active use. (*American Machinist*, 7 December 1911: 1091)

Another writer sought to temper the overenthusiastic application of systems in the following manner: 'Another common fault is in attempting to make the system cover too many departments. While in theory a good system should be logically extended to the limit, it is far better to confine its application to such departments as prove its practical value' (*American Machinist*, 7 December 1911: 1091). Lastly, 'Nor must it be forgotten that much so called efficiency is only apparent and not real. And just as the coal pile or the cost of power is the only real indication of a steam engine's efficiency, so the net bank account is the real test of a system's worth.'

Leon Alford corroborated these observations in his report on the status of management. Alford referred to the 'systematizers' as 'one of the most unfortunate features of this great movement' (Jaffe 1957: 63). In Alford's view, they were 'alleged experts' who promised 'extravagant results' if allowed to install their systems in a plant. Alford accused systematizers of publishing statistics implying exaggerated gains, of undervaluing leadership, of overvaluing the 'system', and therefore of removing individual responsibility for results. Systematizers, he continued, assume that all problems in similar plants are capable of being solved in the same way, and they inadequately appreciate the human factor in industry.

Much of the reluctance to introduce management systems was due to the systems' insensitivity to human beings. As one engineer said, 'We have put too much faith in systems and too little in men' (*Engineering Magazine*, December 1911: 386–92). An editorial suggested that the organization of people should precede the introduction of system and not vice versa:

The forms and procedure are there, but the people are thinking in the old way. They do not follow the system; organization must be developed first. Get the people to think along the new lines, to appreciate their new responsibilities and functions; then provide a system by which they can record and communicate their ideas and wishes and doings. They will use it then, because it is natural. (*American Machinist*, 29 April 1915: 750)

It was suggested that 'any system which dwarfs the natural ingenuity of the workman, or which takes from him his self-reliance, would eventually cripple a shop' (*American Machinist*, 16 April 1908: 610). An editorial in *American Machinist* put it very clearly: 'No factor in organization is of more importance, psychologically, than that of making each subordinate feel that he has his own load to carry; that he is an integral part of the management; that he is really expected to think for himself, and to act promptly and decisively' (*American Machinist*, 15 April 1915: 661).

Nevertheless, the winning version of mechanical system showed little sensitivity to the human actor. The most extreme manifestation of the tendency to exclude the worker from decision-making and to impede his or her self-reliance was the 'planning room', which would serve as the locus of rationality of the firm. As Frederick Taylor instructed, 'all possible brain work should be removed from the shop and centred in the planning or laying-out department' (Taylor 1903; cited in

Clawson 1980: 218). In accordance with these directions, workers received detailed sets of written instructions specifying the tasks they should conduct. From the hearings of the House of Representatives committee which was nominated to investigate the link between the strike at Watertown Arsenal and the introduction of Scientific Management there, it became apparent that workers had no reason to think at all, as Taylor made the production process incomprehensible to them. It was congruent with Taylor's controversial statement, 'You are not supposed to think . . . there are other people paid for thinking around here' (Clawson 1980). At Watertown, a new set of symbols, composed of letters and numbers, had been introduced as part of the management system, and all tools and machines were to be known by these symbols, in place of customary names. The formal rationale for the change was ease of writing; however, in practice, the symbols generated chaos, insecurity, ignorance, and uncertainty on the part of workers and other partici-pants. The ridiculousness and the arbitrariness of the abbreviated system were apparent:

As a matter of policy, workers were not allowed to see the symbols, so they could learn the new names of the tools and machines . . . During the hearings one machinist produced a copy of the symbols which had been passed to him by someone else, proba-bly a tool-room or planning-room worker, though the machinist refused to say. He used the list to establish that the foreman testifying, who had said he no longer had trouble with the symbols, was unable to identify tools which any of the machinists could iden-tify by their common names. (Clawson 1980: 232)

Once knowledge was obtained in the planning room, engineers replaced one system of knowledge with another, swapping workers with engineers in this 'musical-chairs' of ignorance. It was illiteracy and ignorance that Taylor produced in the name of science.

This was not unique to Watertown Arsenal. Observe the following, written by a business manager in a leading electrical equipment company from New York, and published in *American Machinist*:

I was standing by a white-haired man. His age rather interested me. He was punching plates, just pushing them into the machine and punching them. I asked 'What is that plate?' He replied, 'That is P-X-111.' I said, 'You do not understand me. I asked 'What is the plate'?' He said, 'I have just told you.' 'My question was wrong, then,' I continued. 'What do they use it for?' He answered, 'I do not know.' I said, 'How long have you been here?' He replied, 'Twelve years.' (*American Machinist*, 11 March 1920: 551)

The language of engineering rationality, reduced to its formal symbols and syntax, was used to strip machinists of their knowledge, rendering them illiter-ate. It generated a hierarchy of knowledge whereby some people were defined as 'knowledgeable' and others as 'illiterate', some worthy of certainty, others not. These examples troubled engineers who expressed their discontent with systems quite often. Church, discussing the introduction of records and symbols in 1913, suggested eliminating duplication of components and that every element be resolved to its ultimate simplest form. This simplicity needed to be preserved for the future, 'preventing useless and harmful complexity creeping in'. He therefore suggested relying 'on carefully made records, and not on anyone's memory'. Church probably had the experiments in Watertown Arsenal in mind when he added, 'The modern tendency seems to be towards an alarming complexity of symbolization. Mixtures of letters and figures ten units long are not uncommon, such as Lq34967XPG [that] many persons of quite good mental equipment cannot remember.' Most importantly, he argued, 'Symbols needed to be made common knowledge' (*Engineering Management*, January 1913: 487–94).

### 4.3 Additional voices: the battle over the monopolization of management

At the height of its publicity and popularity the engineering-management movement was torn by bitter internal dissensions (Jenks 1961: 445). As early as 1912 Henry Kendall attempted to classify the management movement, making a distinction between 'unsystematized management', 'systematized management', and 'Scientific Management'.[10] The first category referred to the 'hit or miss' and 'more or less' manner in which managerial issues were dealt with in the 1880s (see *American Machinist*, 1 January 1914: 34); the second was composed of engineers consciously engaging in the project of systematization around the turn of the century (described in Chapter 3); and the third referred to Taylor and his followers. In the mid-1910s, in the period after the proliferation of Scientific Management, an additional group of 'efficiency experts' emerged. While the struggle between 'systematic' and 'unsystematic' management was described in the previous chapter, in the following I focus on struggles that took place in the 1910s among these three groups as reflected by the engineering literature: 'Systematizers', 'Scientific Managers' (or 'Taylorites'), and 'Efficiency Engineers'. By focusing on groups rather than on individuals I wish to shed light on alternative historical possibilities that emerged in practice and on their sociological ramifications.

*The contest between systematic and Scientific Management.* Litterer, who was the first to conduct a comprehensive study of the systematic management movement, explained the differences between the two groups. He argued that under 'Systematic Management' organizational issues were viewed as falling into recurring types for which a method or system could be employed. The claim of 'Scientific Management' was based on measurement and experimentation rather than unorganized experience or armchair knowledge (Litterer 1986: 21). Litterer suggested that the systematizers attempted to generate an orderly arrangement of organizational parts, while the Taylorites were not satisfied with that since they wanted to know how well each component performed its task (*Engineering Magazine*, April 1911: 98). Whereas Litterer focused on differences at the ontological level, I would like to highlight the sociological implications: that the contest between these two groups focused on rhetoric, power, and professional domains as well.

In light of the increasing popularity and exclusivity of Scientific Management around 1910–11, management activist Alexander Hamilton Church was concerned that Scientific Management would overshadow the previous body of work produced by systematizers who did not particularly define themselves as experts of Scientific Management: 'Mr. Taylor and his associates have put themselves forward . . . As the inventors or the sponsors of a special system of industrial administration which they term "Scientific Management," thereby obviously implying that all other management is unscientific' (*American Machinist*, 20 July 1911: 108–12).

Church recognized that he and some of his colleagues were losing ground to Scientific Management. While arguing that Scientific Management could not be categorized as science, he made an attempt to gain credibility by attributing some of its public success to previous efforts made by the 'systematizers':

At this date, when 'Scientific Management' has become a popular and favorite theme of the ready pens of the daily journalists and magazine writers, it can not be too clearly pointed out that the modern theories of industrial administration represented by the newly coined term are no magic formulae, but are the fruition of decades of slow and steady progress and of the laborious work of highly trained and experienced investigators. (*Engineering Magazine*, April 1911: 97–101. See also *American Machinist*, 20 July 1911: 108–12)

Not only did Church try to regain credibility, but he also attempted to present an evolutionary account of the development of management science: 'It is hardly too much to say that the evolution of a science of management was inevitable as soon as the scale of industrial operations became so great that no single manager, however naturally gifted, could continue to control personally all the activities of the plant.'

At one level, the argument legitimizes the ambitious mission of the management movement; this is, to be sure, how it would be read today. At the time, it was also meant to discredit the creativity or the success of particular individuals (e.g. Taylor, Gantt, and Gilbreth), and to reject the attempt to depict them as revolutionaries. The version that Church espoused was evolutionary. Management systems were seen as having grown as a result of objective needs. Church attacked Henry Gantt for his claim that the 'general principle' connecting production and cost was a new invention (*American Machinist*, 26 August 1915: 385). Gantt believed that inefficiency had to be rooted out of not only the work methods of workers, but also those of management. He designed a cost system and introduced production charts to set standards for management that would be analogous to the stopwatch standards for the workers (Haber 1964). Church addressed Gantt's work: 'It is to be presumed that Mr. Gantt supposed this discovery to be one either original with himself or at any rate . . . as yet unpublished, and unknown to the world' (*American Machinist*, 2 September 1915: 431).

The debate focused on issues of professional boundaries as well. The question 'who is an engineer?' was at the core of the debate. Church was not an engineer, but an accountant, and he was self-conscious about it. He referred to a previous debate he had had with Gantt: 'As for Mr. Gantt's imputation that my criticism was due to a feeling of resentment in the old quarrel—engineer versus accountant—this is rather amusing.' Church defended his allegiance to the engineering profession: 'I was an engineer before I was an accountant, and as an engineer I obtained a knowledge of what the problem was; but it must be remembered that scientific accounting is a kind of engineering too.' Gantt did not remain aloof. Two months later he responded: 'We were using, under the direction of F. W. Taylor, the machine-factor method of distributing expense several years before Mr. Church claims to have devised it' (*American Machinist*, 21 October 1915: 737).

Attacks on Scientific Management surfaced in the *American Machinist*. In 1911 the magazine published Frank C. Hudson's article entitled 'The Machinists' Side of Taylorism' (*American Machinist*, 27 April 1911: 773). In it, Hudson flatly rejected Taylor's conviction that workers are 'a set of loafers' and argued that Taylor's idea implying a class distinction between employers and employees 'belongs to the Middle Ages'. The author cried out against Taylor's claim that 19 out of 20 men deliberately try to see how little they can do, and concluded that the removal of responsibility from the worker meant the reduction of ambition that eventually would prove detrimental to the workplace. In the same year, the editor of the *American Machinist*, Leon Alford, published a critical essay written by Dexter Kimball, a professor of machine design and construction at Cornell's Sibley College, entitled 'Another Side of Efficiency Engineering' (*American Machinist*, 10 August 1911: 263–5). Kimball concluded that the principles of industrial efficiency were not new by any means and that they offered no real hope for a viable solution to industrial problems.

The 'present state of the art of management' report written by Alford in 1912 revealed the falsehood underlying the argument that the mechanical engineering community was unanimous in its attitude to Scientific Management. Apparently, many of the interviewees—managers, engineers, manufacturers—asked to define the 'new element' in the art of management were skeptical toward Scientific Management. One said, 'I am not aware that a new element . . . has been discovered'; another commented, 'the term "Scientific Management" is a catchword', and stated that, contrary to its pretense, industrial institutions had been scientifically managed prior to Taylor. Others added that 'there is hardly any part of it that has not been practiced by managers for the past 100 years', and that the Taylor system was simply 'an honest, intelligent effort to arrive at absolute control in every department'. 'Management engineering', the report concluded, 'seems more fully to cover its scope than science' (Jaffe 1957: 59–60).

Alford himself deplored the term 'scientific' as being incorrectly interpreted to mean that there is a science rather than an art of management. This was in line with Church's articles in both *American Machinist* (*American Machinist*, 30 May 1912: 857–62) and *Engineering Magazine* (*Engineering Magazine*, April 1911: 97–101).

Despite these differences and internal struggles, these two camps of expertise were not mutually exclusive in their philosophy of management. Both had emerged from the ideology of rational standardization. The systematizers focused mainly on the standardization of organizations as social systems. Scientific management focused on the standardization of the human element in production. The two also shared a common organizational premise: the notion that organization should be conceptualized as a mechanical system. Organizational system was believed to support the function of management in several respects: the need for information (e.g., *Engineering Magazine*, December 1898: 385); the handling of repetitive tasks; freeing managers from time-consuming tasks (see Litterer 1986); and supporting the continuity of management (*Engineering Magazine*, June 1900: 395). One of the main features of Taylor's scheme was a centralized planning department, something the systematizers had promoted all along. Furthermore, many individuals could be classified as both systematizers and advocates of Scientific Management. This is not surprising. While Taylor first presented his principles of management in 1895, the term 'Scientific Management' was given to the efficiency movement only in 1910. Up to that point, the differentiation between 'scientific' and 'systematic' was not yet constructed. It is clear that Taylor based his systems on systematizers' work and he acknowledged their contribution to his lifelong project (Taylor 1903: 201–2, quoted in Litterer 1986: 253; see also Haber 1964: 9).

*The struggle against the new breed of efficiency engineers.* By the mid-1910s there was a proliferation of experts, with and without engineering degrees, selling their services to industry as systematizers. The relationship of these experts— efficiency engineers—to the management movement was ambiguous (Jenks 1961; Nelson 1974). Old-time systematizers, as well as the Taylorites, felt threatened by these newly emerging efficiency experts.

Ironically, the legitimacy of these efficiency experts and systematizers was first stimulated by the success of Scientific Management. The demand for the services of the new scientific managers was so high that 'a black market of get-rich-quick phonies sprang up' (Merkle 1980: 59). As the Hoxie Committee, nominated to investigate the perils associated with the application of Scientific Management, reported,

The great rewards which a few leaders in the movement have secured for their services have brought into the field a crowd of industrial patent medicine men. The way is open to all. No standards or requirements, private or public, have been developed by the application of which the goats can be separated from the sheep. Employers have thus far proved credulous. Almost anyone can show the average manufacturing concern where it can make some improvements in its methods. So the Scientific Management shingles have gone up all over the country, the fakirs have gone into the shops, and in the name of Scientific Management have reaped temporary gains to the detriment of the real article, the employers and the workers. (Hoxie 1921)

Scientific Management was being attacked by the mid-1910s (partly because of its unprecedented success) and efficiency experts therefore introduced alternative techniques that were essentially Scientific Management in disguise (Guillen 1994). The Bedaux system was the most famous such example (Guillen 1994: 56–7; see also an article by Charles Morrow, a managing editor of the *American Machinist* on 'The Bedaux Principle of Human Power Measurement', *American Machinist*, 16 February 1922: 241). Charles Eugene Bedaux's book, *The Bedaux Efficiency Course for Industrial Application*, was first published in 1917. The basic argument was the call to standardize the time spent on a task by factoring in fatigue—adding 'rest allowance'. Bedaux, naturally, did not see his system as being identical to Scientific Management. He felt that the usual time-study methods had inherent weaknesses. For example, they did not take into account the nature of the strain on the human body (*American Machinist*, 16 February 1922: 241). Over 700 American businesses including GE, which employed 675,000 employees, were advised by the Bedaux Company between 1918 and 1942 (see also Steven 1993).

The popularity of 'efficiency experts' and their catchy techniques seemed to editors of engineering literature to be getting out of hand. An *American Machinist* editorial complained:

No word in the English language has been more abused than 'efficiency,' especially during the past year or two. This has reached the point where those whose business it is to improve shop output and conditions, balk at the name 'efficiency engineer' of which they were once so proud and are using different titles to convey the same meaning. (*American Machinist*, 7 December 1911: 1091)

Taylor tried to dissociate himself from the new breed of efficiency engineers, who made a living selling efficiency kits. In 1910–11, Taylor's disciples formed a closed group that defined their work as 'scientific', to distinguish it from other 'transitory management' and 'fad and fashions' as well as from the old systematizers. The new forum, known as 'The Society for the Promotion of the Science of Management' (after Taylor's death in 1915 the society was renamed 'The Taylor Society'), sought to distance itself from the new systematizers. Members of the society were concerned with the expansion of such 'marginal groups, [of] systematizers uninstructed in the philosophy, science and principles of management, [which were] ignorant of the spirit and so missing the results' (*Engineering Magazine*, April 1911: 952).

The two magazines attacked the new trend. Frederick Colvin, editor of *American Machinist* in the 1920s, commented on the 'crusade' against efficiency engineering during 1902–14:

The much overworked word 'science' was bandied about . . . by people who had not the slightest idea what it actually means. Science was in a fair way to becoming another religion or cult, if one could judge by the columns and columns of space devoted to the popularized variety in the increasing number of Sunday supplements . . . [This trend] brought in its train a fair number of charlatans and thimbleriggers who figuratively set up their medicine shows in the public square and sold flummery and hocus-pocus in the name of science to the uninformed multitude. . . . Very early in the game, the *American Machinist* organized a countercrusade which, while acknowledging the good points of honest Scientific Management, began to debunk the quacks and impostors who posed as efficiency experts. (Colvin 1947: 154)

Given the fact that the *Engineering Magazine* was a staunch supporter of both systematizers and scientific managers, it is also clear why the editors expressed caution in relation to the phenomenon. This was made explicit in the magazine's editorials. During the Eastern Rate Case, Dunlap, its editor, noted the following:

In view of the hasty, imperfectly informed, and not very wise propagandism of efficiency (or 'Scientific Management') undertaken by magazines of general literature, it becomes a duty to those who, like ourselves, have been furthering the movement for more than a dozen years, now to preach caution where heretofore we have had to preach courage. (*Engineering Magazine*, March 1911: 952)

Even as late as 1923, *American Machinist* commented that 'the professional management engineer is still suffering from the discredit brought upon his profession by the flock of quack "efficiency engineers," whose principal efficiency seemed to lie in their ability to separate money from their clients. Most of these fakers failed to weather the business depression' (*American Machinist*, 4 January 1923: 21). The editor sought to save the credibility of management by excluding such experts and techniques from its profession, and denounced the 'clown jokes from the side lines' (*American Machinist*, 3 July 1913: 35).

*Debates within ASME circles.* The issue of translating engineering work to include economic and managerial issues generated controversies within ASME (American Society of Mechanical Engineers) as well. Many society members thought that such issues were improper for a mechanical engineering society, arguing that the society—like the German and French associations—ought to concern itself solely with the technical field. An editorial in *American Machinist* in 1905, which commented on the debate, criticized the efficiency considerations of the Taylor system (*American Machinist*, 26 October 1905: 572). The editorial reflected upon a contest between the wage premium plan advocated by Frederick Halsey and the piece-rate system. The editors argued that they knew no case in the USA where Taylor's ideas had been put into successful use 'except by himself or those who have been associated and largely trained by him'. The reason, according to the editors, might be that his system did not tolerate application by mediocre workers, who formed the majority of the working classes. If only exceptional men can install the system, argued the editors, 'it cannot find large application'. The editors recommended the premium plan rather than the piece-rate system of labor rewards. They believed that for matters of remuneration the premium plan was more humanitarian, simple, obvious, and applicable. In their view, 'it does not aim so high as to miss its mark entirely, as the piece rate system does'.

The rationalization of ASME itself is a case in point. After his nomination as AMSE president, Taylor reached the height of his power within the society. The most ambitious reform he undertook during his reign as ASME president was the simplification and standardization of office routines, applying the principles of Scientific Management to the society itself. He hired Morris L. Cooke and Carl Barth to reform the society's accounting system. However, Taylor's efforts were more costly than he had anticipated. Internal opposition to him grew. One of his opponents, Jesse Smith, was elected president as his successor. The opposition to Scientific Management within the society grew stronger. When Taylor tried to elicit ASME endorsement for the statements of Brandeis and Emerson at the ICC hearing in 1910, he faced a firm objection led by railroad people in ASME. Further, the ASME committee that he had successfully installed refused to endorse his system as being a science.[11] Even Dodge, who chaired the committee and supported Taylor, argued that he was using arbitrary definitions for 'average' and 'first class' workers in standardizing his results (Noble 1977: 273). Eventually, the society refused to publish Taylor's *The Principles of Scientific Management*. Taylor was told that 'the membership does not want manuscript of this kind' (Calvert 1967: 276). Only in 1912 did a special committee of ASME (headed by L. P. Alford of *American Machinist*) report favorably on 'labor saving management' (Jenks 1961). When ASME recognized Taylorism it was already popular among the public, following the four well-known showcases at Tabor Manufacturing Company, Link-Belt, Watertown Arsenal, and the Topeka shops.

Taylor also faced opposition among his own followers. As Frank Gilbreth grew increasingly excited about the motion picture camera, Taylor began to suspect that he was starting to neglect Scientific Management; he argued that Gilbreth did not understand Scientific Management (Haber 1964). Taylor did not accept Gilbreth's claim to have invented 'motion study' as distinct from 'time study'. For Taylor, 'time study' was 'time and motion study'. An actual break between them came when, in response to a complaint from one of Gilbreth's clients, Taylor sent another engineer to replace Gilbreth (Haber 1964: 38). Gilbreth did not attend meetings of the Taylor Society in the period following his clash with Taylor.

The sometimes heated debates among Taylor's disciples after his death strengthened Scientific Management. They served to broaden 'the armory of techniques available to Scientific Management' without changing the central elements in its philosophy. Furthermore, Scientific Management 'became more flexible, and better able to survive when the anti-Taylor reaction set in; in the end, it was this flexibility that, in large part, helped it gain universality' (see Merkle 1980: 49). This can be clearly shown by the *American Machinist*'s increasing support of Scientific Management over the years.

*The debate with the British engineering community.* The American management movement was also struggling with the European engineering community, particularly the British. At the turn of the century Britain had only half of the number of engineers per worker that the United States had (Guillen 1994: 213). Furthermore, very few engineers in England were admitted to upper management positions in industrial firms. Contrary to the enthusiasm expressed by German engineers with regard to modern American management at the turn of the century, British engineers reacted with animosity (ibid.: 214). As Mauro Guillen commented, the institutional tendency in England was against the new management movement which was understood to be an expression of the greediness of American capitalism (Guillen 1994). American management was too rigid, too inhuman, and too anti-labor in the eyes of British compeers.

After spending two weeks at the Ford Plant in Detroit, Frederick Colvin published in 1913 and 1914 a total of sixteen articles in *American Machinist*.[12] These were not well received in Britain. As editors of the *American Machinist* complained, British engineering magazines had 'their coats off and sleeves rolled up'. They 'ridiculed the American engineer for alleged dipping into metaphysics', condemned the management movement as 'inhuman', and 'congratulated British industry upon being free from anything of the kind' (*American Machinist*, 5 February 1914: 257–8). The British engineering magazine the *Engineer* argued that Scientific Management 'would not be tolerated by the workmen of England'. This is because British workers would not submit themselves to 'route cards' or to the teaching of 'the motion master'. American workers 'are not expected to think since the bureau does that for them'. In sum, 'they are parts of a machine'. The *American Machinist* accused the editors of the *Engineer* of ignorance, and castigated them for their failure to visit the USA so that they could learn first hand about these methods. They concluded that, from a selfish point of view, it would be best if the British never corrected these mistakes anyway. British magazines published articles on Scientific Management in great numbers only after 1916, as part of the rationalization associated with the war effort. One-third of the authors, however, were American efficiency experts. Only by the mid-1930s did a new wave of articles on Scientific Management emerge in Britain (Guillen 1994: 222).

The First World War had a legitimizing effect on the systems discourse in the United States. System, efficiency, and Scientific Management came to be associated with bureaucracy, the military, and hence with patriotism. Secretary Meyer of the US navy, who appointed a special commission to investigate efficiency in the navy, stated in 1911 before the Economic Club of the City of New York, 'though not known by name, this has been practiced in the fleet for years, and has brought about a wonderful increase in gunnery efficiency. Scientific Management experts who saw the recent battle practice tell me the battleship is the finest exhibition of Scientific Management they have ever seen' (*Engineering Magazine*, June 1911: 472). During the First World War, 'efficiency became a patriotic duty', and an urgent matter (Haber 1964: 119). One of the regional societies, the Western Efficiency Society, formed in Chicago, was reactivated after the First World War to become the National Society of Industrial Engineers (Jenks 1961).

In 1920, after three long years of effort, four engineering societies (ASCE, ASME, AIEE, and AIMM) succeeded in organizing a conference to determine cooperation on 'non-technical' work, realizing that 'sociological and economic conditions are in a state of flux' as Richard L. Humphrey, the chairman of the Joint Conference Committee, put it (*American Machinist*, 17 June 1920: 1320). The Federation of American Engineering Societies was the most potent vehicle of progressive engineering reform, eventually electing Herbert Hoover as its president. The formation of the federation was defined by the *American Machinist* as 'the awakening of the engineer' to a new sense of the importance and responsibility of the profession (*American Machinist*, 7 October 1920: 686; see also *American Machinist*, 21 October 1920: 782). Herbert Hoover, who was described by Morris Cooke as 'the engineering method personified' (Noble 1977: 286), defined problems of government not in political but in technical terms. According to Hoover, the engineering method was much needed since politics involved 'emotions that confused the data and excited controversy' (Sinclair 1980: 14). He thought that engineering training was the best weapon with which to solve social and economic problems, as well as questions of government. Akin to this ideology, Henry Gantt promoted the idea of the *New Machine*, an elite organization of engineers, which was to transform society by transferring the control of industry into the hands of engineers, the ones who understood its operation.[13]

## 4.4 The opposition of labor and the struggle over legislation

John Dunlap, editor of *Engineering Management*, commented on the objection of acting managers to the introduction of management systems and pointed to a similar opposition of labor unions:

The fatal obstacle in the way of converting the industrial world is the difficulty of making either managers or men (and managers far more than men) friendly to the methods or the ideas the methods are intended to express . . . The unions today are admittedly the most serious menace to industrial stability. Organized labor is usually found alert and implacable—or at least strongly hostile—to the attempt to introduce any of the advanced wage systems. (*Engineering Management*, March 1910: 905)

A brief perusal of the testimonies of labor leaders and labor publications from the Progressive era provides ample evidence that skilled workers viewed modern management as a twin menace: the loss of craft control, and the radical polarization of mental and manual labor. In 1916 a leader of the Molders' Union articulated the opposition in a typical manner:

The one great asset of the wage worker has been his craftsmanship . . . Of late, the separation of craft knowledge and craft skill has actually taken place with an ever increasing
acceleration. Its process is shown in the introduction of machinery and the standardization of tools, materials, products, and processes, which makes production possible on a
large scale . . . The second form, more insidious and more dangerous than the first, is the
gathering up of all scattered craft knowledge, systematizing and concentrating it in the
hands of the employer and then doling it out again only in the form of minute instructions, giving to each worker only the knowledge needed for the mechanical performance
of a particular relatively minute task. When this process of systematizing is complete, the
worker is no longer a craftsman in any sense, but is an animated tool of the management.
(*American Federationist*, May 1916: 365–6; cited in Davis 1983)

It is particularly significant that the flash points of labor strikes during the
early Progressive era were located in the very industries that were being rationalized and systematized. A survey of conditions and complaints in the affected
plants reveals how 'The tactics of systematization (e.g., time study, task setting,
efficiency payments) had systematically resulted in job dilution, speed-up, and a
lowering of wages' (Davis 1983: 87; see also Braverman 1974, for a discussion of
how capitalists used Scientific Management and technology to deskill workers
and to fragment work groups).

The IWW's (Industrial Workers of the World)[14] periodical, the *Industrial
Worker*, repeatedly editorialized the need to contest the 'stopwatch'. Its editorials
on Scientific Management can be surveyed, in a similar manner to *American
Machinist*, to portray its extreme opposition to 'systems'. Labor historians who
have reviewed the *Industrial Worker* (see, for example, Foner 1947; Nadworny
1955; Haber 1964; Dubofsky 1968) find that speed-up, one of the primary goals
of systematization, was repeatedly attacked by the magazine as 'an evil that
should be combated with sabotage' ('Editorial', *Industrial Worker*, 6 February
1913; see also 'Editorial', 28 December 1911, and the articles by Covington
Hall, 16 November 1911, and B. E. Nilsson, 24 April 1913. These sources are
also cited in Davis 1983), while 'speeders' (workers who were 'bribed' by efficiency payments and broke group solidarity) were condemned as 'class traitors'
('Editorial', *Industrial Worker*, 6 February 1913). P. J. Conlon, vice-president of
the International Association of Machinists, summarized the reaction of workers
to 'systems' in his testimony before the Commission on Industrial Relations: 'We
believe that it [Scientific Management] builds up in the industrial world the
principle of sabotage, syndicalism, passive resistance, based on economic deter-
minism. We did not hear of any of these things until we heard of Scientific
Management' (*Commission on Industrial Relations, Report and Testimony* (1915),
i. 874–7).

One of the early issues of contention between the new managers and employ-
ees was apparently workforce layoffs. P. H. Morrissey, president of the American
Railroad Employees, and P. J. Dolan, general secretary of the International
Brotherhood of Steam-Shovel, argued that Scientific Management 'contemplates

the reduction of the operating force by thousands of men', while the unions, according to the editors, want 'more men to lessen their burdens, instead of less men and greater burdens' (*Engineering Magazine*, February 1911: 769–70). The editor of *Engineering Magazine* did not agree, of course: 'It is the old blind cry that labor has always raised against mechanical (i.e., scientific) improvements.' Apparently, 'the stage-coach drivers at the beginning of the nineteenth century opposed the railway with the same objections, with the same earnestness, in almost the same words'. The *Engineering Magazine* explained that efficiency is not about the laziness of workers but is leveraged against superfluous and fruit-less efforts and movements. The causes of inefficiency 'are not generally that the employee does not work hard enough, but that a large part of his work is expended on wholly useless things that do not profit him or any one else'. As far as depriving people of employment was concerned, the editors explained that exactly the opposite was true, for eventually, 'labor which is released from the old wasteful effort is immediately and progressively absorbed by the increasing opportunity for the new and more efficient effort'.

An interesting alliance between employers and the unions was formed around the issues of the introduction of Scientific Management into the government arsenals, and particularly at Watertown (Haber 1964). The military arsenals focused on producing unique items such as complex coast artillery gun carriages in limited quantities, without benefiting from economies of scale (Petersen 1989). Compared with the success of the 'American System' in the private sector, the arsenal seemed extremely ineffective, and politicians who did not support Theodore Roosevelt's administration (1901–9) demanded that the large sums of money in military contracts be channeled to civilian manufacturers (Aitken 1960). These demands always concluded with an appeal that the army arsenals modernize their systems.

Under these conditions, William Crozier, the army Chief of Ordnance from 1901 to 1918—with the backing of Senator Elihu Root who was Secretary of War from 1899 to 1904—supported the implementation of Scientific Management in military installations despite severe political criticism (Petersen 1989). In 1909 Carl Barth and Frederick Taylor offered Watertown a compre-hensive system of Scientific Management. When the workers called a strike in reaction to this interference, both unions and Congress became involved in the matter. The involvement of *American Machinist*, and particularly Frederick Colvin, in criticizing manufacturing methods in the Springfield Armory has been described already. Colvin claimed that operations at the arsenal were conducted at a leisurely speed and this criticism may have hastened the early retirement of Crozier from his position as Chief of Ordnance (Jaffe 1957).

The 1913 annual report of the Chief of Ordnance concerning the operation of modern industrial management in Watertown and in other arsenals (*American Machinist*, 15 January 1914: 125) argued that there was a substantial saving as a result of the application of Scientific Management. The editors of the *American*

*Machinist* added, 'it is clearly in the public interest to extend this work'. In 1914, *American Machinist* suggested that 'the United States Navy Yards could produce a yearly saving equal to the cost of a first-class battleship' if 'modern industrial management' was applied (*American Machinist*, 4 June 1914: 1003). The need for efficiency was considered a public matter since it was linked to national defense. It was also considered a rational program, since it worked to eliminate political favoritism in the hiring, promotion, and discharge of workers in the navy yards.

In a rather symbolic gesture, both the Senate and the House of Representatives passed legislation in 1915 forbidding the use of the stopwatch as a work-measuring device, and as a determining factor in remuneration in the Watertown Arsenal and other branches of government work (Drury 1922; Aitken 1985). Despite Taylor's efforts, both houses of Congress introduced bills that forbade the usage of stopwatches and payment bonuses on government work. Bill HR 8,662 was entitled: 'To prevent the use of a stop watch or other time measuring device on government work, and the payment of premium or bonus to government employees, and for other purchases.' None the less, the congressional hearings concerning the strike at Watertown Arsenal gave Taylor a golden opportunity to present his case for Scientific Management. During the congressional hearing, the opponents of Scientific Management argued that its effect was to 'overwork the men', 'to injure their health', and to 'increase the liability to accident'. Opponents further argued that it 'creates a feeling of unrest among the workingmen' (*American Machinist*, 16 July 1914: 125). The hearings demonstrated that the measurement of time resulted in distortions in the work process rather then increasing efficiencies in it. The editors of *American Machinist*, main players in the field, criticized the 'absurdity' of these objections. First, the premium system had been developed by Halsey some twenty-five years earlier and had been used ever since. Second, time studies were plainly a measuring device. No one would object to 'the use of micrometers or verniers' to aid the work. Third, no machinist was literally forced to exercise either his muscles or his brain. The operation of machine tools takes both time and precision, a fact not lost on employers when considering the use of management systems. The editors extracted a table from the testimony of General Crozier. Based on analysis of ten jobs from Watertown Arsenal, they concluded that the average 'watching time' was rather surprising: 53.4 percent of the whole time. The editors therefore probed: 'Under such circumstances, how is it possible to overwork a man?' The editors concluded that the development of Scientific Management is 'the third great development in our industrial history', after the invention of labor-saving machinery and the development of the interchangeable system.

On 23 July 1914 the editors of the *American Machinist* called upon the 'machinery builders' to protest against political interference in industrial practices. The House of Representatives had voted favorably to support the Dietrick Bill No. 17,800, prohibiting the methods of Scientific Management in government establishments. The bill superseded HR 8,662, which was identical in purpose. It was attached to the army appropriation bill, and extended the prohibition to private manufacturing which contracted with the government. The editorial in *American Machinist* stated that the attempt to prohibit Scientific Management 'is worthy of the dark ages' (*American Machinist*, 23 July 1914: 167).

Looking backward what would we think if the Congress in 1790 had enacted a law prohibiting the use of labor-saving machinery in Government shops? What would we think if Congress in 1820 had passed a law prohibiting the use of American system of manufacture—the interchangeable system—in Government shops? Are the American people going to sit idly by and allow a few agitators and vote-hunting Congressmen to persuade Congress to pass a law [such as this]? (*American Machinist*, 23 July 1914: 174)

*American Machinist* continued in the following issue to campaign against the bill (*American Machinist*, 30 July 1914: 211), claiming that instead of attempting to block the progress of efficiency in the navy, every effort ought to be made to increase it:

Just suppose that every time the president of the Great American Wrench Trust visited one of their shops a man was detailed to throw 21 monkey-wrenches into a well provided for that purpose; 19 for the vice-president; 15 for the general manager; 13 for a director, and when one works manager visits another, 8 perfectly good monkey-wrenches were thrown into the scrap well . . . every stockholder would be up in arms at the useless waste and the price of monkey-wrenches would be correspondingly higher in consequence. Could any officer proposing such a course escape the lunatic asylum? And yet this isn't a cent on a dollar to the cost of the senseless firing of salutes when an officer visits a vessel of the navy.

The *Engineering Magazine* took part in the debate as well. As Dunlap acknowledged in an editorial in 1916, 'Labor leaders have claimed that the movement was primarily intended to exploit labor; managers that it was fantastically theoretical and highly impractical. There was a third class of sophists who claimed that efficiency can only come from a joy in work and that this movement does not inspire that motive' (*Engineering Magazine*, May 1916: 272). In this last sentence, Dunlap referred to the emerging school that emphasized the 'human factor' and 'industrial psychology'.

On several occasions, the editorial office of the *Engineering Magazine* published letters that supported the movement, particularly from employees, employers, and engineers. For example, a machinist who claimed to have worked in the industry for thirty years stated that since he had been exposed to the movement during Brandeis's testimony, he had got more and more interested in it and eventually used his savings to study it. He testified: 'So much do I believe in it that I took the few dollars which I had saved and secured admittance to a course in Scientific Management at Harvard.' He believed that 'the day is not far off, when the Trades Unions will seek by legislation to protect Scientific Management instead of trying to kill it' (*Engineering Magazine*, May 1916: 272).

Dunlap notified his readers in January 1916 that labor officials in Washington were ready once more to promote legislation against management systems and that the fight had centered again around government shops. Dunlap and his staff referred to the bill proposed by Congressman Tavenner in January 1916: 'A bill prohibiting the most enlightened wage systems ever yet devised by man' (*Engineering Magazine*, April 1916: 1–11). The bill, known as 'House Bill HR 8665', aimed 'to regulate the method of directing the work of Government employees'. Furthermore, suggestions were made to prohibit government 'from letting any contracts . . . to any private establishments where any such systems are in use (*Engineering Magazine*, January 1916: 607–8). The editor argued that labor leaders realized that if the government condemned these methods, they would have a powerful lever to force their objection on other industrial establishments. The editors called upon manufacturers to act immediately in combating possible legislation because in the end, those manufacturers who applied the methods would have the lowest bids in competition for army and navy contracts (*Engineering Magazine*, January 1916: 607–8). Dunlap called for 'prompt action' given that 'we are face to face with a serious and threatening situation' (*Engineering Magazine*, April 1916: 1–11). Dunlap explained the seriousness of the situation:

The labor leaders and labor politicians are deliberately planning to 'put-over' this legislation by trickery and stealth, because they reason that it will strengthen the labor unions and make more labor votes. The domination of the labor unions in Great Britain, especially in engineering trades, is both historic and notorious. They bitterly opposed the introduction of the power loom, the sewing machine, the locomotive, the air brake, the mower and reaper, the type-setting machine, and in fact every great labor-saving device that has ever been invented—upon the stupid theory that 'it would throw men out of work.' This proposed American legislation is of a piece with all such ignorant reasoning, and the definite plan of our labor leaders is to take advantage of this presidential year and force such legislation through Congress without hearing or debate.

Dunlap also informed the readers that a similar bill had been introduced by Congressman Van Dyke on the same date (11 January 1916) to prohibit all time studies throughout the entire Postal Service. In the last Congress, the editor reminded his readers, similar legislation had been incorporated as 'a rider' in an army appropriation bill. This time, the 'ring-leader in the conspiracy to pass this damaging legislation' was Congressman Buchanan of Illinois, 'who is now under indictment by a United States Grand Jury'. Dunlap concluded:

If they succeed, the time may come very soon when, like England, our most vital national interests may be imperiled. Less than a year ago the entire civilized world was shocked by exposure of the fact that, through the arbitrary, dogged, and uncompromising regulations of the British labor unions, the armies in the field were actually short of munitions, while the British, the French, and the Italian navies were seriously threatened with a shortage of coal.

Given the threat of 'anti-efficiency laws' in Congress, a committee of engineers and large manufacturers was established to help defeat the bills. This is notable given the initial conflicts between them over the introduction of management systems. The committee—known as the Committee of Ten to Oppose Legislation Antagonistic to Efficiency in American Industry—represented the leading engineering societies, the National Association of Manufacturers, the National Metal Trades Association, and many local chambers of commerce with the chairmanship of Henry Towne, past president of the American Society of Mechanical Engineers. It included individuals such as W. Herman Greul, secretary; Miner Chipman, John R. Dunlap, Richard A. Feiss, H. P. Kendall, William Kent, W. W. Mason, W. B. Richards, and Sanford E. Thompson (for a description of their memoranda see *Engineering Magazine*, August 1916: 751). Towne, Dunlap, Kendall, Kent, and Thompson were connected with ASME, and with the professional practices of management systems. Thompson, for example, was a consulting engineer with Taylor at Bethlehem Steel and was the inventor of special apparatus for taking time records. Their vested interest in systems was enormous. The committee set an agenda to block the legislation and to disseminate the importance of industrial management, 'exposing the fallacies of this reactionary and dangerous proposal':

We therefore call upon every reader of these pages to at once telegraph or write personally in protest to both your Senators and certainly to the Congressman representing your district. Let your telegrams and letters be brief, pointed and just as earnest as you can word them. Address them personally, sign them personally, and insist that congress shall at least grant public hearings on the measures before they can be put upon the statute books. (*Engineering Magazine*, April 1916: 3)

Dunlap assured his readers that the forces of good were on their side: 'Mr. Louis Brandeis, who has been nominated for the Supreme Court, is on record in unqualified endorsement and approval of "Scientific Management."' This language demonstrates how seductive the logic of Progressivism was. Scientific Management was portrayed as a progressive mode which should help labor, since Brandeis himself was, at least ostensibly, on the side of the workers: 'For years past he has been a voluntary attorney and arbitrator for the labor unions, and it will be recalled that he won nation-wide distinction as attorney for the shippers in their protest before the Interstate Commerce Commission against the large increase in freight rates which the railroads insisted upon having four years ago.'

At this stage, the support of the large private manufacturing establishment and of eminent engineers in favor of the introduction of systems in general and Scientific Management in particular was clearer. Criticism was leveled at the government, which seemed to be being manipulated by 'labor agitators'. Thomas Edison commented that the bill 'is based on fallacy' and 'would be disastrous to labor and to the public'. Edison said in the language of Progressivism, 'the worst enemy of all the workers is an inefficiently managed shop'. E. M. Herr, president of Westinghouse Electric & Manufacturing Company in East Pittsburgh, said, 'This bill is reactionary and bad for both the interests of the government and its employees . . . [The bill] is pernicious and should be defeated.' Coleman Sellers Jr., president of William Sellers & Co. in Philadelphia, called the measure 'vicious'. Henry Sharpe, treasurer of Brown & Sharpe Co. in Providence, argued that critics of Scientific Management 'are either theorists, cranks, or those who have axes to grind, including the leaders of so-called organized labor' (*Engineering Magazine*, April 1916: 1–12). William L. Ward, president of Russel, Burdsall & Ward Bolt & Nut Co. in Port Chester, New York, pleaded: 'use the utmost skill and energy, abolish all slap-dash methods of manufacturing, abolish all waste of effort, waste of material, waste of plant investment, and organize our industries on common sense, scientifically efficient lines.' Ward argued that industrialists were 'hampered by unwise restrictions' that are caused by the fact that 'Government enacts laws to discourage effort.' In Chapters 5 and 6, I describe the manner by which labor opposition was used by engineers to further the language of systems and to convince the manufacturers' community of its urgent necessity.[15]

### 4.5  Transforming management into a science

In the minds of the systematizers who wrote about organizations, they were collectively engaged in making a scientific field (for a strong defense of 'industrial engineering' as a science, see *Engineering Magazine*, May 1910: 251). Having established a mechanical model of organizations—both as a description of reality and as a prescription for practical work—their texts suggested that this model should replace the old set of rules ('which have served their day') and establish the modern principle that industrial order is 'the first law of the universe' (*Engineering Magazine*, June 1900: 395). Whereas the machine image offered harmony and order as its basic ingredients, the systems image suggested wholeness, interdependency, and accountability (*American Machinist*, 1 January 1891: 7). The editors of *American Machinist* suggested that 'there is not a man, machine, operation or system in the shop that stands entirely alone. Each one, to be valued rightly, must be viewed as part of a whole' (*American Machinist*, 3 March 1904: 294–6). This delineation was later extended to include an array of methods and organizational tools, such as accountancy techniques, wage plans, production control, and communication devices. The system, with its many overlapping features, became the ideological cement of organizational thought.

Following the First World War, management became recognized as a scientific field. Two parallel processes were instrumental to this outcome: the acceptance of management systems by government, politicians, and labor representatives, and the universalization of its body of knowledge. The engineering magazines—and later management periodicals—had a prominent role in the shaping and disseminating of such perceptions, and in the 'manufacturing of consent' regarding systems. The editors of the magazines proved to be, throughout the years, prominent gatekeepers of the profession. They devoted great effort to delegitimizing amateur attempts to practice management (e.g. *Engineering Magazine*, September 1916: 849–54), and to differentiating 'scientific' from 'non-scientific' (e.g. *Engineering Magazine*, March 1911: 952).

The 1912 report of the ASME committee, headed by James Dodge, on the 'present state of art of management', written by Leon Alford, documented trends in the development of 'industrial management' as a science (*American Machinist*, 7 November 1912: 757–62). The report marked the rapidity with which literature on management had been accumulating. Alford mentioned a directory which included 500 titles on business management, and argued that 75 percent of them had been written within the previous five years. He pointed to popular interest in management, evidenced by the large number of articles published in the daily papers and popular magazines. Alford also informed ASME members that engineering techniques were eventually accepted by parties who had previously objected to them. He mentioned 'the suddenly intensified interest in the subject on the part of employers and business executives in many lines of activity'. In 1915 Dunlap observed that the efforts were successful in placing 'industrial management among the recognized sciences'.

The science of organizations was placed close to sociology: '[It] has been termed a smaller sister of sociology, as a science of human nature ... Organization as a science teaches the art of so uniting and directing these working forces as to produce the most desirable composite effect' (*Engineering Magazine*, January 1912: 481–7; for a general discussion about the link between management and sociology see Chapter 7). Mentioning the thirtieth anniversary of Towne's presentation in ASME, Dunlap argued that Towne can be 'indisputably ranked as author of the first proposition that industrial management should be recognized as a distinct science' (*Engineering Magazine*, April 1916: 12–16). Towne, who responded to this statement in a rejoinder, recollected that it had occurred to him at the time that this was an opportunity to create and develop 'a true science of industrial management'. He explained that in this case, as in the case of the physical sciences, the Baconian system was applied, namely, the study of existing facts, the testing and proving of these by experiment, the recording and analysis of the information so gathered, and 'the deduction from such data of basic principles which, when properly stated and collated, shall constitute the foundation for a true science' (*Engineering Magazine*, April 1916: 12). The management movement was therefore already busy constructing a narrative regarding its history and founding fathers. That is to say, it was already engaged in canonization as early as 1915. John Dunlap and Hugo Diemer, a professor at the Pennsylvania State College, devoted their efforts to constructing the historiography of management. They wanted to see 'a distinct literature devoted to industrial economy' (*Engineering Magazine*, May 1915: 163–6). That same year, Diemer explained that industrial management was 'logical, systematic and scientific' (*American Machinist*, 27 March 1913: 507). The Society of Industrial Engineers was established in 1918, and promptly published its professional code.

Leon Alford crafted in 1916 another report on the status of industrial management for ASME. His 1912 report had been critical—or at least ambivalent—towards Scientific Management, arguing that there was little evidence to prove that it was truly a science. In his 1916 report, Alford provided the legitimization of management as grounded on scientific foundations. Identifying a 'need of a scientific study of everything connected with production', Alford argued that 'the management investigator uses laboratory methods to discover facts for immediate use'. As management consultant Robert Kent stated: 'It should be remembered that time study is, in effect, a laboratory experiment' (*American Machinist*, 6 December 1923: 839). Frank J. Oliver, Jr., of the editorial staff of *American Machinist*, acknowledged that reports and records of such experiments are to be kept since 'knowledge is power' (*American Machinist*, 18 October 1928: 601–5).

By the end of the First World War the early ASME debates, dealing with the engineers' role regarding managerial issues, had been settled. In 1919, the Society of Industrial Engineers elected its officers and a board of directors. Among them were engineers, university professors, and editors from the technical press—people such as Russell Bond, editor of *Scientific American*, and Charles Buxton Going, who had earlier resigned from the editorial office of *Engineering Magazine*. Among the university representatives were Dexter S. Kimball, dean of the College of Engineering at Cornell University, Joseph W. Roe, a professor from the Sheffield Scientific School at Yale University, and W. E. Hotchkiss, director of the School of Business Administration in the University of Minnesota. The list of engineers included Frank Gilbreth, Harrington Emerson, C. E. Knoeppel, and Dwight T. Farnham. These individuals formed the industry–university network of engineering management.

A year later, the society prepared the agenda for the annual meeting in Cleveland. One of the main issues was the codification and standardization of professional principles (*Industrial Management*, October 1919: 328–30), and the standardization of professional language. As the official document stated, the society aspired to professionalize the field 'with a view to ensuring mutual understanding, to realize the necessity for definitions of such words as "schedules," "planning," "dispatching," "turnover" and the like' (*Industrial Management*, October 1919: 328–30).

These statements set the tone for developing a professional jargon that in time became the mainstream language about management. ASME founded its Management Division in 1920, which grew, by 1922, to become the largest ASME division (Merrick 1980). A ten-year study of engineering education in the 1920s revealed that more than half of engineering graduates, five or more years after graduation, were in management careers rather than practicing the traditional engineering specialty of their academic curricula (Merrick 1980). The practice and discourse of management had assumed lives of their own, dissociated from their political and ideological origins. During the 1920s *American Machinist* continued its mission to increase the legitimacy of industrial management and its experts. For example, the magazine asked twelve of the best-known consulting management engineers—among them Frederick Miller, Dwight Merrick, Charles Knoeppel, Wallace Clark, Dwight Farnham, and Harrington Emerson—to provide the readers with standards of management (*American Machinist*, 4 January 1923: 21–7).

In this chapter I have shown that the newly born management movement nurtured by the engineering community faced enormous opposition from within as well as from without. There was, however, yet another major problem in the way of management systems: industrial unrest. In the next chapter I explain how engineers and management activists turned the problem around and used industrial unrest to their advantage. The struggles described in this chapter and the subsequent ones suggest that the efforts of the systematizers to develop managerial systems should not be viewed simply as an extension of capitalist thought (see also Stark 1980). It was a much more complicated ideological process. The relevance of labor politics to this process, as the following chapters show, cannot be overemphasized.

## Notes

1. It should be noted again that Chandler, Williamson, and Edwards represent very different theoretical perspectives. Chandler assigns a prominent role to technology and market needs; Williamson to the cost of transactions and to trust and uncertainty among different organizational participants; and Edwards contradicts the peaceful picture of evolutionary theorists by applying a neo-Marxist view according to which employers introduced organization systems in order to control labor. Nevertheless, they all share the two assumptions which I challenge in this chapter.
2. Conflictual perspectives on the nature of industrial rationalization have been proposed by Kolko 1963; Fligstein 1990; Roy 1990, 1997; Guillen 1994.
3. The conflict within managerial circles (to be shown below) refutes the theory of cyclical changes in managerial rhetoric over the course of the century (see Barley and Kunda 1992). This theory suggests that in each historical era one can identify a clear and coherent managerial ideology. Given the evidence about internal dissensions, it is clear that each historical period should not be viewed as ideologically homogeneous, and should not be viewed as representing a coherent scheme. Management activists are not all cut of the same cloth and the description of one dominant ideology per period conceals variations and conflicts that took place within each period. Abrahamson's data (1997) support this contention which runs counter to Barley and Kunda's argument about the repeated shifts between rational and normative rhetoric.

4.  The firm is the Scovill Manufacturing Company. See Yates 1989: 195.
5.  Boltanski provides a similar argument regarding *les cadres* in France (1990: 348). Likewise Urwick (1929: 58) describes the inability of British employers to comprehend the advantages of engineering-based management (see Lash and Urry 1987: 179).
6.  A methodological note is in order here. Throughout this chapter I back up the argument that capitalists opposed systems by drawing primarily on evidence from engineering magazines. Such evidence is oblique as the magazines were themselves agents in the field and their representation of such opposition is no doubt biased in some ways. Where possible, I tried to corroborate my findings with external documents (i.e. company files or employers' testimonies, and labor history documents). However, it is extremely difficult to come by more direct evidence of the objection of employers, particularly since such objection existed against the thrust of the winning historiography. For supporting evidence on the opposition of capitalists to systems, see also Nelson 1974, Merkle 1980, and Guillen 1994). There is evidence from other countries, too, of the resistance of employers to introducing management systems. Luc Boltanski, describing the cadres in France, names employers among their adversaries. My reading of the engineering magazines is offered here once more as a 'deconstruction', or reading between the lines, of the winning version. It is reasonable to assume that the references to employers' opposition in, for example, the *American Machinist* would reveal only the tip of the iceberg of the actual opposition.
7.  Watson worked in the iron industry (e.g. Morgan Iron Works and Novelty Iron Works in New York), in machine shops (e.g. Lowell, Mass.), and was on the editorial staff of the *Scientific American*. He later established the *Mechanical Engineer*, known later as the *Engineer*.
8.  Bell was a professor of physics and applied electricity at Purdue University and the editor of the *Electrical World* during 1890–1. His specialty was power transmission and heavy electric-railway work.
9.  Weber was a mechanical engineer with experience in Europe and in the United States, worked as superintendent in Allen Paper Car Wheel Works in Pullman, Illinois, and was a partner in the Lawrence Machine Co. in Lawrence, Massachusetts.
10. See Henry P. Kendall, 'Types of Management: Unsystematized, Systematized and Scientific' (1912). Cited in Litterer 1986: 104.
11. Members of the committee were: James Dodge (chairman), Leon Alford (secretary), D. M. Bates, H. A. Evans, Wilfred Lewis, W. B. Tardy, H. R. Towne, and Vaughan. Jaffe (1957) argued that at least Dodge, Towne, Tardy, and Evans were favorable toward Scientific Management.
12. Colvin had known the Ford Motor Company since 1907 and he became fascinated with the four-cylinder Model T that was inaugurated in 1909.
13. For example, he suggested the establishment of employment bureaux for better placement of employees according to their abilities and the institution of 'public service banks' to extend credit on assets of personality and capability rather than property. See Haber 1964: 47.
14. The Industrial Workers of the World—the 'Wobblies'—were an American labor

organization with a socialist vision that existed between 1905 and 1920 and had an active role in many plant strikes. See Dubofsky 1967.

15. For a similar approach, albeit in a different period, see Harris 1992. He discusses the role of language in constructing management reality in the context of labor relations in the 1940s.

# 5

# Engineers, Labor Politics, and American Exceptionalism before 1900

In no other country in the world are the relations between employers and employed as uniformly pleasant as in the United States. Nor is there any other country in which both proprietors and workmen are as jealous of their well known rights. Strikes often occur, but it is seldom that one of them is virulent.

(American Machinist, 26 January 1884: 8)

There is no such thing in this country as a working 'class' . . . Except it be a distinction between reputable citizens and loafers.

(American Machinist, 16 January 1886: 8)

We will not use the hackneyed and obnoxious expression 'the working classes'.

(American Machinist, 18 December 1886: 8)

Beginning in the 1870s, severe industrial unrest shook the United States for more than fifty years. This period roughly coincided with the period known as 'labor homogenization' (1890–1930) (Gordon, Edwards, and Reich 1982), so called to denote the forging of a homogeneous proletariat from the heterogeneous pre-industrial workforce. 'Labor homogenization' represented employers' desire to achieve control, order, and stability in industry. In retrospect, the introduction of management systems was congruent with that goal. The translation of systematization from the technical to the social realm strove to subject the 'workforce' to the same pattern of standardization and routinization that was applied to instruments. The notion of the 'human element' was thus instrumentally appropriated by the engineers. The systematizers might have phrased their intentions as 'individualizing' the job and 'rationalizing' the firm, but the more important implication of that rhetoric was the fragmenting, serializing, and deskilling of jobs to the greatest extent technically possible. The unspoken promise to the employers was evidently not only about efficiency, but about control. Systematization strove, and to a large extent succeeded, to turn the organization into one 'closed system', subject to engineering manipulation.

Organizational systems were expected to rationalize employment relationships, standardize behavior, and increase predictability of internal and external transactions (Kolko 1963). Systems experts developed 'drive systems' that helped break the control of craft workers over their work and entailed the increased use of records, accounting systems, and engineering techniques. In this manner, systematization appeared to take politics out of the labor struggles and offer a technical framework for dealing with tools, machines, and workers alike.

However, it would be imprecise to view systematization as merely a feature of 'labor homogenization' and engineers as obedient organs of capitalism. As argued in Chapter 1, this view has at least three shortcomings. First, the rise of industrial systems was by no means peculiar to capitalist society, but characterized socialist and communist economies as well (e.g. Bendix 1956/1974). Second, there were substantial variations in the political culture, labor strife, and economic ideologies in the USA during the period known as homogenization (1880–1930); each of these had a different effect on capitalists and on industrial relations. Third, it would be misleading to view industrial engineers as 'mere servants of power' (Jacoby 1985). Engineers and management consultants promoted their own agenda as middle-class professionals, and developed priorities that were often different from those expressed by capitalists or government officials. It seems that management systems threatened the power of both employers and unions (see Chapter 4).

Engineers were convinced that social issues should be approached by applying the same method that had proven fruitful in material affairs. To them, 'rationality' and 'science' were critical resources in establishing their professional goals and credibility. Steeped in this engineering-based ideology, they viewed organizations as machine-like systems; they proceeded to popularize this conception in professional circles and in US industry.[1]

As I have shown in the previous chapter, there was no monolithic power behind systematization. The engineers' activities were driven by the desire to make their work scientific and professional, rather than by the desire to promote industrial capitalism *per se*. At the same time, one cannot gainsay the economic and political puissance of large capitalist employers. The political culture and economic ideologies that grew in the USA during the period of 'labor homogenization', therefore, also need to be inspected. Specifically I refer to variations in the intensity of labor unrest, variations in the public interpretation of the conflict, and the transition from nineteenth-century industrial practices to the Progressive era. The textual-historical analysis presented in the following two chapters aims to depict these political variations and to examine how they shaped the institutionalization of the theory of organizational systems over a period of more than fifty years. The analysis is concerned with how politics, economics, and professional ideologies are intertwined and complementary. Along these lines, I do not wish to evaluate the ontological status of the propositions and claims presented in the engineering texts. Nor do I seek to challenge the validity of these propositions as universal truths about organizations. Rather, the historical analysis addresses the manner in which professional experts solidified their claim to 'objective and positive knowledge'. I attempt to link the content of this knowledge, its language, and timing of appearance with the broader ideological fabric that made the production of this knowledge possible.

Rather than subscribing to existing narratives, which tend to be parsimonious and linear, I try to rethink here the shaping of systems ideology in the political context of labor unrest. This perspective unwraps the power/knowledge package of systems theory and practice at the point(s) of production and onward, treating it as a complex set of interactions between professionals' 'search for truth' and the political economy of the period. I therefore historicize the magazines' 'will to knowledge' and trace the dynamic interplay between power and knowledge within a political context.[2] This historicization follows two periods, which themselves represent two historical paradigms: American Exceptionalism and the Progressive era. The rise of systematization *vis-à-vis* these two paradigms is the subject of the following two chapters. During the late nineteenth century, industrial unrest found expression mainly in the idiom of American Exceptionalism. The severity of the labor struggle was denied and the events were attributed to non-American sources. This denial derived from the Exceptionalist rejection of class structure in America. During the early Progressive period, industrial struggle was no longer denied but rather recognized as the 'labor problem'. This 'problem', as well as its proposed solution, was expressed in terms of systems. However, despite a partial retreat from the language of Exceptionalism, the two engineering magazines did not cover industrial unrest in a more detailed or accurate fashion. While qualitative changes in the way industrial unrest (and later, the 'labor problem') was constructed did occur, the larger picture (in the magazines and among the public whose views they represented) was one of denial and neglect. The agenda of systems produced a depoliticized view of history in general and of labor struggles in particular. It was a kind of epistemological myopia on the part of engineers, and I trace its expression within the magazines. During Exceptionalism, the class structure was depoliticized; during Progressivism, bureaucratization was depoliticized.

## 5.1 Industrial unrest in the United States, 1877–1932

The United States is a peculiar case in the history of industrial conflicts. Despite the fact that its labor movement has been among the least radical, the intensity of its industrial violence and unrest has been very high compared with that of other countries (Edwards 1981; Voss 1993). Whereas there are no consistent measures of violence involved in industrial disputes, labor history reveals numerous violent episodes. Among the best-known ones are the 1877 nationwide railroad strikes, the Southwestern Railroad strike during 1885–6, the Haymarket bombing in Chicago in 1886, the encounters in the metal mines in the Cœur d'Alene region in Idaho in 1892, the Homestead struggle of 1892, the Pullman boycott in 1894, the 1902 anthracite strike, the Colorado mine disputes in 1903–4 and in 1913–14, and the steel strike of 1919 (Adamic 1983). Between 1911 and 1916, violence in many industries and locations was at its peak. In general, labor violence involved more attacks on property whereas violence originated by employers was mainly characterized by attacks on individuals (for the qualitative depiction of industrial struggle I rely mainly on Goldstein 1978).

Business corporations were able to usurp government functions for their own ends as a result of the power they gained in the thirty-five years between the Civil War and the beginning of the twentieth century. In the absence of government regulation, companies were able to consolidate capital, integrate markets, form monopolies, and employ political leverage (McCraw 1984). Employers' strategies to repress labor unrest—known in industrial circles as the 'labor problem'[3]—were diverse. In many industries, employees were congregated in company towns under the complete dominance, control, and surveillance of the owners. Manufacturers used private police and private armies to combat organized labor. The arsenals that some corporations used were astonishing. Republic Steel had ten times as many gas guns and over twenty-five times as many gas shells as the Chicago police department. Its armory included over 500 revolvers, 64 rifles, 245 shotguns, 143 gas guns, over 4,000 gas projectiles, and over 2,700 gas grenades (Goldstein 1978). Such a usage of arsenals and private forces had no precedent in European industrial history.

In the strong alliance between industry and government in repressing labor unrest, local police, state militia, or federal troops were often sent to help employers. In fact, several historians have argued that 'in no other Western democracy have employers been so much aided in their opposition to unions by the civil authorities, the armed forces of government and their courts' (Lorwin 1933: 355; cited in Goldstein 1978: 4). On many occasions, such as during the 1919 steel strike in Pennsylvania, police deputized for employees who continued to be paid by the company. During the 1927 coal strike, the Pittsburgh Coal Company paid $800,000 for the so-called Coal and Iron Police (Goldstein 1978). During the period 1877–1937, the national guard was called out at least 250–300 times to interfere in labor disputes; almost always, it acted as strikebreakers (ibid.: 14). The courts likewise reflected the attitude of business toward labor (ibid.). For example, following the railroad riots in 1877, conspiracy prosecutions were revived by the courts after thirty-five years of dormancy. Following the Haymarket Riot in 1886, there were more legal conspiracy cases than during all the rest of the century (ibid.). Ironically, the courts started to use the Sherman Anti-Trust Act of 1890 in order to regulate the labor movement, although it was initially legislated to limit the excessive power of big business.

Consistent data on industrial violence are unavailable;[4] however, official records on strikes and on the number of workers involved in strikes have been kept since 1880 (see Peterson 1938). A strike may be defined as 'a collective refusal to work under the existing conditions of employment, and represents a

state of overt conflict between workers and their employer' (Edwards 1981: 289).
A comparison of the annual frequency of strikes (standardized for the number of
non-agriculture employees) during 1880–1932 suggests that the figure gradually
rose during the 1880s, fell in the 1890s, but then rose again to peak levels during
the Progressive era. It remained high until 1918–19 and then experienced a
dramatic decline in the 1920s, reaching a low point in 1929.[5]

While the frequency of strikes is one index of the intensity of disputes
between labor and employers, the average number of strikers per strike refers to
their scope and severity. The official figures reveal that, following a period of a
relatively constant level of worker involvement in strikes during 1880–1909,
their number started to peak around 1910 and gradually reached its highest level
during the years 1919–22.[6] Similar to the frequency of strikes, the number of
workers involved was at its lowest level around 1929.[7] Fig. 4, which is based on
statistics published by the US Department of Labor, displays the trends for the
time-period 1880–1932 (see also Table 3). Data for the two measures, strikes and
workers per strike, are standardized using a common index (1927=100). Both
measures indicate that unrest gradually increased after the beginning of the
1880s and reached its highest level during the so-called 'Progressive era'. The
number of strikes, and the numbers of workers involved in strikes, in the USA
between 1900 and 1920 were much higher than in Germany, Britain, or France
(Guillen 1994). Note that information for the years 1905–14 is missing in this

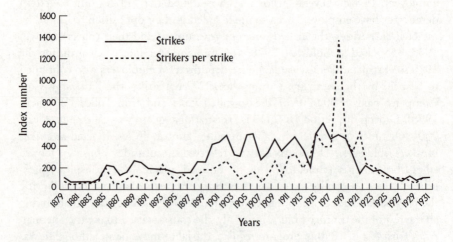

**Fig. 4.** Trends in labor strikes in the United States, 1880–1932

*Note*: Annual number of strikes; and average number of strikers per strike relative to labor
force participation (millions).

   See Table 3 (p. 159) for complete data.

*Source*: Peterson 1938.

figure, as no data on strikes were collected at the national level in the USA during this period.[8] This omission is conspicuous, particularly since it was a period when strikes constituted the main issue on the American social agenda. A similar omission was taking place in the engineering periodicals.

The coverage of labor struggles in *American Machinist* and *Engineering Magazine* over the entire period of 1879–1932 reveals that it was proportionally small and gradually declining.[9] Fig. 5 describes this trend (see also Table 4).

It is intriguing to juxtapose the two figures, namely, strikes and their coverage. Prior to 1895, 15 percent of the non-technical volume in both magazines was devoted to coverage of industrial unrest. After 1895 the yearly average coverage sharply declined to 7 percent, and to 2 percent after 1900. In *American Machinist* alone the decline was even more severe: 4 percent in 1895 to 1 percent after 1900. During the Progressive era there were years with virtual silence.[10] Particularly disturbing was the omission in the coverage of industrial unrest between 1911 and 1916, when a wave of labor disputes of unprecedented intensity swept the nation. In fact, the years 1911–16 were ranked 'among the most violent in American history, except the Civil War', and violence was almost a daily occurrence (Taft and Ross 1969). None of these tragic events was reported in either magazine. In the next chapter I will argue that during these years the

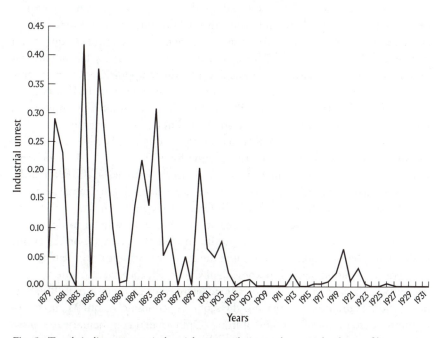

**Fig. 5.** Trends in literature on industrial unrest relative to the annual volume of literature on management, 1879–1932

*Note*: See Table 4 (p. 160) for complete data.

labor problem was reconstructed in terms of systems. Strikes were presented as technical problems, begging a solution by way of a better engineering system.

It was under the supervision of editor Frederick Miller that the politics of labor relations first drifted away from the pages of *American Machinist*.[11] Neither he, nor his traveling reporters, who wandered from one town to another across the country and helped spread new machine-shop methods and organization systems, mentioned labor unrest or cared to focus on it. To be sure, Miller held truly progressive ideas about the 'labor troubles'. For example, he argued once that 'autocracy in industry is irreconcilable with democracy in government', and believed that 'the old driver method of industrial management will no longer do' (*American Federationist*, January 1921: 41). However, he also perceived strikes as 'contagious and infectious', and equated 'the strike spirit' with 'Bolshevism' (*American Federationist*, June 1922: 684). In 1906 Frederick Miller expressed his apolitical approach to the labor–capital cleavage: 'A distinguishing feature of public life in America is that it has not been customary for workingmen and their employers to divide on questions of politics' (*American Machinist*, 5 April 1906: 465).

Leon Alford, editor of *American Machinist* between 1911 and 1917, attributed a minor role to labor relations. Only in 1919, after his editorship, did he pay larger tribute to the issue (Jaffe 1957: 89–101). As an editor of *Industrial Management*, he was then ready to admit that 'at the present time there is a general feeling of uneasiness and unrest throughout our entire industry'. Alford addressed the members of ASME, reminding them: 'Strikes are so frequent and widespread that it is doubtful if a single member of this Society has not at least been inconvenienced during the present year by the temporary cessation of some function of industry upon which he is in some degree dependent' (*Transactions of the ASME*, 41, 1919: 163–86). By the time this late awakening took place, however, the politics of labor was already edited out of both magazines.

Wunderlin has provided a plausible interpretation of the dynamic of this omission among professional experts (Wunderlin 1992). During the 1902 coal mines strike, economist Jeremiah W. Jenks, an active figure in USIC, felt that the miners needed to publicize their case. He wrote to Ralph Easley, the secretary of the Chicago Civic Federation, that he 'intended to write on the coal strike for a prominent magazine of very large circulation'. But Jenks wanted to do so as a disinterested scientist. As Wunderlin put it: 'Instead of a discourse on the events of the strike, Jenks proposed to examine the economic structure of the hard coal industry. The public needed to know, Jenks believed, the extent of the consolidation of coal properties and the railroad ownership of them' (ibid.: 80). The description of the riots was beyond the scope of economic vision. Management engineers were in a similar frame of mind. Opinionated commentary and 'plain coverage' of political events were replaced by a disinterested discourse on organizational systems. John Hill, publisher of *American Machinist*, expressed this credo very clearly a few years later, during a dispute with his printing workers:

In the first place let it be known that our papers are purely technical. They discuss only those subjects relating to the business they represent, and avoid labor disputes and labor news. Each of our three papers is published to disseminate information about the work at hand—the real making of machinery, generation of power or the extraction and milling of ores . . . Our papers have been fair to employee and employers because we have not taken sides. (*American Machinist*, 8 February 1906: 199–200)

When labor unrest was discussed during these years, it was mostly in relation to the experience of other countries (see, for example, *Engineering Magazine*, December 1911: 403; *Engineering Magazine*, March 1913: 833–41; *Engineering Magazine*, March 1913: 929–31; *Engineering Magazine*, June 1913: 414), or in relation to the introduction of systems and managerial techniques (*Engineering Magazine*, January 1913: 597–8). This perspective provided a new prism through which a solution to industrial unrest could be found. During the same period, British employers and managers defined industrial unrest as a major social and political issue on their agenda. As Guillen observed, the pages of the leading British management journals were 'filled with articles, statements and notes on the problems of labor unrest' (Guillen 1994: 212).

A glaring feature of the engineers' depoliticized, 'objective' coverage of the labor problem was their (ab)use of statistics. This elimination was in itself paradoxical since it took place in a political and professional culture that encouraged the gathering of data and figures. Elimination of strikes statistics characterized the engineering magazines, the government, and the capitalists. Recall that no data on strikes were collected at the national level during the years 1905–14. As one economist referred to this omission, 'unfortunately our strike statistics were then allowed to lapse for an eight-year period' (Douglas 1923). This is despite the existence of an independent Federal Department of Commerce and Labor founded in 1903, which was supposed to submit reports on labor statistics. While the reasons for the omission are not entirely clear, it is particularly noticeable given the intensity of labor strikes during this period (e.g. Adams 1966; Montgomery 1974; Goldstein 1978). Strike data were also subject to additional distortion through the application of ideology by major employers. The Rockefeller Foundation, established in the midst of the bloody clashes between labor and capital during 1911–16, served as a theoretical arm of industrial capitalism (Howe 1980; Slaughter and Silva 1980). From its inception, the foundation devoted resources to combat the challenges that unrest posed to capitalists. After the 'Ludlow Massacre'—the peak of the 'civil war' between the Rockefeller coal company and the union in 1914—the Rockefeller group recruited William Lyon Mackenzie King, a Canadian labor specialist, to engage in an 'objective' study 'to promote industrial peace'. King depolarized the conflict by implicitly restricting labor's strike strength. He recommended 'compulsory investigation', which forbade employer lockouts and worker strikes until a government investigation 'has found the facts of the dispute' (Slaughter and Silva 1980: 72). It was clear, however, that during the investigation production would not stop, and the workers were thus deprived of their most effective weapon—the strike.[12] Research and statistics, therefore, were presented as a major scientific and objective tool by both engineers and politicians, while being continuously used and manipulated by them in the service of their own interests.[13]

In the balance of this chapter I demonstrate that, despite their claim of objectivity and political neutrality, the engineering magazines drew on the rhetoric of American Exceptionalism, making the political ramifications of labor struggles insignificant. They deemed strikes unnecessary, attributed unrest to migrant labor and foreign subversive philosophies, and denied the existence of a working class in America.

## 5.2 Claims to objectivity and political neutrality

From their inception, both *American Machinist* and *Engineering Magazine*[14] evoked an ideology of objectivity and political neutrality. In 1877, Jackson Bailey, the first editor of *American Machinist*, proclaimed that his 'editorial opinions are not for sale' and that 'We shall always act independently, not holding ourselves under the least obligation to give "favorable notices" of anything under review, but rather to elicit the plain truth whether it be favorable or unfavorable.' In October 1879, the editor restated his position 'that nobody has ever paid the publishers of *American Machinist* one cent for anything inserted in its reading columns' (11 October 1879: 8). A month later, Bailey addressed the labor struggle and made it clear that 'The *American Machinist* takes no political grounds in favour of, or against any existing party' (*American Machinist*, 1 November 1879: 8. See also *American Machinist*, 22 July 1886: 3; *American Machinist*, 6 November 1886: 8; *American Machinist*, 13 November 1886: 6; or in the fiftieth anniversary issue of the *American Machinist*, 19 May 1927). On the fiftieth anniversary of *American Machinist*, the publisher, James H. McGraw, praised this long-standing philosophy and its translation into practice: 'Mr. Bailey's thought was of a newspaper that would reflect accurately the events in its field, without fear or favour, and he made of his thought a vital force that was greatly needed in the metal industry of his day' (see *American Machinist*, 19 May 1927: 824). Committed to these lines of accuracy, objectivity, and political neutrality, editors regularly criticized what they perceived as distorted descriptions of events covered by other periodicals and newspapers (e.g. *Engineering Magazine*, September 1892: 759–64; *American Machinist*, 30 August 1884: 3). An editorial in *American Machinist* referred to a lack of objectivity in reporting on wage changes in the metal industry:

Whenever a large manufacturing establishment makes a reduction of wages the fact is telegraphed all over the country as a matter of general news, and it appears in most of the daily papers. But when an advance of wages is made, the matter is seldom considered of sufficient importance for an associated press dispatch. Why? (*American Machinist*, 30 August 1884: 3)

In a complaint about the 'injustice of the prison labor contract system', the editors said: 'By keeping comparative silence upon this question, the leading political newspapers have lulled the working men into a feeling of fancied security, most of them, probably, holding the view that it is not so much of a weighty question after all' (*American Machinist*, 1 November 1879: 8). This position was extended to the question of industrial unrest. For example, in 1894 *American Machinist* did not take sides with regard to the wave of coal strikes: 'The coal strike now in progress in this country is in its present and possible effects one of the most disastrous that has ever occurred . . . We confess to being unable to decide the question of right and wrong as between the operatives and operators, and have absolutely no side in the matter' (*American Machinist*, 7 June 1894: 8).

Consistent with the position of ostensible neutrality, the magazines often criticized all parties for wrongdoing in industrial disputes (e.g. 'The Tap-root of Industrial Discontent', *Engineering Magazine*, August 1891: 498–504). Furthermore, as was the case throughout the formation of the management movement,[15] they attempted to dissociate themselves from any connection with big capital, as the editor of *American Machinist* once stated: 'A Michigan man writes us asking for "the address of Vanderbilt and George Gold." We don't know the parties. They are not on our subscription list' (*American Machinist*, 27 September 1884: 8).

In 1891, the *People*, a New York-based socialist publication,[16] attacked *American Machinist* for being a 'bosses' organ'. The editors rejected the 'silly attack upon us . . . a very cheap but favourite form of argument', and took the opportunity to present their philosophy regarding the evils of monopolies and the advantages of a truly free market:

If oppressive monopolies were abolished, and every man given an opportunity to fully employ such talents and abilities as nature has given him, there would then be no serious suffering from personal and inexcusable folly, and we believe that with freedom from such oppressive monopolies, competition instead of being the awful thing imagined by the socialists, will prove the most beneficent of social forces. (*American Machinist*, 16 November 1893: 8)

The editors imperiously concluded: 'Whether we are a bosses' organ or the workingmen's organ (we have been accused of both) this is our belief, and with this statement of it we leave the subject.'

Despite this, political 'neutrality' should be viewed within its larger context. In the next section I assess the merit of this position and attempt to show that reports in the magazines were guilty of severe misrepresentations and omissions. One source of misrepresentation was grounded in the ideology of American Exceptionalism. Despite the magazine's attempt to be factual, some events remained 'unpresentable'. I focus on the magazine's omissions not out of interest in plotting the reliability and validity of journalistic reports. Rather, I attempt to demonstrate that while the development of systems cannot be understood without the internal dynamic of the engineering profession, their action was also informed by the ideological parameters of the larger political context.

## 5.3 The legacy of American Exceptionalism

During the last three decades of the nineteenth century, there were three peaks in industrial violence: 1873–8 (e.g. the Molly Maguires in the anthracite coal-fields of eastern Pennsylvania and the 1877 general railroad strike), 1886–7 (e.g. the Missouri Pacific Railroad), and 1892–7 (e.g. Homestead, Cœur d'Alene, or the Pullman strike). Goldstein has argued, 'Each period was dominated by fears on the part of conservative elites that American workers were becoming infected by foreign subversive theories' (1978: 23). Strikes were perceived as unnecessary and dangerous. During periods of intense strikes, the media were flooded with descriptions of alien agitators, communists, and red revolutionaries. Trade unionists, socialists, 'anarchical socialists', and communists became equated one with the other (Merkle 1980). The agitation of foreign 'anarchists' threatened the very essence of the American republican heritage. Politicians, manufacturers, and the public at large feared labor unrest. The potential danger to property, to the state, to the civil order, and to the free market was real. It was in this vein that the national commissioner of education asserted that 'public schools could train the child to resist the evils of strikes and violence' (Goldstein 1978: 33).

In 1878, the House Committee on Education and Labor—worried by the political threat posed by labor radicalism—investigated the condition of European labor. Any resemblance between American and European class struc-ture was denied:[17] 'We are not a nation of capitalists and laborers; we are a nation of republican citizens. Let us, then, ignore these dividing lines, and each accepting that position for which his capacity best fits him, work upward and onward in the scale of respectable citizenship, doing that which is best for all.' These features of self-identification, which highlighted the uniqueness of the American experience and denied the existence of a class structure in the USA, were the legacy of a national ideology held throughout the nineteenth century. At the core of this ideology was a distinction between the 'old' and 'new' worlds. Many Europeans believed that the United States was the first classless society (Hughes 1989a), and that America had 'the best form of government yet devised by man' (*American Machinist*, 28 June 1894: 8). As Tocqueville sensed in his visit to the USA, something other than class feelings emerged in the new world where people grew increasingly alike (Diggins 1992). Americans were not aware of estates, as Europeans were, nor was there an entrenched aristocracy. Tocqueville believed that in the absence of class enmity (which characterized the middle class and the working class in Europe), all people became increasingly indistinguish-able (ibid.). This ideology intertwined with the Puritan ideas of America's holy mission, the hope that the American Republic would last forever, and the expec-tations for economic opportunities. American Puritanism portrayed an ideal of a self-made individual—a 'frontiersman' who was self-employed (Guillen 1994: 32). Wage labor was implicitly criticized as a waste of time, a temporary stage in the trajectory to an independent economic position and to the accumulation of Wealth. This philosophy, incidentally, resembled the Social Darwinist ideas of competition and survival of the fittest (see Bendix 1956/1974; Guillen 1994).

In the context of industry, Europeans and Americans developed similar ideas about America. As Hughes describes, Weimar Germans who 'discovered America' believed that they had found a modern land in which there was peace between labor and capital, steadily rising wages, and unprecedented prosperity. In a similar manner, James See, an American correspondent for *American Machinist* who wrote under the pseudonym of Chordal, believed, 'Our American systems of labor-saving machinery and devices are probably ... The most marvelous and perfect in the world' (*American Machinist*, 5 May 1883: 4).[18]

The main period that reoriented the language of Exceptionalism was the Gilded Age, which Ross dated roughly from 1877 (the year of the violent rail-road strike) to 1897 (the end of the great depression of the 1890s) (Ross 1991, 1993). But this reorientation did not mean that its legacy disappeared altogether. Traces of Exceptionalism were evident in the publications of both magazines, *American Machinist* and *Engineering Magazine*, throughout the last two decades of the nineteenth century.

## 5.4 The rhetoric of labor unrest prior to 1900

### 5.4.1 Strikes are foreign to the American experience

One year after the publication of the 1878 report of the House Committee on Education and Labor, the editors of *American Machinist* denied the prevalence of strikes and pointed to a major difference from Britain: 'One of the greatest evils of the manufacturing industries of Great Britain has to contend with that of organized strikes of workmen. This evil prevails to some extent in our own country, but not to the same degree as across the Atlantic' (*American Machinist*, 15 March 1879: 8). In 1880 the editors again criticized labor strikes in England and portrayed them as uncommon and 'woefully wrong': It is nothing of an extraordinary character to hear of a strike of 5,000 or 10,000 operatives in a single trade in England ... No intelligent individual need be told that there is something woefully wrong in the social, industrial or governmental system under which such labor upheavals become events of almost common occurrence' (*American Machinist*, 16 October 1880: 8).

This optimistic position—implying that American history might be immune to such phenomena—can be contrasted with a British view of the events in America. In 1879, an editorial in a British engineering magazine determined that labor upheavals took place in America and that there was nothing uncommon about it: 'That America has already undergone great crises, such as few young countries have ever known . . . That she has suffered from strikes and trade disputes equal in extent and mischief to those of England—all these facts prove that, like an unusually strong child, she has had her "eruptions" early, and with remarkable violence' (*American Machinist*, 19 July 1879: 6).

This depiction, which equated the British with the American experience, was, of course, different from the one suggested by the editors of *American Machinist*. The latter expressed firm objections to strikes ('strikes are always to be deplored', *American Machinist*, 15 May 1880: 8) and lockouts. The editors criticized unions for using the method of strikes and condemned employers who black-listed employees: 'As a rule, strikes are unwise expedients which can be prevented' (*American Machinist*, 25 September 1880: 8). The editors expressed this position regarding strikes and lockouts most firmly:

Referring to recent editorials in the *American Machinist*, every opinion that we have ever expressed upon any of the questions that from time to time arise between employers and workmen, has been uttered from one unvarying standpoint; namely that 'strikes' and 'lockouts' alike are unnecessary and prejudicial to the true interest of both parties . . . The influence of the *American Machinist* is, and always has been, against 'strikes' from any cause, or against forced conclusions of every kind, and in favor of peace and industrial progress. (*American Machinist*, 9 June 1881: 8)

In 1894 the editors of *American Machinist* made a definite and clear statement that strikes were barbarous and belonged to the pre-modern period: 'without attempting to write either side up or down, we can, in common with many others, see nothing but cause for regret in the fact that so near the year 1900 the barbarous practice of trying to settle labor disputes by strikes is necessary' (*American Machinist*, 7 June 1894: 8).

When the garment workers in New York went on strike in 1894, *American Machinist* (acting exceptionally) supported their cause.[19] Nevertheless, the editors qualified their support and reiterated an old position: 'The *American Machinist* has, on general principles, opposed itself to strikes' (*American Machinist*, 13 September 1894: 8). In 1895, when a strike was settled peacefully, the editors of *American Machinist* praised the parties for resorting to 'reason' which proves 'worth more than acres of theorizing and moralizing, and infinitely better than abuse and fighting' (*American Machinist*, 14 March 1895: 208). The magazine expressed belief in individual rationality: 'It is true that there are a great many men in the world who are unreasonable, selfish and narrow minded, but the majority of men are not so, and, in our humble opinion, there is no greater proportion of them among workmen than amongst other classes of men.' This use of the Enlightenment notion of 'reason' is very different from the one developed during the Progressive era, according to which human nature does not conform with reason, which justifies the introduction of rational systems. Even as late as 1902 the argument was made that 'The class of leaders who bring on strikes or of managers who cause lockouts will be as finally discredited and retired as the class of rulers who plunge into wars. To doubt it is to deny the plain history not only of industry but of all civilization' (*Engineering Magazine*, November 1902: 264).

The rejection of strikes as indigenous phenomena was not peculiar to engineering circles. It was characteristic of most middle-class professionals. A field in which one might expect to find an unbiased coverage of strikes is labor statistics. Carroll Wright was chief of the Massachusetts Bureau of Statistics of Labor from 1873 and a federal commissioner of labor from 1885 (Leiby 1960). The establishment of the federal Bureau of Labor in 1885 was mainly stimulated by the labor disturbances between 1883 and 1887, the depression of 1883, and the rising power of the Knights of Labor. The essence of Wright's creed was that the statistician must be impartial, though he might also hold his own opinions regarding the events.[20] Industrial disputes appeared to Wright in the 1880s to be 'incidental, annoying, and unprofitable effects of the introduction of the factory system, and to be a passing phase of divine discontent' (Leiby 1960: 152). In the 1887 volume of the bureau on strikes and lockouts, he concluded that strikes did not benefit the wage earners, that they tended to deprive the workers of work, that they led to the demoralization of workers, and that unions were not strong enough to overcome the evil of violence (Leiby 1960: 154).

### 5.4.2 The European connection to anarchism

Opposition to strikes was not only an outcome of American Exceptionalism, but also a result of what the middle class perceived as anarchistic threats to social order. Engineers in particular believed that anarchism as a form of philosophy should be abolished. Philosophy was justified only as long as it guaranteed productive behavior: 'Philosophy is a good thing so far as it pays cash down. When philosophy teaches the hired girl to scatter clothes-pins all over the backyard, one or the other of them should be discharged' (*American Machinist*, 25 October 1879: 7).[21]

The concern with rational order is exemplified in an 1894 editorial statement which deals with the role of the state, the law, and civil society: 'All, except anarchists, or the more euphemistically termed individualists, will agree that a civilized people must maintain some form of government, and that behind this government there must be a potential force, a force capable of compelling obedience to laws and respect to the rights of others when necessary' (*American Machinist*, 28 June 1894: 8).

The year 1886 was labeled by historians as 'a revolutionary year', 'the year of the great uprising of labor', and the 'great upheaval' (Goldstein 1978). Andrew Carnegie, chief spokesman for the industrial community at that time, referred to the 'most serious labor revolt that ever occurred in this country'. Carnegie blamed just about everybody for the unrest: capital (for being frightened into panic), leaders of public opinion (for losing self-control), political economists (for being far removed from everyday affairs), and magazines (for being filled with plans involving radical socialist changes) (Carnegie 1886*b*/1992). During this year, membership in the Knights of Labor—which called for the abolition of 'wage slavery'—increased to its largest number ever: 729,677 members, compared with 111,395 in 1885 and 71,326 in 1884. The 1 May strike turned out to be the largest nationwide strike in American history, and there was growing leeway for 'anti-capitalist' attacks.

The centre of the strike movement was then in Chicago. On 4 May 1886, the IWPA (International Working People's Association) conducted a meeting to protest against the aggression of the Chicago police, which operated 'as though it were a private police force in the service of the employers' (Goldstein 1978: 38). Just as the meeting was about to adjourn, 180 policemen appeared and demanded that the meeting be dissolved. A bomb was thrown into police ranks, and police shot into the crowd. Seven policemen and an undetermined number of civilians were killed. Thirty-six people were indicted as connected with the bombing. The prosecution did not present the case as a murder trial but rather as a contest between the well-ordered society and the evil of anarchy (Goldstein 1978). Defendants were found guilty and all (except for one) were sentenced to death. The repression that followed the Haymarket bombing pushed union members to reject associations with revolutionary ideas and to display obedience to the law.

Goldstein has argued that the Chicago police deliberately strove to keep the anarchist menace alive since local businessmen contributed money to supplement policemen's salaries to combat anarchism. He argued that when the business community cut off the money in 1891, the police began to make new raids to show that the danger was still in effect. An editorial in *American Machinist* supported this interpretation:

The Chicago police are shown up in a very bad light by recent revelations concerning their dramatic, not to say outrageous, interference with private rights in forcing their way into assemblages of workingmen and compelling them to display American flags in their meeting. It has been stated, and corroborated by reliable citizens, that this was done solely to induce a renewal of $100,000 annual subscriptions from wealthy citizens of Chicago for the 'suppression of anarchy,' subscriptions which had been paid for several years, but which the subscribers to had begun to have doubts as to the propriety or necessity of. (*American Machinist*, 4 February 1892: 8)

The editors concluded:

It is beginning to dawn upon the minds of many people that there has been and is now far less anarchy in Chicago than the police of that town would like to have believed, and that there would be far less of it if it were not for the idiotic performances of some of the police themselves. It should always be remembered that when a policemen or a Pinkerton guard exceeds his lawful authority and violates private rights, he becomes by practice, if not in fact, an anarchist himself. (*American Machinist*, 4 February 1892: 8)

In these editorials, the editors of *American Machinist* did not endorse anarchism, but rather expressed a desire for stability in industry in general and metal shops in particular. This explains their objection to any kind of instability. On one occasion the editors reminded the readers that fully armed 'private detectives' in industrial disputes should not be allowed (*American Machinist*, 12 February 1887: 8). On another occasion (1891) *American Machinist* warned that giving every man the right to protect his own property is 'genuine red flag anarchy'.

Carried to its logical conclusion, this would give to every individual the right of making himself a walking arsenal, and shooting every one whom he supposed designed to interfere with any of his belongings. In modern civilized society the individual . . . has the right to demand adequate protection from the constituted authorities. . . . A resort to force to gain more property is no less anarchy than the resort to force to gain the first dollar's worth of it, and it would seem as though men who had property rights worth protecting would think twice before setting an example of lawlessness, which when carried to its logical conclusion, disregards all property rights, and, in fact, all rights but those secured by brute force. (*American Machinist*, 16 June 1892: 8)

In this statement two points stand out. First, the difference between a capitalist and his workers is but a matter of dollars. Second, employers should be careful before they violate rational law which protects them and their property, as it always did in the history of the middle class and the bourgeoisie (see also *American Machinist*, 24 July 1886: 8).

In 1892 there were again signs of an increasing conflict. The most significant strikes were at the Homestead Pennsylvania Carnegie Steel Works, where Henry Frick was able to break the union; at the silver mine Cœur d'Alene in Idaho; at the Buffalo railway; and in the coal mines of Anderson County in Tennessee. The anarchist scare was heightened after several violent events such as the attempt, by the Russian-born Alexander Berkman, to assassinate Henry Frick and the huge strike wave of 1894 including the famous one in Pullman, Illinois (Goldstein 1978; Adamic 1983).

The events at Homestead assumed warlike proportions (Burgoyne 1893/1982). In July, the editor of *American Machinist* referred to Frick's usage of force in Homestead:

We do not believe—we have never believed—in the employment of Pinkerton men in the settlement of labour disputes. It always has and always will lead to trouble. They are not a part of the properly constituted civil or military force, and their appearance upon a scene of trouble will always be looked upon as an effort to overawe workmen. If it becomes necessity to settle labor disputes by force of arms, the operating army should be in charge of those properly constituted to superintend it, and not in the hand of men without responsibility. (*American Machinist*, 14 July 1892: 9)[22]

Prior to 1883, 95 percent of the immigrants to the United States came from northern and western Europe (e.g. the British Isles, Germany, and the Scandinavian peninsula). Thereafter, immigration from central and eastern Europe increased rapidly. By 1907, over 80 percent of the European immigrants came from Austro-Hungary, Italy, Russia, and the Balkan nations.[23] The new immigrants were primarily (Greek or Roman) Catholic and Jewish, and not Protestants. They were also predominantly composed of single males rather than families, and over a third of them (compared with around 3 percent of previous immigrants) were illiterate (Noble 1977: 57). These immigrants seemed not always to meet the 'imperatives of industry' with their 'medley of foreign tongues and customs' and their 'preindustrial' work habits (ibid.: 58). Furthermore, rarely did the immigrants from southern and eastern Europe make it to engineering and other professional circles.[24] The juxtaposition between the 1886 Haymarket bombing (and the subsequent trial) and these characteristics of the rising immigration waves from central and eastern Europe intensified the association between aliens, anarchy, radicalism, and violence. Anarchists and immigrants alike were referred to—to quote an extreme statement—as 'the very scum and offal of Europe' or 'Europe's human and inhuman rubbish' (Goldstein 1978: 41).

Along these lines, *American Machinist* assumed a negative stance toward

The importation of ignorant and degraded foreigners to take places which American workmen could not be induced to fill . . . Not only do we believe that the importation of such people is bad for the American workmen whom they displace, but bad also in many ways for the employers who import them, as many of these employers have discovered to their sorrow. (*American Machinist*, 19 February 1891: 8)

In an editorial from 1891, the explanation was made quite clear: 'The cheap Hungarian labor so freely imported a few years ago has proved anything but a blessing. This class of labor appears to be particularly given to rioting on every possible occasion . . . Such men can only be a curse to any country, and this is especially true of this country. Better let them go home' (*American Machinist*, 8 January 1891: 7; see also *American Machinist*, 15 January 1891: 10; *American Machinist*, 19 February 1891: 8; *American Machinist*, 12 March 1891: 12).

In a similar vein the editors reprinted quotes from the *Jersey City Evening Journal* referring to 'this wild mob of foreign laborers, armed with clubs, knives and revolvers, [who] made an attack on English-speaking workmen'. They labeled them as 'ignorant foreigners' few of whom can speak the language (*American Machinist*, 15 January 1891: 10). It seemed clear to them that 'The ugliest strikes of workingmen that occur in this country are of men who are not citizens' (*American Machinist*, 12 March 1891: 10). Likewise, it was said that 'there were in this country a class of immigrants—most of them imported—who had but little idea of gaining an end except through the exercise of brute force' (*American Machinist*, 30 April 1891: 8). In sum, labor unrest threatened the stability, not to say the very existence, of the rising industrial world. In order to deny the existence of a domestically produced class warfare (as is shown next) it became linked with foreign labor and European anarchist theories.

### 5.4.3 There is no class struggle or class structure in America

Despite the undeniably violent events, *American Machinist* saw no parallel between these events and those that were taking place (or had taken place) elsewhere: 'In no other country in the world are the relations between employers and employed as uniformly pleasant as in the United States. Nor is there any other country in which both proprietors and workmen are as jealous of their well known rights. Strikes often occur, but it is seldom that one of them is virulent' (*American Machinist*, 26 January 1884: 8).

This editorial from 1884 reveals an implicit attempt to deny any similarity to the class struggle that other countries had experienced. In the same year, *American Machinist* published a full-fledged lecture delivered by a clergyman known (according to the editorial) for his broad liberal views:

There is no reason for antagonism between capital and labour; there is no reason why manufacturers and workmen should be hostile to each other. Their interests are identical. If I have five cents and you have one cent, I am a capitalist and you are not, and if I put my five cents to such use as that you can earn something by it, and I also, then my capital is a benefit for both of us. (*American Machinist*, 27 December 1884: 2)[25]

Accordingly, numerous attempts were made to convince the readers that capital was not an enemy of labor (e.g. *Engineering Magazine*, February 1894: 626–63). The editors of *American Machinist* stated, 'There is no such thing in this country as a working "class" . . . Except it be a distinction between reputable citizens and loafers' (*American Machinist*, 16 January 1886: 8) and, therefore, 'We will not use the hackneyed and obnoxious expression "the working classes" ' (*American Machinist*, 18 December 1886: 8). Even after the events of 1885/6, America was still perceived as a classless society. As *American Machinist* suggested: 'Labor employs capital just as certainly as capital employs labor' (*American Machinist*, 15 May 1896: 6).

The editors of *American Machinist* commented on an observation of a British visitor who 'surprisingly' noticed the existence of classes in the USA (*American Machinist*, 10 October 1903: 1370): 'even granting all this as to class distinctions here, they are not as offensive as in England.' Furthermore, they suggested that wealth did not automatically grant class superiority. In this country, they said, 'we have plenty of people who, chiefly because of wealth, consider themselves superior to others, but the others do not acknowledge the distinction'. According to this view the existence of class distinction is subjective and depends on the acknowledgement of the so-called lower classes. When German sociologist Werner Sombart delivered a lecture in St Louis in 1904 on the 'industrial proletariat' in modern society, it was translated to American audiences as 'industrial group' (Ross 1991).

Following the violent events on the Texas and Illinois railroads in 1886, the editors of *American Machinist* still argued that 'Happily, the general relations between employees and managers of most other railroads in this country do not exist in that chronically strained condition so long observable on the Gould railroads of the Southwest' (*American Machinist*, 24 April 1886: 8).

In November 1886, the Pennsylvania Bureau of Industrial Statistics published its thirteenth annual report. Among other things, the report acknowledged:

if we take into consideration the fact that during the past year there has neither been a commercial panic nor an appreciable revival in business, the number of strikes and lockouts may be regarded as phenomenal. . . . If prudence is observed by all classes, and just rights maintained and advanced by well-chosen arguments, based upon acknowledged truth, an era of unexampled prosperity, national and individual, is before us. (*American Machinist*, 13 November 1886: 6)

In 1892 the picture was not as rosy as it had appeared to be in descriptions of previous years, but the uniqueness of the American experience was still preserved. *Engineering Magazine*, for example, argued that 'During the past twelve months, we have seen civil war. Troops have been called out, martial law proclaimed, and indictments for treason, murder, and conspiracy found by grand juries; lives and property have been destroyed and reckless threats made of still worse to come—and all this in the midst of the greatest nation that ever existed in the history of the world and in an epoch of unparalleled prosperity' (*Engineering Magazine*, December 1892: 411–19). The fingerprints of the self-satisfied Exceptionalist ideology—conveying 'limitless opportunities' and greatness—were still apparent in this slight awakening from the dream (see also *Engineering Magazine*, August 1891: 498–504).

## 5.5 American Exceptionalism and the role of the state

In Chapter 2, I demonstrated that the engineers appealed for government involvement in the application of standards. This was not the case as far as labor relations were concerned. In this section I show that engineers rejected government involvement in the market, and also rejected the empowerment of large capitalists. Theirs was a market perspective in which the brokerage and virtue of engineering would play a role. An editorial in *American Machinist* explicitly argued, 'It must be evident both to the workman and the employer, that not to government, but to themselves, must they look for any important improvement of their condition.' A writer in *Engineering Magazine* stated, 'Whatever else may be needed to solve the problem of industrial discontent, we certainly do not need a stronger government' (*Engineering Magazine*, July 1894: 459–65). The author reflected upon European thought and suggested that given the social disorders and strikes, 'we can readily understand why it should be thought in Europe that the remedy against events of the kind is to be found only in the use of those repressive agencies which are believed, in European countries, to be most effective. Strong government is there thought to mean the control of both the purse and the sword.' In the United States, however, the situation was entirely different: 'We have never held that the control of either the purse or the sword makes what we can call strong government, although it may be admitted to make repressive government. We have held to the contrary from the very beginning, that it was an element of weakness.' Engineers stated that 'the public good is not best served by centralization of commercial power'. And the editors put their economic philosophy unambiguously: 'We have no sympathy with that rabid school of political economists who desire to fix a limit, by governmental authority, to the growth of private industrial enterprises. Such an enactment would be in the highest degree antagonistic to the spirit of our free institutions, which permit a man to rise from the most humble position to the highest pinnacle of commercial success' (*American Machinist*, 20 December 1879: 8).

During the 1870s and the 1880s the rhetoric of *laissez-faire* in industry was strong. The logic of a self-regulating market precluded interference with supply and demand processes, and guided the editors' position regarding labor relations (e.g. *Engineering Magazine*, July 1893: 460–7). For example, one of the reasons for opposition to the employment of cheap convict labor was its interference with free market competition (e.g. *American Machinist*, 1 November 1879: 8; *American Machinist*, 26 July 1879: 8; *American Machinist*, 2 February 1884: 8; *American Machinist*, 26 June 1886: 8; *American Machinist*, 9 August 1894: 10–11). In one occurrence, the employers in a Tennessee coalfield introduced convict labor to break a strike. Militia soldiers who were deployed to restore peace after violence erupted expressed sympathy with the workers. The editors of *American Machinist* justified the workers: 'State troops were sent to help the contractors, and uphold the law of the State. The miners met the State troops, and the latter capitulated and consented to be sent home. All of this shows, not that the soldiers were cowards, but that they believed the free miners were right in objecting to convict competition' (*American Machinist*, 30 July 1891: 8).

It was also emphasized that, based on a market perspective, employers should avoid harsh treatment of labor disputes and allow strikes to take place (*American Machinist*, 18 December 1886: 8). In contrast to their condemnation of strikes on different occasions, the editors supported employees' right to strike, and they favored the decision made by the United States Court of Appeal in Chicago to reverse a previous verdict that there 'could be no such thing as a lawful strike' (*American Machinist*, 11 October 1894: 8).

One aspect of the rhetoric of Exceptionalism was the positive potential mobility of workmen based on the belief that there were no, and should not be, absolute and rigid classes. It was argued that the distinction in the new world was not between those 'who have' and those 'who have not', but rather between those 'who have', and those 'who will have'. The transition between these categories would be made, it was argued, if high wages were given to the workmen. Indeed, in the last two decades of the nineteenth century the most frequently mentioned solution to the problem of unrest—a solution which was based on Ricardo's labor theory of value—was the advancement of wages (*American Machinist*, 3 April 1880: 8; *American Machinist*, 11 October 1879: 8; *American Machinist*, 15 November 1879: 8; *American Machinist*, 3 January 1880: 5; *American Machinist*, 29 November 1879: 8; *American Machinist*, 10 January 1880: 3; *American Machinist*, 28 February 1880: 5; *American Machinist*, 13 March 1880: 5; *American Machinist*, 2 August 1894: 7).

In 1879, the editors of *American Machinist* reacted to a statement made by a machinist, published in the annual report of the Massachusetts Bureau of Statistics. The statement said, 'The idea that a man can get rich, without hard work of some kind, must be given up. Thirty three years of hard work; and yet far from being rich is my condition.' This bold , meritocratic statement opposed the foundation of American Exceptionalism. The editors stubbornly argued that 'In this country opportunities are afforded the workman to rise higher and higher, and who shall say he should not use his opportunities? . . . There is no limit fixed by the market to the amount of wages a mechanic shall receive' (*American Machinist*, 15 March 1879: 8). Likewise, the editor of *Engineering Magazine* praised the 'enlightenment age' and 'immeasurable stores of natural wealth and its absolutely unlimited opportunities for unemployed labor' (*Engineering Magazine*, September 1992: 759–64). Wages were considered the force that would stimulate mobility in a free market-like society.

This market approach, when applied to industrial unrest, had implications. It coincided with the Exceptionalist ideology according to which capitalists and laborers were portrayed as equal citizens with equal access to market exchange. Laborers were only temporarily in this position. The advancement of wages was supposed to be a weapon: to promote them from their humble position upwards. If indeed this was the case, there was a need for stability and protection of economic achievements. Thus, property needed to be respected and employers needed to teach their employees 'the justness and honesty of protecting the property of their employers with the same interest displayed in guarding that which belongs to themselves, believing that securing the welfare of the business from which we derive our livelihood is certainly advancing our own' (*American Machinist*, 19 July 1884: 8). It was argued that property is the outcome of success achieved by the fittest (*American Machinist*, 22 May 1902: 725).[26]

On several occasions the magazines strove to make a clear distinction between capitalists and 'monopolists':

It is desirable, it seems to us, that a sharp line of demarcation should be drawn between the capitalists or the manufacturer on the one side, and the monopolist or manipulator on the other. Sometimes the same man may assume all these characters, but it is our belief that the manufacturer, pure and simple, is in these days being charged with oppression, extortion and other sins, of which he is in no wise guilty, simply because the distinction is not made. (*American Machinist*, 28 June 1894: 8)

Along these lines, they expressed fear of excessive power exerted either by the big monopolies or by the unions, and argued that industrial combinations impaired the mechanism of free competition (e.g. *American Machinist*, 20 September 1879: 8). The editors referred to the monopolies as the 'soul-less domination of industrial power', called for their aggression to be repelled, and likewise reprimanded the 'evils of trade-unionism and strikes' (*American Machinist*, 20 September 1879: 8; see also *Engineering Magazine*, August 1891: 498–504). In an essay from 1879 the editors put forward their political and economic platform condemning the excessive power of the 'robber barons':

Railroad management has been gradually drifting into the control of a few universally-recognized magnates—the Scotts, the Vanderbilts, the Garretts and a few others—whose slightest whim may affect the well-being of ten thousand subordinates. In some localities manufacturing and mining operations are centralized under the autocracy of a few wealthy individuals. For examples we need only mention the Bonanza Kings of the Pacific Slope, Mackey, Flood, Sharon, Fair &c, and the two or three dominant families of Fall River, who, with 'their sisters, their cousins and their aunts,' rule absolutely nearly every important productive and financial business in the city. (*American Machinist*, 20 September 1879: 8)

Also consider a similar critique of Gould:

He seems to think he has the same right to allow the traffic of several thousand miles of railroad, of which he has control, to lie idle indefinitely while trying to make the strikers surrender unconditionally, that the owner of a private manufactory has to shut down whenever he has a dispute with employees until he is satisfied to resume. Such an unrestrained power in the hands of one man would be a serious danger to our free institutions. (*American Machinist*, 24 April 1886: 8)

Concentration of wealth was held to be detrimental to the public good, and non-compliant with the 'true theory of government' which strives 'to secure the greatest good to the greatest number' (*American Machinist*, 20 September 1879: 8). The editors thus established that both employers and employees should have the opportunity to exercise their civil rights. They taught that labor relations should be based on a free contract in which 'either party may terminate the connection', or in which 'the right of employers to conduct their business in their own way, and of "scabs" to replace "union" men, is sacred' (*Engineering Magazine*, September 1892: 759–64).

Given the historical origins of the market idea (and the Exceptionalist ideology), the social and political theory that was developed in the United States was narrow (compared with that of Europe).[27] In Europe, liberalism started as a progressive, critical approach, and once established it started to be undermined by socialism. In the USA, on the other hand, liberalism developed as a conservative ideology: 'In America, the ends have been given, given both in the ideological sense and also, and much more forcefully, in the very constitution of the society itself. To mount an argument against them has been to mount an argument against America and thus, to mount an argument that immediately disqualifies itself from serious consideration as a relevant argument at all' (Hawthorn 1987: 195).

The editors of both magazines, as well as other professional engineers in industry, attempted to avoid taking a stand in the conflict between capital and labor. This 'neutrality' was a platform for becoming a legitimate speaker in the prospering industrial world. The engineers saw and presented themselves as applying neutral tools and reason rather than interfering with existing conflict-ual gives and takes. Such conflicts, however, were later also used to enhance the dependence of employers on objective professionals who could offer rational solutions and impartial positions to the conflict. This is how they sold engi-neering-based managerial systems to reluctant employers.

## Notes

1. This argument challenges conventional wisdom that attributes the emergence of systems, in both theory and practice, to functional and economic necessity. Nobel (1977), for example, attributes the rise of system to safety considerations. He argues that a series of boiler explosions in the 1850s accelerated the attempt to standardize boiler specifications which also resulted in organizational stan-dardization. Chandler (1977) argues that the systematization of operations in the railroad industry was a response to a series of train accidents in the 1840s and 1850s. Additional explanations attribute the rise of systems to firm growth, advances in technology, or geographical dispersion. Most of these explanations are instrumental in nature. They suggest that the rise of systems was a response to increase efficiency or reduce uncertainty of employers and managers. From the discourse analysis presented here it is apparent that the functional necessity rhetoric was also used by the systematizers to justify systematization. To be sure, I do not deny that industrialists and engineers operated in environments rife with technical and economic uncertainty. This study, however, is concerned with the sociological processes that cultivated the discourse about systems and enabled it to become pivotal in organization thought.

2. In Michel Foucault's genealogical analysis (e.g. Foucault 1975, 1977, 1979) the 'will to know'—which symbolizes 'reason' and 'rationality' in the ideology of Enlightenment—masks a form of political power which needs to be deconstructed.

3. In the late nineteenth century, the term 'labor unrest' referred to the struggle between labor and capital. The way it was defined represented the employers' point of view. At the turn of the century it was replaced by the term 'labor prob-lems', extending the definition to issues such as 'turnover' or 'soldiering' (loafing) from the employers' point of view and issues such as 'stable employment', 'child labor', and 'working conditions' from the employees' point of view. See Kaufman 1993: 4.

4.  Except for descriptive case studies or partial data. See Goldstein 1978.

5.  As far as the raw number of strikes is concerned, 1917 can be singled out as the year with the greatest number of strikes (4,450), followed by 1916 (3,789), 1903 (3,648), and 1919 (3,630). Data in Fig. 4 are standardized for the year 1927.

6.  The highest average of workers per strike occurred in the years 1922 and 1919 (1,450 and 1,146 respectively).

7.  Shorter and Tilly (1971) combined both measures (annual frequency of strikes and number of workers involved in strikes) to introduce the concept of 'strike waves' which indicates periods of a high level of conflict. A wave occurs 'when both number of strikes and the number of strikers in a given year exceed the means of the previous five years by more than 50 percent' (Edwards 1981: 28). Applying this definition to the period in question, only three years qualified for inclusion as wave years: 1886, 1887, and 1903.

8.  In order to complete my analysis, I relied on proxy statistics provided by Griffin (1939) for the missing years. Griffin's method was evaluated by Edwards (1981) who found that the trend predicted was by and large valid. In an attempt to validate this argument I estimated that the correlation coefficient between the national level and the state of Massachusetts was .88 for 'strikes' and .86 for 'workers involved in strikes'.

9.  Measured by the volume of text devoted to unrest and standardized by the entire yearly volume.

10. Years of no coverage of unrest in the *American Machinist*: 1906, 1908, 1913, 1914, 1915, 1917; years of no coverage in the *Engineering Magazine*: 1905, 1908, 1909, 1910, 1912, 1914, 1915.

11. It is quite interesting that his biography, put together by a group of five ASME members among whom were Wallace Clark, Fred Colvin, and Morris Cooke, suggested that Miller did 'pioneer work in the field of labor relations' (ASME 1941: 9) or was 'a pioneer in the handling of labor troubles' (ASME 1941: 17). They probably referred to his experience in settling the strikes at the Remington Co. while serving as a general manager.

12. King also accepted company unions as more realistic and democratic than trade unions or national unions. Company unions, however, were restricted to the workplace and their actions were less dangerous since they were local and therefore less likely to lead to class warfare.

13. See Breslau 1998 for a similar argument regarding labor market construction. The politicization of labor data is evident in engineering magazines. The magazine *Industrial Management* envisioned 'labor audits in industry' composed of 'officials going up and down the country probing to the bottom of the sources of unrest'. Ordway Tead, 'How to Study Labor Unrest', *Industrial Management*, February 1918: 133–4. The scientific method was suggested as a technique of control in the guise of a disciplinary analysis. As was further suggested in *Industrial Management* in 1918, 'The success of these several agencies will be endangered and their usefulness minimized if there does not exist for their use a precise weapon of search, a nice instrument of inquiry with which they can probe to the seat of existing but concealed irritation.'

14. Throughout the analysis I refer to both of them as 'the magazines.' Recall, however,

that for about twelve years (1879–91) *Engineering Magazine* did not exist. All the materials from this period pertain to *American Machinist*.

15. Taylor, for example, attempted to prevent the participation of employers and employers' associations in the Taylor Society (Haber 1964: 32).

16. The *People* was established in New York in 1891 with Lucien Sanial as editor-in-chief. It replaced the *Workmen's Advocate* which Sanial edited from 1889 as the official journal of the Socialist Labor Party of America. Sanial resigned in 1892 and was succeeded by Daniel De Leon, who served in office until 1914.

17. US, Congress, *State of Labor in Europe: 1878* (1879), 39. Cited in Merkle 1980: 17.

18. Hounshell (1989) provided a materialist interpretation to this ideology. He suggested that both Hegel and Marx noted that 'as long as land was abundant in the United States, class divisions would not be great'. Hounshell suggested that this 'safety valve' thesis has 'motivated two generations of historians'.

19. One should not get the impression that strikes were always automatically condemned. There were exceptions. For example in 1881 (*American Machinist*, 21 May 1881: 8) the editors of the *American Machinist* mentioned the bakers in Chicago who demanded to work twelve rather than sixteen hours per day. The *Machinist* justified the strike: 'Men who are required, in any employment, to work two hours out of every three, from Monday morning till Saturday night, should be encouraged and assisted by the public at large to strike for a reduction of the hours of labor. When such cases are brought to public attention, the great mass of citizens need no urging to bestow their sympathy in the right direction.'

20. See also Carrol D. Wright's article on 'The Value and Influence of Labour Statistics', *Engineering Magazine*, November 1893: 134–44.

21. On the other hand, the *American Machinist* also argued in the years to come that the terms 'anarchy' (*American Machinist*, 30 August 1894: 8) and 'conspiracy' (*American Machinist*, 10 April 1902: 533) were attached too easily to workers whenever they went on strike or resisted employers' control.

22. See also 'The "Pinkerton Bill" ', *American Machinist*, 19 March 1891: 11; *American Machinist*, 9 February 1891: 2; *American Machinist*, 1 December 1892: 8.

23. By 1900, 13.4 percent of the population in the USA were foreign-born whites. Faulkner 1951: 103.

24. William E. Wickenden, *Report of the Investigation of Engineering Education* (1930). Cited in Noble 1977: 58.

25. 'Although the lecture had special reference to the Moulders' union and the stove interests of Troy, the extract we make here are quite as applicable to other manufacturing interests in other localities' (*American Machinist*, 27 December 1884: 2).

26. Jenks denies that this was the case, arguing that it is hard to ascribe such ideologies to industrial engineers. Nevertheless, Jenks himself admits that 'It is true that social evolution of the broadly Spencerian character was widely assumed to prevail, and was sometimes explicitly asserted as justifying the progressive transformation of the shop.' Furthermore, 'Dunlap himself and his staff writer Arnold were articulate social Darwinists' (1961: 439).

27. For a strong critique of the free market idea as a natural entity, see the classic book by Polanyi (1944/1963).

TABLE 3. *Labor strikes in the United States, 1879–1932*

| Year | Strikes | Workers per strike |
|------|---------|--------------------|
| 1879 | NI | NI |
| 1880 | 762 | 299 |
| 1881 | 477 | 273 |
| 1882 | 476 | 334 |
| 1883 | 506 | 336 |
| 1884 | 485 | 341 |
| 1885 | 695 | 371 |
| 1886 | 1,576 | 388 |
| 1887 | 1,503 | 292 |
| 1888 | 946 | 172 |
| 1889 | 1,111 | 234 |
| 1890 | 1,897 | 197 |
| 1891 | 1,786 | 185 |
| 1892 | 1,359 | 176 |
| 1893 | 1,375 | 209 |
| 1894 | 1,404 | 491 |
| 1895 | 1,255 | 324 |
| 1896 | 1,066 | 233 |
| 1897 | 1,110 | 375 |
| 1898 | 1,098 | 240 |
| 1899 | 1,838 | 235 |
| 1900 | 1,839 | 309 |
| 1901 | 3,012 | 187 |
| 1902 | 3,240 | 213 |
| 1903 | 3,648 | 216 |
| 1904 | 2,419 | 237 |
| 1905 | 2,186 | 138 |
| 1906 | 3,655 | 105 |
| 1907 | 3,724 | 135 |
| 1908 | 1,957 | 107 |
| 1909 | 2,425 | 186 |
| 1910 | 3,334 | 247 |
| 1911 | 2,565 | 145 |
| 1912 | 3,053 | 318 |
| 1913 | 3,574 | 279 |
| 1914 | 2,736 | 229 |
| 1915 | 1,593 | 569 |
| 1916 | 3,789 | 422 |
| 1917 | 4,450 | 276 |
| 1918 | 3,353 | 370 |
| 1919 | 3,630 | 1,146 |
| 1920 | 3,411 | 429 |
| 1921 | 2,385 | 461 |
| 1922 | 1,112 | 1,450 |
| 1923 | 1,553 | 487 |
| 1924 | 1,249 | 524 |
| 1925 | 1,301 | 329 |
| 1926 | 1,035 | 318 |
| 1927 | 707 | 467 |

| Year | Strikes | Workers per strike |
|------|---------|--------------------|
| 1928 | 604 | 520 |
| 1929 | 921 | 313 |
| 1930 | 637 | 287 |
| 1931 | 810 | 422 |
| 1932 | 841 | 386 |

*Note*: NI = no information.
*Source*: Peterson 1938; Griffin 1939.

TABLE 4. *Literature on industrial unrest relative to the annual volume of literature on management, 1879–1932*

| Year | Percentage unrest (*AM* and *EM*) | Percentage unrest (*AM*) |
|------|-----------------------------------|--------------------------|
| 1879 | 0.054 | 0.054 |
| 1880 | 0.289 | 0.289 |
| 1881 | 0.230 | 0.230 |
| 1882 | 0.024 | 0.024 |
| 1883 | 0.000 | 0.000 |
| 1884 | 0.418 | 0.418 |
| 1885 | 0.013 | 0.013 |
| 1886 | 0.377 | 0.377 |
| 1887 | 0.234 | 0.234 |
| 1888 | 0.098 | 0.098 |
| 1889 | 0.007 | 0.007 |
| 1890 | 0.010 | 0.010 |
| 1891 | 0.136 | 0.098 |
| 1892 | 0.217 | 0.145 |
| 1893 | 0.138 | 0.035 |
| 1894 | 0.311 | 0.242 |
| 1895 | 0.049 | 0.059 |
| 1896 | 0.079 | 0.009 |
| 1897 | 0.003 | 0.006 |
| 1898 | 0.053 | 0.107 |
| 1899 | 0.000 | 0.000 |
| 1900 | 0.206 | 0.250 |
| 1901 | 0.066 | 0.031 |
| 1902 | 0.052 | 0.102 |
| 1903 | 0.079 | 0.052 |
| 194 | 0.023 | 0.031 |
| 1905 | 0.002 | 0.005 |
| 1906 | 0.012 | 0.000 |
| 1907 | 0.013 | 0.003 |
| 1908 | 0.000 | 0.000 |
| 1909 | 0.000 | 0.000 |
| 1910 | 0.000 | 0.000 |

| Year | Percentage unrest (*AM* and *EM*) | Percentage unrest (*AM*) |
|------|------|------|
| 1911 | 0.001 | 0.000 |
| 1912 | 0.001 | 0.002 |
| 1913 | 0.022 | 0.000 |
| 1914 | 0.000 | 0.000 |
| 1915 | 0.000 | 0.000 |
| 1916 | 0.005 | 0.005 |
| 1917 | 0.006 | 0.000 |
| 1918 | 0.010 | 0.016 |
| 1919 | 0.025 | 0.041 |
| 1920 | 0.065 | 0.053 |
| 1921 | 0.011 | 0.009 |
| 1922 | 0.033 | 0.054 |
| 1923 | 0.006 | 0.009 |
| 1924 | 0.001 | 0.002 |
| 1925 | 0.001 | 0.002 |
| 1926 | 0.006 | 0.009 |
| 1927 | 0.003 | 0.000 |
| 1928 | 0.000 | 0.000 |
| 1929 | 0.001 | 0.000 |
| 1930 | 0.001 | 0.000 |
| 1931 | 0.000 | 0.000 |
| 1932 | 0.001 | 0.001 |

*Note*s: *AM* = *American Machinist*; *EM* = *Engineering Magazine*.

# 6

# Taming the Shrew: Systems and Labor Politics during the Progressive Period

Progressivism was not one coherent scheme but, rather, an amalgam of ideas and ideals that converged under a single label (see Hofstadter 1955; Hays 1957; Kolko 1963; Haber 1964; Kloppenberg 1986). The movement, led by middle-class, well-to-do intellectuals and professionals, was stimulated by the power of giant industrial corporations and by corruption in politics, and had a large impact on diverse sectors such as government, industry, education, and art (e.g. DiMaggio 1991). Progressives demanded redistribution of wealth by means of welfare legislation and rebalancing economic power through antitrust legislation (Hays 1957). The Progressive period was advantageous to the development of systems for at least two reasons. First, it provided legitimization for the roles of professionals in the public sphere. It was a period of unprecedented proliferation of new class technocrats such as educationalists, social workers, psychologists, doctors, government bureaucrats, health care specialists, lawyers, accountants, and, of course, engineers. Second, it was congruent with the agenda of systems, which seemed, on the face of it, to promote progress and equality.

Progressive culture and big systems supported each other, slouching toward an economic coherence that would replace the ambiguity of the robber barons' capitalism through bureaucratization and rationalization. Progressivism, like systems, facilitated industrial growth. Yet the Progressive era also 'brought' with it increased labor unrest. At the turn of the century, industrial unrest became recognized as a potential threat to the future of American democracy. The control of labor became an important goal for the industrial firms, which stood at a crucial crossroads in their attempt to stabilize business conditions and to develop legal business practices.[1] Reflecting this situation, a report of the United States Industrial Commission (USIC) from 1902 expressed these fears and emphasized the importance of political stability (Wunderlin 1992: 40).

The chaos and ambiguity associated with industrial unrest seemed to engineers to be solvable with the application of management systems. Mechanical engineers perceived themselves as gatekeepers at the junction between politics and economics, and they offered 'management systems' as a solution to industrial upheavals and political instability. The first stage in this project of engineering rationality was to acknowledge the severity of labor–capital relations. In sharp contrast to the attitude which obtained during nineteenth-century Exceptionalism (Chapter 5), industrial conflict was recognized outright during the Progressive period as 'the labor problem'. This acknowledgement was congruent with the democratic spirit of Progressivism, which was prima facie pro-labor. As far as Progressivist engineers were concerned it was crucial to make the phenomenon visible and to be explicit about its severity. The more apparent the problem, the more urgent the need to find a solution and the greater the saliency of systems. In this chapter I delineate this process from the denial associated with American Exceptionalism to the designation of labor unrest as a managerial problem. As will become clearer toward the end of the chapter, the liaison between the engineering ideology of systems and labor unrest was dangerous. It incorporated unrest into the mechanical scheme of engineers and blurred its ideological significance. Thus, while it paid due attention to the problem, it also diffused its significance. It is not surprising therefore that the Progressive period has received confusing—even contradictory—accounts in American history (Kolko 1963).

## 6.1 Exercising management: from industrial unrest to 'the labor problem'

At the turn of the century industrial peace did not seem to be at hand. The violence was escalating, resulting in at least three periods of public concern over an anarchist scare: 1901–3, 1908–9, and 1914–16. The fact that American labor was turning 'radical and subversive' was undeniable. At this stage, professionals became more vocal in their insistence that America face its industrial unrest and provide viable solutions. The annual meeting of the American Economic Association provided a special forum for the assessment of labor relations and the unrest. In 1902 E. R. Seligman, the president of the American Economic Association, rejected the Exceptionalist ideology: 'We have been largely living in a fool's paradise. There is nothing peculiar or inherent in our democracy.' He rejected the idea that 'This country has in some way a distinctive mission to perform, and that we are marked off from the rest of the world by certain inherent principles, relative indeed, in the sense of being peculiar to America, but eternal and immutable in their relation to ourselves' (Ross 1991: 149).

Likewise, economist Francis Walker admitted that 'Americans could no longer expect divine providence to exempt them from the laws of classical economics' (Ross 1993: 105). He perceived that America was following a more universal—as opposed to idiosyncratic and 'exceptional'—course of history. Public acknowledgement of the severity of events, and the rejection of Exceptionalism, came also from the presidential office. The establishment of the USIC (United States Industrial Commission) in 1898, which provided the initial setting for the formulation of labor theory in the Progressive era,[2] followed attempts to push for a public inquiry into industrial relations. In accordance with the Progressive spirit, the Interstate Commerce Commission justified its regulatory activities as a 'constructive coordination' (Hamilton and Sutton 1989). The USIC intended to bring forward a comprehensive examination of American economic institutions. The editor of *Engineering Magazine* published in 1900 the 'New York Agreement' between the National Metal Trades Association and the International Association of Machinists as an attempt to demonstrate that 'labor troubles' can be adjusted by 'common sense' agreements. A year later, John Dunlap suggested that 'it is distressing to find within twelve months that the fears, rather than the hopes, have been realized' (*Engineering Magazine*, July 1901: 586).

The wave of fears and the red scare started in 1901 with the assassination of President William McKinley. The hysteria following the assassination resulted in the arrest of anarchists throughout the country and in legislative acts against immigration. Most significant was the passage of a law in 1903 that barred entrance to immigrants who 'believe in or advocate the overthrow by force and violence' of the US government. During 1902 and 1903, several states passed legislation to outlaw anarchy. The 1902 anthracite coal mines crisis—in the midst of public hysteria—heightened public attention to the consequences of political turmoil and social instability. Realizing that American society had become more polarized, and that his political future could be dependent on his handling of the strike, President Roosevelt actively intervened to bring it to an end. He also instructed a commission 'to inquire into, consider and pass upon the questions in controversy in connection with the strike in the anthracite region, and the causes out of which the controversy arose' (Wunderlin 1992: 83).

Five years later there was another nationwide wave of anarchist-labor scares.[3] One sign of the increasing anxiety was Roosevelt's decision to send federal troops to Nevada during a relatively peaceful strike. In 1908 the Department of Commerce and Labor announced a major campaign to deport alien anarchists. In 1908, Roosevelt sent a message to Congress announcing, 'compared with the suppression of anarchy, every other question sinks into insignificance' (Goldstein 1978). These public acknowledgements constituted a departure from the rhetoric of Exceptionalism and had the potential to set the stage for a less rigid attitude toward the inequities that industrialization produced.

The events during the next five years (1910–14) resembled those in the 1880s, in which people feared for the very survival of American society. On 1 October 1910, an explosion destroyed the building of the *Los Angeles Times* and twenty persons were killed. The bombing followed an incident where the LA police interfered with a series of strikes and union parades. The Progressive magazine *Survey* devoted an issue to the case and the word 'war' was used often to describe the general atmosphere (ibid.). Another disturbing event was the 1912 strike at Lawrence, Massachusetts. It involved policemen trying to stop a parade. A woman striker and a 15-year-old boy were killed, and martial law was declared, followed by a decision to make all public meetings illegal. In 1913, seventy-two persons, mostly children, died in a panic that was set off by an anonymous person at a Christmas party. The climax of industrial upheaval took place in March 1914, when state militia attacked and burned a miners' tent colony at Ludlow, Colorado. The struggle was about the harsh disciplinary actions of the large corporations, wages, the introduction of management techniques, the 'labor process', the right to strike, and the right to unionize. Three unarmed strikers were taken prisoner and shot while under guard. The events that followed this massacre resembled a war. Altogether, seventy-four persons were killed when federal troops tried to restore order in what was known as the Ludlow Massacre.

Particularly worrisome to employers was the growth in union membership. In the 1890s there were half a million union members. The number rose in 1904 to 2 million, in 1919 it reached 4 million, and in 1920 there were 4.8 million unionized workers (Bendix 1956/1974). Employers started a campaign against unions and distributed blacklists of activists among industrialists, known as the 'open shop' campaign. Their position was that trade unions should not press employees in a particular workplace to join them. This position was adopted by *American Machinist* as well. During a dispute with the printing workers, John Hill, publisher of *American Machinist*, stated his position regarding the 'closed shop' strategy of the unions: 'For me it is the violation of a religious principle.' He also exposed his Exceptionalist position: 'The closed shop means the changing of all this to the foreign standard, where a workman is always a workman, where ambitions are still-born and hope is dead.' An editorial from April 1906 repeated this position, arguing against the entrance of unions into politics: 'A distinguishing feature of public life in America is that it has not been customary for workingmen and their employers to divide on questions of politics' (*American Machinist*, 8 February 1906: 199–200).

However, contrary to Hill, many engineers saw the anti-union open shop militancy as 'alien to the rationalistic approach of industrial engineers' (Jenks 1961: 438). Violence on either side was senseless and needed to be regulated and moderated without resort to power. Rather than choosing militancy, engineers advocated rational and mechanical techniques to resolve the labor problem (e.g. *Engineering Magazine*, April 1903: 99–100). As ASME president E. D. Meier urged, the abuses of capital had driven labor into 'protest, dangerously near rebellion'. He thought that 'the remedy lies in placing engineers in all responsible positions in these great industries'. The engineer would find the 'sane middle ground between grasping individualism and Utopian socialism' (Layton 1971: 66–7).

During the years 1914–16 there was violence almost every week. Following the attempts to assassinate John D. Rockefeller and bomb St Patrick's Cathedral in New York City, there was again an anarchist scare. The three best-known events were the Joe Hill case,[4] the Moony case,[5] and the 'Everett Massacre'.[6] During the First World War, anarchism and patriotism became more closely connected. Democratic President Wilson condemned the anti-war movement and made implicit accusations against immigrants. He imputed that 'the masters of Germany' were using 'liberals . . . socialists, the leaders of labor' to 'carry out their designs' (Goldstein 1978: 107). In the period following the war, government involvement in industrial disputes took a different shape. Goldstein argued that whereas in the 1870s–1900 the federal government entered the stage only at the tail end of local disturbances, after the First World War repression was actively 'managed' by the federal government (Goldstein 1978). Furthermore, as a result of the red scare, Congress dismantled most progressive wartime economic measures. The government abolished the US Employment Service, cut back housing projects, and returned the railroad to private ownership. In July 1919, Congress appropriated special funds for the Justice Department to prosecute radicals. It was not unusual for labor unions and politicians who sided with them to be labeled as 'internal enemies' (William H. Barr, president of the Lumen Bearing Co., Buffalo, New York, in the *American Machinist*, 10 June 1920: 1256) 'unprincipled men', 'merely demagogues' or 'enemies of the United States', part of a 'campaign to disturb and demoralize the social and economic conditions of the country', and the 'disease of unjustified unrest' (Elbert H. Gary, president of the American Iron and Steel Institute, in the *American Machinist*, 1 July 1920: 14). President Wilson stated that 'we are now facing a danger greater than war itself', and called for a President's Industrial Conference. Indeed, such a conference was held for two and a half intense weeks, though in the end it was dismissed when the labor group headed by Samuel Gompers walked out of the session (see *Industrial Management*, November 1919: 419–22). In December, the President convened a second conference in Washington to remedy the failure of the first one. It was a smaller and more compact body of representatives of three groups: the public, employers, and labor. The conference presented a national plan for industrial arbitration but did not make any comment or statement as to the causes of industrial unrest. Engineer Henry Gantt acknowledged that industrial unrest was growing, but 'the answer is that this is not a problem for theorists, who deal largely with words only, but for men of the engineering type of mind, who deal mostly with things, and seek the solution of problems on their merits' (*Industrial Management*, August 1919: 89–94).

It was only later, in the 1920s, that the hysteria settled down. Union membership declined from 4.8 million in 1920 to 3.6 million in 1923. The number of strikes in 1928 was at the lowest level since 1884. In the early 1930s, labor relations became relatively peaceful. As a commentator in *American Machinist* reflected in 1932, 'As we think back over the last two years, we begin to thank our lucky stars at the absence of serious labor trouble in the United States. It is high time that the workingman be recognized and even rendered a nation's gratitude for his understanding, his loyalty and his considerable forbearance' (the writer was C. J. Freund, an apprentice supervisor in the Falk Corporation. *American Machinist*, 14 January 1932: 43).

Disillusionment with Exceptionalism and the search for universal institutional arrangements had appeared in the engineering literature since the beginning of the Progressive era.

All this started with a recognition of the struggle. As the editors of *Engineering Magazine* said in 1903: 'The present greatly disturbed condition of the relations of employers and workmen is more than sufficient justification for the space given to labor questions' (*Engineering Magazine*, May 1903: 256). Elsewhere they stated, 'The whole industrial world seems to have been seized with the strike madness. On every side we hear of labor wars and rumors of labor wars, and there are those who take the gravest view of the situation' (*Engineering Magazine*, June 1903: 415). Leon Alford, editor of *American Machinist*, argued that the tension in industrial relations started in the 1880s, but the problem did not become acute until 1905.[7]

In 1902, the editors of *American Machinist* quoted employers in Ohio commenting on 'the great danger' facing American industry. The employers used harsh words in their attack on the unions: 'The greatest, most tyrannical and most unlawful trust the world has ever known, guided as it is by the hands and minds of trouble-breeders, agitators, socialists, anarchists, without regard to law and order or the rights of others ... Aided by unscrupulous politicians' (*American Machinist*, 15 May 1902: 695–6). *American Machinist* used this paragraph to falsify the 'criticism' of a European counterpart who claimed that America did not have a labor problem: 'A copy of this report should be kept on file in the offices of some of our esteemed foreign contemporaries whose editors and contributors evidently think that no labor organizations worth mentioning exist in America and that the problem of dealing with them does not present itself to the American employer.' According to *American Machinist*, American corporations and the American system were successful despite unrest, not because of the lack of it.

With the growing acknowledgement of industrial struggle, unions were gradually recognized too. But union leaders needed to be enlightened, as the editors of *American Machinist* said patronizingly: 'There is much for them yet to do, first, in educating their more backward members in sound ideas of right and wrong, of reason and justice, and of sound industrial economy; there is much to do in perfecting their organization and discipline and the sense of responsibility' (see *Engineering Magazine*, August 1901: 749).[8] Furthermore, while in the 1880s *American Machinist* denied that there was a working class in America (*American Machinist*, 16 January 1886: 8), by the 1900s it was fully acknowledged. In 1904 the editors provided strong support to a controversial statement (published in a book by John Mitchell entitled *Organized Labor*) suggesting that 'The average wage earner has made up his mind that he must remain a wage earner' (*American Machinist*, 28 January 1904: 130). They co-provided a strong support to the claim that America had a class structure: 'We believe that the statement ... Is correct, regardless of what its consequences may be. It is senseless to shut our eyes to plain fact simply because we deplore it or the consequences that may follow it.'

In 1908, Charles Eliot, president of Harvard University, told the Harvard Teachers' Association that American society 'is divided, and is going to be divided into layers whose borders blend, whose limits are easily passed by individuals, but which, nevertheless, have distinct characteristics and distinct educational needs'. Progressivist Ellwood Cubberly wrote that schools 'should give up the exceedingly democratic idea that all are equal, and that our society is devoid of classes' (Tyack 1974: 188). He explained that 'increasing specialization has divided the people into dozens of more or less clearly defined classes', and 'the increasing centralization of trade and industry has concentrated business in the hand of a relatively small number'. He concluded that 'The employee tends to remain an employee; the wage earner tends to remain a wage earner' (1974: 189).

Concurring with this position, both magazines published materials by individuals who identified themselves as workmen, capitalists, and managers, representing a range of class distinctions (e.g. *Engineering Magazine*, May 1903: 253–5). *Engineering Magazine* commented on the resistance of 'organized labor' and linked it to Gantt's proposal to introduce individual wage systems (see Gantt 1910). The editor provided a clear class-based explanation for that objection: 'They have a deep-rooted suspicion of every attempt, however benevolent, to weaken that defence (as it seems to them) by introducing gradations within the class and so in some way introducing differences of interest among different members and breaking up the class cohesion' (*Engineering Magazine*, March 1910: 905). These quotes show that awareness of class structure was now strong within engineering circles.[9]

In recognition of the struggles, class structure, and unions, *Engineering Magazine* made an attempt to convince the capitalists that trade unionism was an 'inevitable outgrowth of modern conditions' (*Engineering Magazine*, September 1904: 977–9). The tenor of recognition of trade unionism was strong, almost surprising: 'It is a primordial instinct . . . An instinct older than the swarming of the bees or the herding of the wild horses.' The editors urged the readers to see trade unionism and the rise of organizations as part of a single phenomenon:

The factory system first facilitated the formation of the union by bringing the great company of workers together in the closest personal contact, next held up to them the example of successful organization and its corporate ownership and management, and finally supplied the imperative motive by accentuating the frequency, the suddenness, and the weight of those economic shocks to which the wage-worker has unfortunately always been most exposed. (Ibid.)

Furthermore, 'Enlightened unionism is no more necessarily selfish and arbitrary than enlightened corporate management . . . For it can no more be "smashed" than the use of machinery or the whole system which developed from the use of machinery could be smashed.' This position, which also finds in it little justification for government intervention in industrial affairs, did not necessarily mean that all unions' actions were to be approved. Dunlap, for example, wanted to reform labor: 'The unions can not be suppressed: but their false economic theories can and must be exploded, their false leaders retired, their false aims corrected, their false pretensions curbed.' To be sure, both magazines continued to condemn violence and threats to property and 'liberty' (*Engineering Magazine*, June 1903: 416). However, rather than resorting to uniqueness and Exceptionalism, the magazines now conceptualized the unrest using a more universal framework.[10] There was a growing number of references (since the early 1890s) comparing labor conditions and strikes in the USA with other countries, mainly European (*American Machinist*, 29 September 1892: 8; *American Machinist*, 30 January 1902: 151; *Engineering Magazine*, March 1902: 903; *American Machinist*, 1 May 1902: 645; *American Machinist*, 26 May 1892: 3; *American Machinist*, 5 May 1892: 8–9; *American Machinist*, 28 August 1886: 7; *American Machinist*, 29 November 1900: 1126; *American Machinist*, 17 March 1898: 208; *American Machinist*, 17 August 1922: 280c). Apparently, 'The whole industrial world seems to have been seized with the strike madness' (*Engineering Magazine*, June 1903: 415). Reference to other countries was an implicit sign of departure from the narrow ideology of American Exceptionalism. These references emphasized the similarities of American society to the experiences of other countries rather than its uniqueness. Class struggle was now conceptualized as an inevitable stage in the process of industrial progress (e.g. *Engineering Magazine*, March 1902: 903).

In keeping with this ideological transition, federal commissioner of labor Carroll Wright reformulated his position regarding strikes. The rise of organized labor in the 1880s, with the more frequent resort to strikes and the 1877, 1883, and 1885–6 strikes, forced the subject to his attention. In his 1906 book *The Battles of Labor*, Wright traced the labor problem to the ancient and medieval periods: 'It was an aspect of human evolution, not a frightening new development in the nineteenth century.' And Dunlap said: 'It becomes plainly evident that the labor question has become the paramount problem before every American manufacturer' (*Engineering Magazine*, November 1916: 146). This realization brought home the conclusion that labor problems should be studied:

In the light of this development, and in preparation for the steady work of education and enlightened study of labor problems which lies ahead of all employers and employment managers, it affords us special pride and pleasure to announce that beginning with our January number we shall establish as a special feature of this Magazine a department to be entitled: Employment Managers' Department. (*Engineering Magazine*, November 1916: 147)

Among its subjects were the sixty-eight different problems that the Employment Managers' Association gathered in Boston in 1916, which the column treated under the title 'how to hold the restless young man and woman'. The 'labor problem' was now conceptualized as deserving the attention of employers, and engineers took up the challenge of dealing with it. Articles in *American Machinist* often referred to engineers as a 'third party' in industrial disputes, hammering on the public interest (e.g. *American Machinist*, 14 September 1922: 416–17), and vicariously creating a 'non-partisan' zone of rationality from which the engineer could participate in the conflicts between capital and labor. This can be understood within the parameters of engineers' vision of the new industrial order.

## 6.2 Progressive engineers and the new vision of industrial capitalism

Although Progressivists and engineers shared common ground—i.e. the belief in mechanization, the scientific method, and efficiency, and the fear of labor unrest—it is important not to lose touch with the substantial differences that remained between them (Layton 1971: 64). Engineers showed no sympathy for such mainstream Progressive concerns as referenda or direct primaries. They perceived many reformers as 'agitators', 'utopists', 'demagogues', and 'dilettantes' (Haber 1964; Kloppenberg 1986). More importantly, Progressive reforms carried an ambivalent attitude toward organizations (not to say an anti-organizational bias) whereas engineers were, for the most part, corporation employees (Kaufman, Zacharias, and Karson 1995).[11] The growth of business did not threaten to displace engineers, but rather to open up future possibilities for their careers. Therefore, engineers accepted the structure, power, and ideological principles of business and big corporations. They believed in better management, more efficiency, and no government control. Some even argued that the modern corporation was the product of an evolutionary law discovered by Spencer, and it was the engineer's duty to defend the corporation from government regulation. The mergers and consolidations movement at the turn of the century strengthened and expanded the bureaucratic orientation of engineers.[12]

This bureaucratic orientation was in accord with the attempt by institutional economists (e.g. Francis Amasa Walker and Carroll D. Wright) to push *laissez-faire* aside and to accommodate economic theory to industrialization—'the age of big business' and 'the decline of *laissez-faire*'.[13] It was a revolt against the older social and economic order which advocated free market competition. The individuals responsible for these visions—mainly John Commons, Jeremiah Jenks, and Dana Durand—were not only academic economists but were also active participants in public inquiries into industrial relations during the Progressive era.[14] The two competing perspectives, which became explicit during the hearings and the reports of the USIC, set the parameters for the academic and public discourse on industrial order during the Progressive era (Wunderlin 1992: 26). Both perspectives, however, accepted the existence of large corporations.

At the turn of the century there was evidence in the engineering literature of a growing support for industrial combinations. After the settlement of the

1900–1 machinists' strike, an editorial declared that 'The *Engineering Magazine* has been persistently hopeful for the future of organization,' stressing that the editors supported all sorts of associations and combinations (see *Engineering Magazine*, August 1901: 749). In 1905, the editors of *American Machinist* endorsed Andrew Carnegie's opinion regarding the ownership of large corporations.[15] They agreed that the ownership or control of public utilities should be in the hands of the public, while matters which 'can be freely carried on by private individuals or corporations without infringing the rights of the public should be so carried on'. John Dunlap justified the idea of a 'freedom for the action of natural laws' (*Engineering Magazine*, July 1902: 594).

Along these lines, *American Machinist* argued that there was 'too much railing against "capital" and "capitalism" ', and suggested making a distinction between two types of monopoly. One, the legitimate type, emerged out of the severe competition to lower prices especially when such companies had no control over the supply of their raw materials or the transportation of the finished product. For this type, 'We do not see how any reasonable complaint can be brought against them, no matter how large they may be.' The second, the illegitimate type, referred to monopolies whose rights have been 'granted' or 'given away by thoughtless or corrupt representatives of the people'. In this case, 'it is monopoly and not capital that is the offender' (*American Machinist*, 9 August 1900: 1).[16] The editors of *American Machinist* reiterated their distinction between monopolies that were injurious to the public welfare, and companies which were perfectly legitimate competitive business enterprises no matter what their size. The editors summarized their position, 'This is written simply as explanation against being regarded as an advocate of socialism' (the motto of socialism as defined by the editors was 'From Each According to His Ability; To Each According to His Needs', *American Machinist*, 4 October 1900: 941–2). The editors quoted results of a 1901 survey conducted by the labor commissioner of Minneapolis among a large number of workers. The survey examined the interest of labor in the issue of mergers and trusts. The commissioner reported that the majority of workers believed that large organizations were beneficial to wage earners since they provided more certain employment and higher wages (*American Machinist*, 10 April 1902: 533). *American Machinist* concluded:

For three centuries the Anglo-Saxon has been instinctively opposed to monopolies . . . Only very recently have we awakened to the fact that there are certain natural monopolies that should be maintained as such and subjected to regulation to keep them within bound. Among them are the telephone, transportation means of various kinds, water supply, and gas and electric light and power services. The danger, of course, is that those natural monopolies will be over-regulated, as some have been. But better a short period of too much regulation than that destructive competition should wipe out the services altogether. (*American Machinist*, 14 January 1926: 74)

At the administration level, reactions to the large corporation were diverse. Both Theodore Roosevelt and Woodrow Wilson believed that the power of the big corporations should be restricted by federal government. Roosevelt envisioned a 'new nationalism', a greater America integrated by economic and social reforms at the national level. Wilson had no such imperialist aspirations. He espoused a 'new freedom' philosophy, which spoke of a restoration of the old freedom that had existed (or that was believed to have existed) prior to the monopolization of the market by the 'robber barons'. It should be noted, though, that neither president opposed 'big business' as such. As long as monopolies and trusts achieved their position 'honestly' and obeyed the law, they posed no threat to society (Wunderlin 1992; Kaufman, Zacharias, and Karson 1995). This trend toward the recognition of the new industrial order was also recorded in the magazines, a recognition that paved the way for the formation of the visible hand ideology in industry within which systems ideology seemed inevitable. By the 1920s, the bureaucratic corporation was accepted as the central organization in the American economy (Chandler 1977; Glover 1980; Kaufman, Zacharias, and Karson 1995). The relative number of administrative employees rose from 7.7 percent in 1899 to 18 percent in 1929 (Bendix 1956/1974: 214; Guillen 1994: 36).

'Management Systems' were congruent with the ideology of Progressive engineering. Engineers were at the right place at the right time. They neither manipulated nor cheated labor and capital. They strongly believed in their project and in their role in the growing zone in between labor and capital. Engineers capitalized on the severity of labor unrest in order to 'sell' the agenda of systems as a solution to the 'labor problem'.

However, one must appreciate the dialectical—Janus-like—nature of the relationship between labor unrest and management systems. On the one hand, labor unrest was used by mechanical engineers to promote the rhetoric of systems. Through the introduction of systems, engineers feathered their own nest: they provided a role for the engineer as an organization expert and constituted his position as a legitimate speaker in the industrial discourse. The empirical evidence, both quantitative and qualitative, clearly points to the intensification of the systems discourse in periods of intense strikes. On the other hand, it was through the filter of the systems perspective that labor unrest was, in turn, viewed and conceptualized as a purely mechanical, rather than political, issue. Many engineers were convinced, or at least so they argued, that unrest could be formulated in technical terms, and solved with the tools of engineering.

### 6.3 The constitution of labor unrest as a problem in mechanics

Concern over labor unrest had been evident in the industrial world since the beginning of the century. Writers realized the unpredictability associated with human behavior and its magnification during times of unrest: 'The human element cannot successfully be bound by the same iron-clad rules as a machine and will always be something of a variable quantity' (*American Machinist*, 7

December 1911: 1091). They nevertheless believed that human nature had to be rationalized in order to generate predictable and desirable outcomes. The concern with the stability of social order and the disobedience of workers was made rather bluntly by a manufacturer who would have preferred dogs to be employed in his business, since 'They never go on strike for higher wages, have no labor unions, never get intoxicated and disorderly, never absent themselves from work without good cause, obey orders without growling, and are very reliable' (cited in Goldstein 1978: 8).

Mechanical engineers, empowered by the success of machine technology, were keen to offer the same ideology for dealing with unrest. 'Systems' appeared both practical (a 'great mechanical invention') and essential (as a social philosophy) (e.g. *American Machinist*, 27 March 1913: 507). Leon Alford, editor of both *American Machinist* and later of *Engineering Magazine*, pleaded that industrial engineers be involved in the effort to improve relationships between employers and employees (Wren 1972: 184). C. E. Knoeppel, an active writer in engineering magazines, insisted that the problem of industrial unrest should be dealt with in ASME, since 'Neither employees nor employers could give it the proper attention; only the engineering world could do that' (Jaffe 1957: 101). The Committee on Aims and Organization within ASME considered the solving of industrial unrest an integral part of the society's future objectives (Sinclair 1980: 121). John Dunlap, editor of *Engineering Magazine*, complained that 'the whole scheme of production is subject to constant, wasteful, and brutal interruption because of the inability of the two elements—employer and employees—to work in any kind of harmony'. He concluded that there was something wrong with industrial philosophy, which was 'so marvelously effective on the mechanical side and so complete a failure in dealing with the workman' (*Engineering Magazine*, September 1904: 977).

This position was reiterated most clearly in the New York local section meeting of ASME in September 1919. The executive committee discussed industrial unrest, and argued that following the war 'Employers are in an attitude of uncertainty in regard to the future of their own business, the policies they should adopt toward labor and their relations with the public and the government' (*Industrial Management*, October 1919: 340). Under these conditions, engineers could work toward the well-being of people: 'The engineering profession is the bridgehead between the two opposing groups in industry . . . The engineer alone speaks the language of both these groups and hence he should be the interpreter of each to the other . . . Therefore, from his ranks will come the remedy.' Similar statements were made elsewhere. In an open letter to the Aims and Organization Committee, Henry L. Gantt said that 'If a conflict in industry is to be avoided engineers must take the initiative in harmonizing the interests of owners and workers' (*Industrial Management*, April 1919: 332). 'The only men in the community who understand the needs of the nation, desires of the workmen and power of the productive force, are the engineers. If they do not take the initiative and devise methods which will harmonize the interests of the owner and the worker we shall have a conflict, the result of which cannot be foreseen.'

Labor unrest and other political disagreements of the period were treated by mechanical engineers as simply a particular case of machine uncertainty to be dealt with in much the same manner as they had so successfully dealt with technical uncertainty. Whatever disrupted the smooth running of the organizational machine was viewed and constructed as a problem of uncertainty. *American Machinist* argued: 'Labor troubles are found throughout the United States, and will continue to disturb business until a satisfactory solution of the problem is found, and this condition of affairs makes prosperous times extremely doubtful and uncertain while they prevail' (*American Machinist*, 8 January 1887: 2). A glimpse at the application of mechanical ideology to quell unrest is provided by another writer:

The habit hitherto has been to regard metals and the other materials of manufacture as certain and reliable elements to be dealt with, while human nature has been regarded as the uncertain and capricious element. But as we grow wiser and go deeper into things we find that all material which we handle is more or less uncertain . . . On the other hand, the assumed uncertainties of human nature are largely dissipated as we learn its proper manipulation. (*American Machinist*, 8 February 1894: 6)

This was the prevalent overtone during the industrial turmoil of the Progressive era. Already in 1903, John Dunlap stated: 'There is no more vital need today than that of applying to the labor question the same enlightened common sense which has lately revolutionized machine-shop equipment and practice' (*Engineering Magazine*, May 1903: 161–7). Also in 1903, Charles U. Carpenter of the National Cash Register Company proposed:

The 'labor problem' now confronting us cannot be solved until the same principles of organization that have been such great factors in commercial success are brought to bear upon it. Manufacturers generally, though they have recognized the seriousness of the situation for some time, are just beginning to realize the necessity for a general and comprehensive plan of organization. (*Engineering Magazine*, April 1903: 1–16; see also *Engineering Magazine*, April 1918: 326)

*American Machinist* explained, 'The real cause of the present-day unrest lies in the fact that there is no unit of measurement which both employers and employees can use' (*American Machinist*, 12 February 1920: 331–5). The ideological work presented here reduces unrest to a problem of measurement.

Leon Alford offered several solutions to the labor problem (*Transactions of the ASME*, 41, 1919: 163–86), none of which made mention of the political dimension of labor unrest. As his biographer argued, 'Alford was fearful of the view stating that labor unrest was fundamentally a "struggle for control" ' (Jaffe 1957: 98). Labor unrest was not framed as an ideological issue but as a technical one. This was ratified in *American Machinist* by John Calder, director of modern production methods in a business training corporation in New York City: 'Can the complicated phenomena vaguely termed "labor troubles" be taken out of politics? We believe the answer is in the affirmative' (*American Machinist*, 24 April 1919: 807). *Engineering Magazine* said in August 1916, following numerous strikes: 'Strikes are a disease, hence curable' (*Engineering Magazine*, August 1916: 748). But the magazine also offered a cure: 'Look where you will, labor troubles and unstandardized working conditions are concomitant phenomena.' The cure is in the system. In short, the strife between capital and labor was ideologically neutralized by mechanical engineers who had taken industrial unrest as given in order to apply engineering rationality to it.

### 6.4 The link between unrest and management systems

> There is no more vital need today than that of applying to the labor question the same enlightened common sense which has lately revolutionized machine-shop equipment and practice.
>
> (*Engineering Magazine*, May 1903:161–7)

Students of management can be categorized into roughly three types. First are those historians who overlook industrial strife, such as Chandler and Waring (Chandler 1977; Waring 1991). Chandler, for example, attributed the rise of management to technology and market needs, neglecting the politics of labor altogether. Second are neo-Marxist sociologists such as Braverman, Marglin, and Edwards (Braverman 1974; Marglin 1974; Edwards 1979), and neo-Weberian sociologists such as Bendix and Guillen (Bendix 1956/1974; Guillen 1994), who have claimed that labor unrest is relevant to the development of management, though they provide no consistent quantitative evidence to support their argument. In the third and more ambiguous category are Barley, Kunda, and Abrahamson (Barley and Kunda 1992; Abrahamson 1997). These writers attribute shifts in managerial discourse to upswings and downswings of economic long waves or performance gaps. Although they conclude that labor unrest does not provide a consistent explanation of surges in rational and normative managerial ideologies over the course of the twentieth century, they acknowledge that Scientific Management, which they accurately consider a rational ideology, 'flowered when strikes were more common than any other time' (Barley and Kunda 1992: 389). While the scholars mentioned above linked labor unrest with the introduction of systems, my perspective regarding the nature of this linkage is different. I argue that engineering rhetoric, rather than class structure, is the 'engine' behind this linkage. I claim that engineers used intensified periods of labor unrest to sell the agenda of management systems to reluctant employers and the public at large.

Once engineers positioned themselves as arbiters between labor and capital, and framed unrest in mechanical terms as a problem of technical uncertainty, the introduction of systems to handle the human element became both logical and natural. However, the opposing parties (employers and workers) had first to be convinced or coerced into accepting this paradigm. An editorial in *Engineering Magazine* rejected the use of non-rational power in work relations, and established a link between 'rational methods' and 'labor unrest' (*Engineering Magazine*, March 1913: 929–31). The editorial warned readers that '[a] Few rebels can intimidate, sabotage and demoralize an industry', and that it is important 'to foster more intelligent measures for the betterment of industrial conditions, and to spread the philosophies of hope which hold a brighter promise for both employers and employees'. The editor of the magazine proposed distributing educational literature on management. In his own words: 'Is there any literature more broadly important to humanity, more directly significant to engineers who are the leaders of material civilization, than the literature of "industrial management"?'

In 1892/3 *Engineering Magazine* published a debate regarding the causes of the 'labor troubles' (or the 'civil war' as it was labeled in several instances). The contributors often linked labor troubles to the necessity of a system to solve them (*Engineering Magazine*, January 1893: 569–76). One engineer argued that employers' objectives were not to be obtained by extortion but rather by a 'better system, by improved machinery and processes, by the application of sound economic laws. What really is the principle underlying the relation of employer and employed, whether or not the employed know it, or the employer means it? The system, the exacting rules.' This position was made applicable for all versions of systems: wage systems, accounting systems, production control, or organizational systems. Systems were seen as enabling a new economic order with greater precision and better organization. This linkage between systems and strikes was supposed to legitimize and advance the engineering solution to labor unrest (*Transactions of the ASME*, 23, 1901–2: 361; cited in Calvert 1967: 239).

The logic that prompted the necessity for organizational systems was made even clearer by Frederick Taylor. Taylor boldly asserted that his differential piece-rate system could put an end to labor unrest:

There has never been a strike by men working under this system, although it has been applied at the Midvale Steel Works for the past ten years; and steel business has proved during this period the most fruitful field for labor organizations and strikes ... The moral effect of this system on the men is marked. The feeling that substantial justice is being done renders them on the whole much more manly, straightforward, and truthful. They work more cheerfully, and are more obliging to one another and their employers. (Taylor 1903: 183, 185)

Taylor further suggested that the laws of management systems would be impartial and above class prejudice.

In 1904 Henry L. Gantt explained why an organizational wage system (as compared with inside-contracting) was necessary. He argued that workers chose salaried work since they prefer to sell their time rather than products (*American Machinist*, 19 May 1904: 654; *American Machinist*, 20 October 1904: 1394–6).

Nevertheless employees try to remain the owners of their time by not allowing employers to introduce time studies. Gantt saw the solution to this tension in a system based on scientific methods and which applied scientific principles of management.[17] Studies of profit sharing at the Ford Motor Company and at McCormick provided evidence that accounting-based incentive plans were implemented to reduce labor resistance (Oakes 1988: 270).[18] Harrington Emerson noted in 1904 that he 'cannot but regard disputes over wages as the effect rather than the cause of unsatisfactory and unscientific relations between employer and employee' (*Transactions of the ASME*, 25, 1903–4: 878; cited in Calvert 1967: 239).

Whereas I do not argue that engineers promoted management systems with the intention of oppressing labor, the rise of systems discourse with emphasis on order and harmony during the years 1890–1930 was in accordance with labor 'homogenization'. Homogenization was associated with rationality, order, and integration. Homogenization was possible through the participation of engineers, which facilitated the production of 'drive systems'. These entailed the generation of record systems, job design, accounting procedures, production control, and time and motion methods. Efficiency experts claimed to be neutral and objective. They looked to 'neither capital nor labor but to some force outside both' to bring the needed social efficiency. They argued that 'the efficiency systems had uncovered the underlying harmony of society and their spread was inevitable' (Haber 1964: 60). These engineering techniques were used to monitor, control, and discipline workers.[19] While a neo-Marxist explanation would focus on such a linkage, my perspective extends it with what I believe is a broader focus on the professional ideology of engineers (Larson 1977; Freidson 1986; Abbott 1988). For the neo-Marxist writers the discourse and methods of organizational systems were used to shunt labor unrest, in the mechanical sense of sending a railway wagon from the main track onto a siding. Engineers saw and advertised their role as keeping the main track clear. Nevertheless, the actual implication of their project, however neutrally presented, was to expand their power and span of control.

Henry Varnum Poor, editor of *American Railroad Journal*, described in his editorials the workers' resistance to discipline. He justified organizational systematization and thought that tighter control was required to 'bring order from chaos' (Wren 1972: 90). Poor saw 'no other way in which such a vast machine can be safely and successfully conducted' (see Chandler 1956: 155). In 1908 the editors of *Engineering Magazine* introduced an article by George F. Stratton on the 'division of responsibility and authority in the General Electric company's shops', and invited more discussions of successful organization systems (*Engineering Magazine*, January 1908: 569–76). Such articles 'will show how, in these vast works, an army of men is kept in orderly and productive employment on a multitude of operations, all moving harmoniously to the completion of the desired product'. The harmony that the editors referred to was the harmony of the machine functioning. The terminology of harmony and cooperation was used quite often. In the midst of the 1913 industrial violence, Hugo Diemer suggested that 'unification', 'cooperation', and 'common good' are essential elements in time of unrest. To him, organizational system consisted of 'the uniting' of individuals and groups 'in such a manner as to cooperate for the common good' (*American Machinist*, 27 March 1913: 507).

An editorial in *American Machinist* as late as 1922 argued that when the worker has been shown that he is getting a fair share of the profits, then 'the entire organization will pull together in peace and harmony', and 'the problem of the age' ('the industrial modern Sword of Damocles') will have been solved (*American Machinist*, 2 November 1922: 705). Furthermore, it was argued that principles of efficiency unite people and make them believe in a common cause: 'The efficiency of men loyal to a common cause, and to one another, is very much more productive than their mechanical efficiency alone, and an organizer should do everything in his power to make conditions favourable to the growth of this spirit' (*American Machinist*, 27 March 1913: 511).

Although engineering did not operate out of a motive of helping capitalists to discipline workers, in effect it helped depoliticize the language of oppression. The syntax of systems discourse, which appeared neutral and harmonious, translated the politics of unrest into a technical, ostensibly apolitical, language. Engineering methods were appropriated to convert political issues into soluble technical problems (see Habermas 1970). In a programmatic essay justifying the establishment of personnel departments (probably one of the first ever), Charles Carpenter linked them with labor troubles: 'It is my belief that all great departments of industry must have their departments of labor, if serious friction is to be avoided and wisely adjusted.' Labor departments met employees 'fairly, firmly and promptly'. Therefore, 'this department should be in control of the labor question with full authority to settle all questions that the men and foremen cannot settle'. Furthermore, in terms of personnel to fill up positions in the labor department, 'mechanical experience is very desirable' (*Engineering Magazine*, April 1903: 1–16).

Similar reasons were involved in the description of the employment department of the Westinghouse Electric & Manufacturing Company (*American Machinist*, 23 June 1904: 832–3). Hiring and selection ought not be left to the foremen, who might be influenced by emotional motives. 'The selection of relatives and general favouritism' was a trouble common enough among foremen. Using this justification, the advantages of a rational system were emphasized.

At Midvale, Taylor encountered workers' attempts to limit production. This interference, which Taylor labeled as 'soldiering', appeared to him as the crux of the labor problem (Layton 1971: 136). Taylor designed a system that attempted to transcend dependence on particular individual supervisors.

The shop (indeed the whole works) should be managed, not by the manager, superintendent, or foreman, but by the planning department. The daily routine of running the entire works should be carried on by the various functional elements of this department, so that, in theory at least, the works could run smoothly even if the manager, superintendent, and their assistants outside the planning room were all to be away for a month at a time. (Haber 1964: 25)

Taylor linked the system to 'labor troubles': 'One of the chief advantages derived from the above system is that it promotes a most friendly feeling between the men and their employers, and so renders labor unions and strikes unnecessary.' In a similar vein, Hugo Diemer reported on a conference organized in 1911 by H. S. Person, the dean of the Tuck School of Business Administration of Dartmouth College. Person, who in 1913 became the president of the Taylor Society, invited several guest speakers, including Taylor and Gantt, to talk about business efficiency and management. The speakers concluded that the greatest gain under the system was 'the establishment of more cordial relations between employee and employer' (*American Machinist*, 9 November 1911: 899–900). In July 1913, James Dodge, an ex-president of the American Society of Mechanical Engineers and chairman of a subcommittee on administration in the society, asseverated that Taylor's system was a solution to labor unrest. 'It is known to all that industrial unrest comes from the lack of agreement as to what shall be the division of the earnings.' If all parties involved can accept a 'mental revolution' through the introduction of Scientific Management, all parties will benefit and 'the artificial barrier' between employers and employees 'is removed for all time' (*American Machinist*, 3 July 1913: 42). This quotation illustrates the sophistication and authority with which engineers had come to promote their managerial role. It is interesting to compare the engineers' rhetoric to what Bauman says about what he calls 'the character of postmodern authority structures', which 'cannot demand obedience by invoking explicitly its putative right to command. Commanding as such has been discredited as oppression . . . An effective authority must not appear to be an authority—but a helpful hand, a well-wisher, a friend' (Bauman 1992: 196). At the beginning of this century, well before 'postmodernism' became a catchword, engineers were using a similar discourse in order to promote their structure of authority.

Engineers refrained from taking sides. They were there to service the mutual interest of employers and employees, or rather for 'the system'. Henry Gantt said, for example, that the best time for the introduction of systems was 'not when labor trouble is brewing, but when things are running smoothly and employer and workman have confidence in each other' (*American Machinist*, 19 May 1904: 654). Efficiency, it was believed by Progressive reformers, would lower costs and raise wages and therefore check the 'greed' of the employer and the 'laziness' of the employee. They believed that the interests of the capitalists and labor would converge and there would be no need to resort to class conflict. The editors of *Engineering Magazine* believed that the methods introduced by Gantt regarding the training and compensation of workers 'Would remove the present chief cause of antagonism between employer and employed' (*Engineering Magazine*, February 1910: 653).

A few years later John Dunlap supported Taylor's, Gantt's, and Diemer's position. He argued that in places where 'the true spirit of Scientific Management has come to permeate an organization, labor troubles are almost as rare as planetary collisions' (*Engineering Magazine*, August 1916: 748). He mentioned that in the industrial center in Syracuse in 1915 strikes were rampant. There was only one plant were strikes did not take place, and 'in that one Scientific Management prevails . . . The workers are so satisfied that agitation has absolutely nothing to feed upon.'

If Taylor's work is significant in the history of management, it is not because of his technical contribution. It was the link between his methods and industrial unrest—the missing and 'invisible' political link—that made him so disproportionately visible in the history of management. As Merkel put it, 'Taylorism's strength lay not in its patented mechanisms, its mnemonic and accounting systems, but in its patented mechanisms as a device for social control and a strategy of social action in times of unrest' (Merkel 1980).

According to the engineering rhetoric to which Taylor, Gantt, Diemer, Dunlap, and others were but a few contributors, the properties of the machine-like system were expected to transform chaos into order, ambiguity into certainty, and irrational into rational behavior, as in the following quote:

The difference between music and noise, between an army and a mob, between a wagon-train and a stampeding herd of cattle, between righteousness and wickedness, is that *standards and schedules* have been evolved for music, for an army, for a wagon-train, for righteousness; none, for noise, for a mob, for a stampede, for wickedness. (*Engineering Magazine*, April 1911: 23–32 (emphasis is mine) )

Standardization provides orderliness: 'A spirit of orderliness is inculcated into the working force and there is 'better attendance, greater promptness, more attention to work, better workmanship and less spoilage' (*American Machinist*, 28 June 1923: 939).

This rhetoric of order and system minimized the political significance of unrest, since the standardization solution 'is simply a question of method, the application of a few simple rules' (Litterer 1961*b*: 473). The mechanical model was expected to replace 'the old set of rules, which have served their day', and to establish the modern principle that order is 'the first law of the universe . . . The nearer our approach to it, the more harmonious will our arrangement work' (Litterer 1961*b*: 475). It follows, therefore, that if engineers used labor unrest to justify the introduction of systems, this rhetoric became more intense as labor unrest intensified. Quantitative analyses support this expectation (for a detailed description of these analyses see Shenhav 1995). Simple correlations show that systems discourse was positively related to the number of strikes. It also shows that the volume of literature on management issues increased as the number of strikes increased. I employed time series regression analyses using system as the dependent variable, and several variables were simultaneously included in the analysis. I found discourse on systems to be significantly higher during the Progressive era (as has already been shown in Chapter 3). It was also significantly related to the professionalization of mechanical engineering: the greater the number of ASME members, the higher the proportion of systems thinking.[20] In addition, the number of strikes had a significant effect on the appearance of organizational systems.[21]

Fig. 3 in Chapter 3 showed that there was a decline in the discourse on systems beginning towards the end of the Progressive period. There are two interpretations regarding this decline. First, it might be an artifact of the data sources. During this time, another engineering spin-off journal, *System: The Magazine of Business*, was started. It is possible that the overall count of articles appearing in the journals with the addition of *System* would yield a steady state or perhaps even an increase in the proportion of entries on systems rather than a decline. However, the decline can also be understood as a reaction to the rise of industrial psychology as an independent managerial discourse. Psychology is to replace sociology as the ally of management.[22]

## 6.5 Industrial psychology on the rebound

Before 1912–13, engineering, accounting, and economics were the only bodies of knowledge relevant to systematic management. If considerations of the 'human factor' were at all involved, they were based on philosophy, ethics, and religion (see Jenks 1961; Noble 1977; Guillen 1994). At the beginning of the century, in parallel with the intensification of systems discourse, there were already discussions about the human side of production. For example, in 1908 an article in *Engineering Magazine* entitled 'Personalism in Railroading' suggested a more human and democratic approach to managing organizations (H. W. Jacobs in *Engineering Magazine*, June 1908: 404–11). Another article said, 'In industrial organization the human element is vastly the most important factor, and that increased efficiency is to be obtained principally through the stimulation of the personnel by a system of individual reward' (*Engineering Magazine*, December 1908: 329). Frederick Colvin reported in 1911 that the Chicago & Northwestern Railway had secured a low cost for locomotive repairs without elaborate management systems, but rather with the personality of managers and the recognition of individuality among workers which secured 'the heartiest co-operation all along the line' (*American Machinist*, 7 September 1911: 439–40). Colvin signified the forthcoming shift between the rationality of systems and the psychology of the workplace:

No iron-clad set of rules, or system, can insure [success] . . . For such rules ignore the main factor which makes for either success or failure—the personality of the manager and of his men . . . The policy of being human in business, of treating employees like human beings rather than like inexpensive and readily replaced parts of the inanimate equipment, or worse, can be shown, and over and over again has been shown to be profitable. (*American Machinist*, 31 August 1911: 393–5)

In 1913 Hugo Muensterberg published his *Psychology and Industrial Efficiency*, in which he assessed the value of psychology to industrial affairs. As the editors of *American Machinist* commented then, 'The word "psychology" has always carried with it an air of mystery' (*American Machinist*, 10 July 1913: 77). In 1915 *American Machinist* published an article by C. B. Lord, a superintendent in electrical manufacturing, titled 'Personality in the Shop: Psychology of the Foreman' (*American Machinist*, 25 February 1915: 315). Articles during this period dealt with all sorts of human characteristics. One proposed 'hiring men on basis of physique and skill' (*American Machinist*, 8 January 1914: 51–4); another 'standardizing the characteristics of men' (*Engineering Magazine*, December 1916: 308–23). Yet another, entitled 'Personality in the Shop: Psychology of the Female Employee', said, 'When properly understood women and girls make efficient employees for light and repetitive mechanical work' (*American Machinist*, 15 April 1915: 593–4). Before and during the First World War, the literature on industrial psychology peaked (Bendix 1956/1974; Baritz 1960. For examples, see *Engineering Magazine*, September 1915: 801–8; *American Machinist*, 31 May 1917: 934). Industrial psychology was used for military hiring, for training, and also as an instrument of labor control in industry. As one manager said: 'You must know the thoughts of workers if you are to treat them right. You must know their desires, their home environments, their relaxations—everything about them' (*Engineering Magazine*, March 1918: 197–8).

In 1918 *Engineering Magazine* established a regular section on 'Employment and Labor Maintenance'. Industrial psychology was applied to several domains: first, to the emerging role of employment managers (e.g. *Engineering Magazine*, August 1918: 145–6),[23] and second, to the hiring and selection of employees. The editors referred to the 'science of character analysis' (*Engineering Magazine*, June 1918: 498–9). Third, there was a concern with turnover (e.g. 'Why Men Leave their Jobs', *Engineering Magazine*, August 1918: 147–8), including the development of questionnaires and other instruments (*Engineering Magazine*, September 1918: 239–47) of human engineering and physical factors (e.g. *Engineering Magazine*, November 1918: 367–71; *Engineering Magazine*, November 1918: 372–4), and with 'organizational culture'. One article, for example, observed that in order to create 'the spirit of the organization' one should start from the top: 'For in most cases the sorrows, as well as joys, at the bottom are only a reflection of the top' (*Engineering Magazine*, August 1918: 117–18). Another article recommended 'making employees read the plant paper by telling about their babies' (*American Machinist*, 19 August 1920: 363). Another said that shops need to have in-house magazines 'to make work in the plant easier, more intelligent and more pleasant' (*American Machinist*, 15

January 1920: 120–1). *American Machinist* said on a different occasion: 'Men like to read intimate items about their work and to see their names in print' (*American Machinist*, 19 February 1920: 385–8). In 1920, an editorial in *American Machinist* appropriated psychology as another domain of engineering. The editor said that one of the most important functions of a production engineer was psychology (*American Machinist*, 15 July 1920: 134).

Closer examination of *American Machinist* reveals that the percentage of items associated with industrial psychology was ten times as large during 1913–20 as in the earlier period, 1879–1912 (see Table 5). As for *Engineering Magazine*, there were very few items on industrial psychology prior to 1916. In 1916, the percentage was approximately 2 percent, but it rose to 22 percent in 1917 and to 28 percent in 1918. During the First World War and thereafter, the literature on industrial psychology was teeming (e.g. *Engineering Magazine*, September 1915: 801–8; *American Machinist*, 31 May 1917: 934; *American Machinist*, 28 June 1917: 1107). In addition to the motives presented above, Wunderlin argues that interest in industrial psychology was stimulated by economic considerations. In 1919 economist John Commons asserted that machinery and factory organization 'are continually approaching a limit of diminishing returns' (Wunderlin 1992: 132). According to Wunderlin this realization urged managers to examine the human side of the labor process, 'to find a new way to squeeze out hidden profits'. In fact in the 1920s and 1930s a heated debate developed regarding the motivation of workers and as a result a battery of tests and testers emerged in industry to investigate their attitudes and aptitudes (Lash and Urry 1987). However, the findings also suggest that industrial psychology might have replaced, or at least added to, the logic of systems, as a solution to the 'labor problem'.[24]

Some of the writings on industrial psychology directly addressed 'labor troubles'. Commenting on an article written by an engineer about cooperative systems, the editors of *American Machinist* praised the writer for paying attention to 'the human element in engineering' and for improving chances for 'identifying the interests of workmen with those of their employers and doing away with many of the causes of misunderstandings and of friction which exist under the present system' (*American Machinist*, 15 November 1894: 8). Engineers were not

TABLE 5. *Average percentage of items (per year) associated with industrial psychology and human relations*

| Period | American Machinist | Engineering Magazine |
|--------|--------------------|-----------------------|
| 1879–1912 | 0.005 | 0.002 |
| 1913–20 | 0.050 | 0.280 |
| 1921–32 | 0.025 | NI[a] |

[a] No further information on industrial psychology was coded after 1921 in the *Engineering Magazine*.

alone in their exploitation of unrest to establish their professional authority in industry. Psychologists and psychiatrists, among other professionals, followed. E. E. Southard, the director of the Massachusetts State Psychiatric Institute, introduced the role of the psychiatrist as a 'modern specialist' in dealing with labor unrest (*Industrial Management*, June 1920: 462–6). The writer asked, 'What is unrest?' His answer paved the way for the role of the psychiatrist:

The theory that group experiences leads to group thought, which in turn leads to group action, may be sound theory for a portion of industrial phenomena, but individual experience, individual thought, and even individual action are also factors in industrial situations . . . The psychiatrist is rather more likely than any other expert to know how the main lines of unrest will run . . . The psychiatrist has always been a specialist in unrest;—unrest, to be sure, confined within asylum walls, particularly. In company with the psychiatric social worker, the modern psychiatrist has under more or less definite supervision, large numbers of the so-called psychopathic personalities, being persons who are not insane in kind or degree to warrant their commitment to institutions, but who are psychopathic enough or in such wise as to benefit from community supervision . . . Unrest on the part of the individual is the big problem of the psychiatrist—year in and year out he comes in contact with the finest, as it were, and the most brilliant examples of unrest, namely, certain patients in his wards. (Ibid.)

The director provided several psychiatric causes for improper behavior in the workplace and removal from payroll. Among other things he named those who 'did not like supervision . . . Resented criticism . . . Work too hard, agitator, carelessness, dishonesty, drinking, fighting, indifference, insubordination, too slow.' These entries suggested what sort of investigation ought to be carried out by the psychiatrist as a result of the authority given to him in studying industrial unrest.[25]

The Human Relations movement, as an offspring of Industrial Psychology, thrived on industrial unrest too. For example, Elton Mayo attracted attention to himself and to his work through the 'labor problem'. In 1921, while still in Australia, Mayo wrote five articles on the role of psychological research in resolving industrial conflict (e.g. 'Industrial Unrest and Nervous Breakdown'). In recent years the newspapers had been reporting industrial violence in the United States: the murder of mine workers, the use of troops, and the death of a child in clashes between strikers and guards. In 1922 Mayo sent letters to senior executives of Standard Oil where he described 'the application of psychology to social investigation (e.g. the causes of social unrest)'. In a popular article published in 1925 called 'The Great Stupidity', Mayo concluded that the happy future of American industry depends 'upon the intelligence of employers and employers' associations [in] anticipating the unionization of industry, by making it unnecessary' (Trahair 1984). He suggested that through psychological investigation the irrational causes of industrial conflict would be found and brought under 'rational control'.

Mayo believed that extreme industrial struggle reflected the defects of any industrial society. He had a different interpretation of the sources of the labor struggle from his predecessors. Following Malinowski's theory, he believed that individuals were no longer able to identify with their occupations, and no communal support or psychiatric guidance was available to correct for the isolation from family life and the lack of communal ties caused by industrialization (ibid.). In October 1927 Mayo was invited to speak before a group of prominent industrialists at the Harvard Club in New York. The invitation came from the director of Industrial Relations Counselors, an organization that had been formed a year earlier by a group of industrial relations specialists and supported financially (exclusively) by John D. Rockefeller. The original purpose was to keep Rockefeller informed about industrial relations in his firms. Later, additional industrialists joined the club 'to advance the knowledge and practice of human relationship in industry, commerce, education and government' (Trahair 1984: 208). Among the attendees at this lunch meeting was T. K. Stevenson, the personnel director of the Western Electric Company, who recruited Mayo to advise him on the Hawthorne Works at Cicero, Illinois, and later to work with George Pennock, the officer in charge of the famous Hawthorne study. In 1928 Mayo was commissioned by Rockefeller to study problems of industrial relations in Rockefeller's Colorado Fuel and Iron Company in Pueblo. Rockefeller was concerned with the success of his plan to reduce industrial strife in the company's mines and steel works (Trahair 1984).

The implementation of 'industrial relations' studies converged, rather than competed, with the systems perspective. The latter was institutionalized around the First World War, with America's war mobilization and the efforts to coordinate industry, eliminate waste, and remove organizational inefficiencies. The spirit of Progressive systematization encouraged the emergence of a 'visible hand' ideology in industry. The macro-management philosophy of the war experience was adopted to resolve problems of productivity, unemployment, and class conflict. This resulted in a system of public and private linkages in which the government (particularly President Hoover and the Commerce Department) encouraged private business, engineers, and social science technocrats to undertake industrial planning (Hawley 1974; Alchon 1985). This system was welcomed by proponents of modern management. It was also in accord with the interests of the large industrial establishments founded by such people as Carnegie, Edison, Westinghouse, Bell, and Ford. Systematization and standardization were developed along with these corporations' product lines and allowed them to increase control over their respective industrial segments (Noble 1977). Systems provided greater rationality in production and served as a means of labor control, particularly as the level of industrial violence increased. Consequently, there was a substantial increase in systematization and in the number of system-related technocrats such as personnel administrators, corporate lawyers, accountants, and industrial engineers.

Rational engineering systems seemed to provide a perfect solution even for those who held an anti-organizational bias. They assumed that dissimilar and often contradictory causes could be put together to minimize differences, based on the premise that the operation of organizations is value-free and that it transcends participants' ideological positions and political biases. They emphasized the 'whole', usually the need to pursue 'a common goal', and implied the coexistence of parts in a general equilibrium (Lilienfeld 1978). Systems were therefore a social theory of harmony rather than conflict, cooperation rather than tension. They attempted to bind individuals in mutual relations of responsibility and accountability. The system was perceived as a blueprint for rationality, to produce consistency, predictability, and stability.

Application of the war experience in this way forced labor to accept the tenets of modern management as well. In 1919 the AFL issued a statement signed by the principal officers of 110 labor unions: 'To promote further the production of an adequate supply of the world's needs for use and higher standard of living, we urge that there be established cooperation between the scientists of industry and the representatives of organized workers' (quoted in Stark 1980: 104). With state intervention in the conflict between capital and labor during the New Deal period, labor struggle was denied through collective bargaining (Tolmins 1985). Over time, the issues of bargaining were eventually limited to wages, hours, and working conditions. The unions agreed to leave management of the productive sources to professional managers or to owners of capital. In exchange for recognition, labor agreed to limit the number of issues that would result in strikes.

In this chapter so far I have shown how systems were offered as a solution to labor unrest while at the same time appearing to be apolitical and scientifically objective. Engineers paved the way for a seductive structure of authority that was later further institutionalized and formalized within the canon of Management and Organization Theory. In the balance of this chapter I argue that, *vis-à-vis* the institutionalization of systems perspective, the coverage of labor unrest was also edited out of the engineering discourse. Together with its canonization, systems perspective was stripped of the very same politics that had helped promote it in the first place. The final outcome was therefore a truly 'invisible' structure of authority, consisting of a universal regime of surveillance and control with seemingly no political and historical genesis. Describing the final separation of systems from politics, it paves the way for an ideological critique of the depoliticization of management and its related disciplines in America.

## 6.6 The apolitical appeal of systems

The story of the relationship of systems and politics is like a turbulent love affair. I have described in earlier chapters how the project of systems grew itself in response to the political context, particularly *vis-à-vis* labor politics. Under the paradigm of Exceptionalism, when class ideology was denied, engineers ignored labor unrest and promoted the 'American system'. With Progressivism, labor unrest was reconstructed as the 'labor problem' and shunted aside while engineers closed down the system to include both the machine and human elements of the organization. Systems ideology was triumphant precisely because it did not have to cope with unrest anymore. The labor problem was simply edited out of organizational thought; it was relegated to a subdiscipline that branched out in 1919–20, namely, industrial relations. Following the First World War, when management was institutionalized as a scientific, apolitical academic body of knowledge, industrial relations started to emerge as a separate academic field. The first event to symbolize this was the 1919 publication of the monthly periodical *Industrial Relations: Bloomfield's Labor Digest*, edited by Daniel and Meyer Bloomfield, two prominent industrial consultants. The second event was the formation of the Industrial Relations Association of America (IRAA) in 1920. Among its activities, the IRAA published a monthly journal called *Personnel*. In 1920 the first academic program on industrial relations was established under the direction of John Commons in the University of Wisconsin (Kaufman 1993). Similar programs were established in 1921 (Wharton School of Business), 1922 (Princeton University), and 1923 (Harvard University).

The evolution of systems perspective and the coverage of labor unrest have been analyzed separately in Chapter 5. Here I propose to juxtapose the two in order to demonstrate the converse relation between them. Table 6, based on the annual frequency of items associated with 'unrest' and 'system', suggests that there was a converse relationship between the political and the 'non-political' discourses of industrial relations within the pages of the engineering magazines. The table reads as follows: before 1895, 15 percent of the items (on average) were associated explicitly with labor unrest, compared with 7 percent of the items associated with systems. However, after 1901, only 2 percent of the items were devoted to labor unrest, and 37 percent were associated with organizational systems. The table therefore demonstrates that the dominance of the two discourses has been intersected and reversed at the turn of the century, and more particularly during the period 1895–1905.[26] This empirical observation substantiates Locke's conclusion in his *The Collapse of the American Management Mystique*:

[T]he marginalization of labour studies, their separation from the study of management, results from a categorization of study that the very triumph of managerialism has

TABLE 6. *Average percentage of items (per year) associated with unrest and systems*

|  | 1879–94 | 1895–1900 | 1901–32 |
| --- | --- | --- | --- |
| Literature on labor unrest | 0.15 (0.14) | 0.07 (0.08) | 0.02 (0.04) |
| Literature on organization systems | 0.07 (0.06) | 0.35 (0.17) | 0.37 (0.12) |

*Notes*: Analysis is based on data from the *American Machinist* and the *Engineering Magazine*.
    Standard deviations in parentheses.

imposed. Labor has simply become management's problem, one which disallows the disturbing possibility of management being labor's problem as well. By divorcing labor from management studies, the sort of scholarly dialogue necessary to develop a thesis about the collapse of the American management mystique could not easily take place. (Locke 1996: 13)[27]

Despite the fact that the institutionalization of systems discourse and the exclusion of labor relations occurred concomitantly, I should be careful in using a language of causality since the introduction of systems was a typical professional strategy during the Progressive era—probably independent of unrest. But it is clear that, in the minds of those who produced the discourse on organizations, the only solution to 'labor unrest' was to introduce systematization and management systems. Furthermore, the quantitative and qualitative analyses provided thus far suggest that its usage was effective in reframing labor unrest in neutral, non-political terms.

As more systems solutions were offered, the reality of conflict, of power, and of inconsistency was gradually replaced by the world-view of engineers: analytical, consistent, rational, derivable. The editing out of labor problems from the canon of management was ideologically necessary in order to keep what I termed the 'unity of matter' in the organizational field, and the scientific, objective authority of managers. In the discursive field of systems there was no room for human-based contingencies such as 'unrest'. The employees, like the employers, were, after all, designated as rational constituents of the same system. The canon of systematization rhetorically replaced the 'labor problem' with the larger, more abstract notion of 'uncertainty'. As part of its canonization it therefore did away with the politically contingent in order to gain the illusion of the scientifically universal. With the dominance of systems discourse, discussion of unrest became technical. Simultaneously, the explicit link between the two world-views of order (systems) and conflict (the labor struggle) was diffused. This conclusion is both obvious and surprising. On the one hand, labor unrest, mob behavior, violence, and anarchy were threatening concepts and challenged professional authority and managerial control (*American Machinist*, 7 November 1895: 888). On the other hand, labor unrest also provided the contextual justification for introducing managerial techniques, promoting a distinction between managers and non-managers, and advancing the bureaucratization of large firms.[28] Episodes of unrest were used to justify a claim for professional expertise and to promote a particular line of theoretization. The theory of organizations as systems was developed in this context. Obviously, the early management movement was far quicker to establish and use a professional language than the labor unions had been.

Management professionals often argued that their theories and methods were objective and removed from the politics of the labor struggle. They often made the point that their work was anchored in the objective operation of efficiency. As one engineer explained, 'We are realizing that real efficiency knows neither nationality nor locality. We are big enough and broad enough to look at a machine for what it can do instead of inquiring into details of the pedigree of its builders' (*American Machinist*, 16 April 1914: 696). The universal nature of this objectivity can be seen as a strategy to transcend the current. Politics is about 'here and now' and about particular and historical events, while systems are transcendental.

To make way for their systems, engineers had to create a new, professional space between capital and labor. Employers and employees alike were therefore criticized in the engineering magazines, though on different occasions and on different grounds. The answer to power relations needed to be grounded in the application of 'well-defined principles', rational in nature. Rationality and technicality mitigated power. This was because 'the problems of civilization are becoming more and more technical in their character' (*Engineering Magazine*, November 1916: 256). In reference to the Homestead strike, Dunlap offered to determine 'the abstract or algebraic value of the situation, and hence to devise an equation for settling such differences henceforward' (*Engineering Magazine*, September 1892: 759–64). The engineering magazines called striking employees 'explosive workers' with strike-prone personalities. This view reconfigured strikes as matters concerning human nature rather than politics (see *Engineering Magazine*, January 1917: 503–5). 'Explosiveness' was described as an addiction; strikes were thus reduced from being political events of a collective nature to a matter of 'individual character': 'The trouble with working explosively is that the individual addicted to this character of activity won't fit into any decently organized scheme of production. He is a sort of human bomb-shell lacking a timer . . . In the family, he's the juvenile "problem"; in school, the hopeless impossible! and in the shop, the idlest of idle apprentices.'

Social problems were thus allowed to enter the organizational realm only after being dressed in technical terms. Pragmatic solutions were to replace ideological controversies. This was the common impetus behind the many and various endeavors of systematization.

One of the most blatant manifestations of the political pretensions of systematizers was the New Machine—an elite organization whose charter was to transfer control of industry into the hands of engineers. Formed in 1916 and headed by Henry Gantt, its mission was presented in a letter sent to President Wilson, which declared that 'we are jealous and anxious that America shall be made invincibly strong through the rectification of its business system and the release of creative faculties of the people' (*Engineering Magazine*, April 1917: 127–8). The aim was to close the gap between business and politics by sterilizing politics and running the government with engineering tools. The ideology of systems was peddled as a technique which could be run scientifically for 'society as a whole', without involving politics.

Many management historians fall short in realizing the seductive nature of this epistemological transition from the political to the non-political. For example,

Nelson has argued that 'rather than a partial solution of the labor problem, Taylor's system was a comprehensive answer to the problem of factory coordination, a refinement and extension of systematic management' (Nelson 1974: 480). This logic accepts the premise that technical systems are apolitical. Even if we were to accept the argument that Taylor was not genuinely interested in the labor problem, his preoccupation with systems still enabled efficiency experts to divert the politics of class struggle and labor unrest to the technical domain.[29] Whether Taylor and other systematizers intended to divert interest into a different domain, or whether they realized the consequences of their actions, is less important to us.[30] The important point is that systematizers and efficiency experts were able to neutralize political language even when they dealt with wholly political matters.[31] In hindsight, we may wonder about the ease with which engineers could capitalize on politics while yet appearing to be apolitical. The observations of literary critic Irving Howe may provide a hint:

The Americans failed to see political life as an autonomous field of action; they could not focus upon politics long and steadily enough to allow it to develop according to inner rhythms, for it bored or repelled them even as it tempted them . . . One of the most striking facts about American life and literature is the frequency with which political issues seem to arise in non-political forms. Instead of confronting us as formidable systems of thought, or as parties locked in bitter combat, politics in America has often appeared in the guise of religious, cultural and sexual issues, apparently far removed from the contentions of Europe yet difficult to understand except in regard to those contentions . . . Observers of 19th century America, even while reporting the national craze for politics as a 'game' or a means of plunder, also testify to the feeling among educated Americans that neither as public activity nor intellectual pursuit is politics to be regarded as quite legitimate. (Howe 1957: 166, 164)

'Apolitical' politics of the type offered by engineers was therefore appealing both to Americans who believed in the exceptional difference of their country and to Progressives who advocated the business of bureaucratization. There is, however, another interesting point here. Given the ideological stronghold of American Exceptionalism, it is surprising that American scholarship and particularly the social sciences so willingly adopted such apolitical and universal organizational models. American Exceptionalism would offer—in its ideal form—an idiosyncratic model of society, a focus on idiographic methodology sensitive to history and politics. This was not the case, however. The American 'Exception' dictated its own rules. While contrasting itself with the old history, it simultaneously abolished the aegis of history. American Exceptionalism was a flight from history. The American revolution was not a revolution against the ancient regime, as was the case in Europe, but rather an attempt to secure what began in a historical vacuum. To American scholars, 'America seemed already to have reached perfection. The past had been consolidated in a future whose integrity lay in remaining as much like the present as possible' (Hawthorn 1987: 195). This produced a unique sense of time which in essence was ahistorical. Given the perspective that classes did not exist and society was harmonious and rational, the social and political theory that was developed was narrowly defined by the bounds of a 'constructive' liberalism. In Europe, liberalism began as a progressive critical approach, and once established it started to be undermined by socialism. In America, on the other hand, liberalism was established from the very beginning and was never challenged seriously since it was anchored in the very constitution of society (Hawthorn 1987: 195).

Dorothy Ross extends this analysis, explaining that Progressive social scientists who retreated from the logic of Exceptionalism accepted the universal nature of modernity and the progressive evolution of historical forces to which the future of American also subscribed. They found that this progression could be understood and tamed through liberal theories that captured the capitalist market, democracy, and scientific knowledge (Ross 1991: 149). During its formative years (roughly between 1870 and 1929), American economics lost its historicist orientation and emerged modeled after the natural sciences with an emphasis on the positivist methods of inquiry, and the ahistorical direction embedded in the classical ideology of liberalism and individualism. It was a social order based on harmony, not conflict. Ross says:

Progressive era social scientists turned deliberately to the classical liberal tradition to revise their exceptionalist heritage. Liberal theory cast political democracy as the work of sovereign individuals in voluntary association. The scientific enterprise was likewise premised on the rational capacity of individuals. Social scientists returned to these individualist foundations both to set the fundamental character of American society and to provide the basis for a socially harmonious order. (Ross 1991: 153)

In her view, 'the functional interdependence of the market and the increasing opportunities for social mobility' provided for 'the amelioration of conflict'. Engineers and systematizers were both the products and facilitators of that paradigm.

## Notes

1. Goldstein (1978) argues that the balance of power in the beginning of the period was so much on the side of business that on the surface Progressivists seemed to be pro-labor. In fact, only unions that accepted the premises of the new industrial order were recognized.
2. It actually paved the way for many Progressive era and New Deal labor laws (Wunderlin 1992: 69).
3. As Montgomery observed, 'after 1909, strikes and union membership grew rapidly both inside and outside the bounds of legitimacy defined by AFL' (1987: 6). Among the challenging organizations was the IWW (Industrial Workers of the World) which was founded in 1905. For the history of the 'Wobblies' see Dubofsky 1967.
4. The murder of a grocer and his son in Salt Lake City in January 1914. Joe Hill, a labor activist, was arrested, convicted, and executed with no sufficient evidence.

5. A union leader who was arrested after the bombing of a war 'preparedness' parade in San Francisco. The case became a symbol of the capitalist oppression of militant labor.

6. A gun battle that developed in Everett, Washington, in November 1916 in an area where the unions made an attempt to organize.

7. Which Alford attributed to the 'evils' of the 'absentee' directorate of large corporations substituted for ownership control. See Jaffe 1957: 93.

8. Also, in May 1886 the *American Machinist* suggested that the employers should get organized in order to solve the labor problems (see: 'Unions to Prevent Labour Troubles' *American Machinist*, 29 May 1886: 8).

9. This is not to say that there were no exceptions. Even in 1920 Elbert H. Gary, the president of the American Iron and Steel Institute, argued that 'There are no classes in the United States such as have existed in other countries.' That is to say the ideological shift was not necessarily smoothly and neatly packaged. See *American Machinist*, 1 July 1920: 14.

10. Ross argued that disillusionment with Exceptionalism had an important role in shaping American social sciences as they shifted attention from the American peculiarity to the universal course of natural law (Ross 1991). Social scientists accepted the universal nature of modernity, the progressive evolution of historical forces to which the future of American is also subject.

11. However, there were Progressivists (e.g. Dewey, Lippmann, and Croly) who believed that, in certain cases, organizations (i.e. regulatory agencies) might be amenable to economic and technological development. In their mind, government regulation was a logical response to the weak state apparatus during the period of intense industrialization (i.e. 1870–1900).

12. In contrast to engineers and despite significant variation, most Progressive activists (i.e. strong middle-class reformers) agreed that large organizations constituted a social and economic problem for America's future. However, Progressive history in the USA has also received more radical interpretations. Kolko (1963), for example, argued that Progressivism was not the triumph of middle-class defense or of small business over the trusts, but the victory of big business in achieving the rationalization of the economy by establishing political capitalism. Key business leaders realized that they had no interest in a 'chaotic' industry and cooperated with the government to 'tame' this chaos. Regulated capitalism (or 'organized capitalism' as Lash and Urry (1987) have labeled it) was not only directed toward economic losses but also toward political turmoil: violence associated with strikes, the Populist movement, and agrarian discontent.

13. A third generation—the marginalists who were the first to establish academic economics in the 1880s (e.g. Richard Ely, Henry Adams, and Simon Patten)— viewed labor and capital as interchangeable. For that matter all workers were considered identical. This was in line with what is called 'labor homogenization', the process in which the heterogeneous pre-industrial workforce became a single proletariat.

14. Jenks, Commons, and Durand offered historical-institutionalist alternatives to the mainstream neoclassical perspective. They recognized that there were irreversible transformations which the 'old market' had undergone. But they represented at least

two different schools. In Jenks and Durand's organicist view, monopolies emerged naturally and shaped the old market structure. They suggested a limited role for government in the regulation of industrial relations and advocated a strategy of stabilization based on voluntary arrangement between labor and capital (such as voluntary arbitration). For Commons (and, for that matter, for Ely and Adams, too) monopolistic power was derived from political and legal privileges bestowed on corporations by the government. Commons suggested a statist policy to regulate industrial order through the creation of administrative bureaucracies or compulsory arbitration. The consensus by 1901 favored voluntary cooperation, but this consensus collapsed during 1902–4 following the anthracite coal strike. It was realized that labor disputes do not come only from income distribution and level of wages but from efforts to control the workplace and productivity. Open shops and scientific management became benchmarks in the industrial relation system (Wunderlin 1992: 92). See also Howell 1995.

15. Carnegie, whom the editors referred to as 'Andy' (they had been in a honeymoon relationship since Carnegie donated a building as a gift to the engineering societies), 'preserves the youthfulness of his mind', said the editors.

16. 'Co-operative Factories and Monopolies'.

17. Contrary to the argument that I am trying to advance, Jenks did not accept the proposition that writers believed in the link between systems and unrest. He argued that Taylor and Emerson were in a minority 'believing that thorough, scientific application of their principles would eliminate the labor problem' (1961: 437).

18. Nelson corroborated the claim that the earliest incentive wage schemes were products of the growing concern over the 'labor problem' (Nelson 1975: 51).

19. This analysis provides an interesting case in which discursive and non-discursive practices emerged hand in hand with a shared epistemology and identical ideological assumptions.

20. In using this measure, I assume that the new engineers joining ASME over the years were increasingly convinced of the need to emphasize systems thinking. Note that the coefficient for ASME was obtained with a one-year time lag. Similar results for ASME were obtained for the analyses with no time lag (coefficient = .726; SE = .30), and with a two-year time lag (coefficient = .882; SE = .40). No time lags were included for strikes since I assumed that the effect of strikes should register immediately as they occurred.

21. The relationship between strikes and systems had an inverted-U shape. This can be inferred from the fact that the coefficient for strikes is positive and significant and the coefficient for strikes squared is negative and significant. The maximum value of this inverted-U shape is at a level of 2,816 strikes. This was calculated by taking the first partial derivative and setting it equal to zero. It is thus the ratio of the coefficient of strikes to twice the coefficient of strikes squared (16.9/.006). The interpretation of this finding is that more strikes resulted in more items on systems up to a level of 2,816 strikes. Beyond this level, more strikes resulted in fewer items on systems. In 41 years out of the 54-year period between 1879 and 1932, the level of strikes was below 2,816. In these years strikes had a positive effect on the publication of items on systems. Furthermore, the average strike level (1,876 strikes per year) falls within the range of a positive relationship between strikes and systems.

22. Herman (1995) shows that psychology managed to replace sociology as the science of society since it pushed the locus of control onto individual actors, and the 'improvement' of society as a whole was made dependent on individual self-improvement and therapy programs; for the contribution of economics see Locke 1984.

23. On one occasion the *Engineering Magazine* reported that women could be admitted to the courses in employment management given at the University of Rochester and Harvard University. The *Magazine*'s opinion was that 'Without doubt in some of the aspects of labour maintenance women can and will excel' ('Women as Employment Managers', *Engineering Magazine*, July 1918: 66).

24. A similar observation was made by Noble 1977: 263. Also, the interplay between the language of systems and industrial psychology is discussed thoroughly by Barley and Kunda 1992.

25. See also an article by Southard in the April 1920 issue of *Industrial Management*: 'Trade Unionism and Temperament', 265–70.

26. Assuming that the mid-1890s was a turning point in the shift between 'labor unrest' and 'organizational system'. Indeed, several people commented that 1895–1904 was an innovative decade on management-related ideas (e.g. Jenks 1961).

27. Shalev further argues that in American social science 'industrial relations were viewed as a distinguishable subsystem of society relatively detached from the political economy at large' (1992: 4).

28. Both Frederick Taylor (see for example Haber 1964) and Elton Mayo (see for example Trahair 1984) capitalized on the 'labor problem' to promote their industrial philosophies.

29. It is rather intriguing that Nelson himself cites Hoxie's report (the US Commission on Industrial Relations) from 1916, which argued that the Taylorists 'tend to look at the labor end of their work as a simple technical matter' (Nelson 1974: 487).

30. As far as I am concerned, I believe in the relative autonomy of professional experts who aim to make their craft 'more educated', 'necessary', 'demanded', an essential part of the social fabric.

31. This debate with Nelson leaves me, however, with one basic agreement with him. For all practical purposes, Scientific Management was a direct continuation of systematic management.

# 7

# Deus ex Machina: Concluding Remarks

If one wants to pass through open doors easily, one must bear in mind that they have a solid frame: this principle, according to which the old professor had always lived, is simply a requirement of the sense of reality. But if there is such a thing as a sense of reality—and no one will doubt that it has its raison d'etre—then there must also be something that one can call a sense of possibility . . . So the sense of possibility might be defined outright as the capacity to think how everything could 'just as easily' be, and to attach no more importance to what is than to what is not.

(Musil 1953/1979: 12).

What is management? In this book I offer a historical approach to that question, viewing management as ideology and practice. In order to uncover the roots of management, I went back to the period between the Civil War and the Great Depression—exhuming the conflictive and controversial process by which management became an established or institutionalized activity in the United States. Today, American industrialization and its ideology celebrate corporate capitalism and glorify the contribution of professional management to the further advancement of capitalism. The rise of professional management became a progressive symbol of the American industrial way. This ideal, and linear view of management is the product of historical reification; challenging management has required a return to its origins, to the 'scene of the crime', as it were. One could find early assertions of discontent with the rise of management in the writings of Adam Smith, the founding father of modern economics. With the advent of managerial capitalism, however, Smith's admonitions (and similar ones made by his contemporaries) have been forgotten, as has the early conflictive history of American management. Such conflicts and discontents have been largely papered over by the optimistic and progressive historical narrative of modern management and its theoretical handmaiden, organizational and management theories.

My attempt to uncover the roots of management unfolded along three dimensions. First, I documented how the roots of modern American management theory and practice lie in mechanical engineering. The basic contours of managerial ideology emerged from the discourse of mechanical engineering, a discourse that asserted for the first time that management can be turned into a science; that unions are not necessary but should not be eradicated because they can be domesticated by scientific methods; that conflict can be managed; and that efficiency and system are the cure to all industrial and social problems. In formulating such an ideology, the engineers made an argument as to who were the new 'authorized actors' to become managers (Foucault 1979).

Second, I have demonstrated the process by which the engineering approach to management became institutionalized over a period of some five decades, emerging through at least two qualitatively different phases, and was frequently shaped by protracted conflicts between employers and engineers/managers, managers and workers, and among engineers themselves. I provided empirical data about this formative period in the history of American management, connecting it to the shift from Exceptionalist ideology to Progressivism, and accounting for the form by which that change shaped the nature of American management practice. And third, I re-examined the epistemological nexus between the canon of management and organization theories and the early discourse of systematization. This examination showed how the accepted wisdom of business schools employs 'theoretical' concepts whose epistemology hinges on the managerial world-view. It appropriated the engineering discourse while covering its historical sources and complexity under a linear narrative that unfolds from 'closed' to 'open' systems. In conclusion, I summarize the assertions in these three areas, and provide a reflexive analysis of the relationship between sociology and management theory. Toward the end of the chapter I argue that this ideology, which was adopted in the United States, was not the only version of management logic even within the framework of rationality, and was not adopted in the same way everywhere (see Dobbin 1994, and Roy 1997, for similar arguments regarding the social construction of economic policies and organizational realities).

### 7.1 The ideological roots

In the first part of the book I argued that the (legal and financial) 'managerial revolution' had been anticipated by an ideological phase that shaped the actual rise of management. Between the 1870s and 1920s the concept of management was conceived, matured, and developed in American industry. This part of the book portrayed the nuts and bolts of the ideological project of defining, legitimizing, and contesting the managerial discourse through a genealogy of groups of engineers, their social institutions, professional media, and emerging rhetoric.

Ideology was defined as a system of meanings which is manufactured or mobilized in the course of social action. The ideological work of engineers was codified as a project of standardization and systematization by means of analogy, translation, and differentiation. This project blurred the distinction between the social and the technical. Once the boundary was collapsed, the road was open to expand the province of mechanical engineering to additional terrains. Simultaneously, engineers created a boundary differentiating the 'manager' from the 'capitalist' and the 'worker'. In their framework describing management, managers were portrayed not as expressing greed, capriciousness, and unpredictability, but social responsibility, steadiness, rationality, planning, and standardization. These assumptions established the managerial function as a recognized domain in the operation of business.

## 7.2 The conflictive biography of management

My second argument centered on the political context within which management developed in the USA. Chapters 5 and 6 showed how the new ideology proposed by engineers was shaped by the supportive political contexts of American Exceptionalism and, later, Progressivism and the political economy of the First World War. The political context in which the managerial discourse first emerged, roughly during 1870–1900, was a violent and bloody period in US industrial relations, when labor (occupational groups and craft unions) and capital (manufacturers and owners) were engaged in a total war. The managerial discourse pervaded this conflict, eventually helping to moderate it to the auspices of a totally rational language of organizational analysis. Given the initial opposition of many employers to the rise of management, 'labor unrest' was arguably used as leverage to gain legitimacy for systematization. The ideology of systems was understood in the Progressive era as a technique which could be applied scientifically for the good of 'society as a whole'; in this, systems would serve as a 'neutral' and 'efficient' administrative apparatus. Managerial discourse was further defined through conflicts with both workers and capitalists, until it finally emerged as a solution to the problem of 'labor unrest'. It is here that I fully highlight the social and political ramifications of the engineers' efforts to mechanize and systematize organizations. These efforts represented and reproduced the ideological assumption that human and non-human entities are interchangeable and can be equally subjected to engineering manipulation. The natural, objective, 'apolitical' image of management obscured its direct political application. The mechanical systematization of organizational life made it possible, even desirable, for engineers to repress the individuality of workers, curtail democracy, and monotonize behavior.

A central theme in this book has been the conflict between manufacturers and engineers over the management of firms. I argued that the literature on management has failed to make this distinction. Neo-Marxist writers—such as Braverman (1974), Edwards (1979), and Marglin (1974)—have not distinguished between the interests of capitalists and those of managers. For these writers, managers were a capitalist organ with no independent agenda. Even those who made the distinction (e.g. Bendix 1956/1974) failed to demonstrate that their interests were at times antagonistic. This was the case not only in the

United States but also in other countries.[1] The literature on professions carries a different premise, however. Writers such as Abbott (1988) and Larson (1977) provide autonomous roles for professionals but fail to apply this to engineers or managers. Krause (1996), on the other hand, represents a stream of literature that argues that engineering was a category of work and not an occupation acting in its own interest (Larson 1977: 190–207; Krause 1996: 60–7). Krause emphasized that engineers were basically 'employee categories rather than potent political entities'. He further observed a 'complete triumph of the corporate engineers and their particular brand of professionalism' (Krause 1996: 63).

I argue against this position in two ways. First, I claim that engineering was a potent profession acting in its own interest. Mechanical Engineering ideology provided a golden opportunity for American and European engineers to advance their professional prestige in the industrial era (Rabinbach 1990: 241). Second, what seems now a common interest between capitalists and engineers/managers is a socially constructed ideology developed by engineers as part of their struggle for professional jurisdiction. Engineering did not automatically accept the premises of capitalists; management emerged in conflict with traditional capitalism and its economic logic was at odds with the logic of capitalists. The identification between the two groups and their ideologies is now taken for granted, and therefore warranted a genealogical analysis to unearth the origin of the relationship.

My objective in this book was therefore to challenge the simplistic view according to which the systematization of organizations between 1880 and 1920 was the product of employers' efforts either to rationalize production (e.g. Chandler 1962, 1977) or to control labor (Marglin 1974; Stone 1974; Edwards 1979). I demonstrated that the practice and discourse of organizational systems was often promoted against the interest of industrial employers. The conflictual nature of the introduction of organization systems into industry was also apparent in the bitter disagreements that took place within engineering circles. The empirical materials upon which this study is based offer a non-evolutionary history of rationalization and rationality. Obviously, this argument does not resonate with naive scientific realism arguing that the appearance of managerial capitalism was economic and not political in nature.

## 7.3 The canonization of management and organizational principles: 'system', 'rationality', and 'uncertainty'

My third argument returns to the managerial ideology charted in the outset, treating it as a canonized body of knowledge which has become a self-sustaining structure with self-propagating logic. I treat the origins of the management discipline as 'a self-constituted class of experts who, through their talk, can establish truth or falsehood' (Burrell 1988: 223). I suggest that much of management and organization theory is epistemologically and theoretically infused with the ideological parameters that were born during the efforts to establish the legitimization of management. Emerging from the rhetoric and practice of mechanical engineering, these efforts gradually turned into an intellectual project with the deliberate aim of establishing a scientific body of knowledge about organizations. It was the birth of a new language, the creation of objects of knowledge, the generation of images through which reality is filtered. There would have been no room for the twentieth-century managerial revolution without the widespread readiness to accept the spirit of these arguments.

The concepts of mechanical engineering, and later of management, were canonized in a language game called 'Organization Theory'. Made up of sociologists, political scientists, psychologists, management specialists, and economists, it was (and is) known by additional labels such as 'organization studies', 'organization science', or 'organizational sociology'. Sociology is a core member in this interdisciplinary enterprise. Despite their extensive efforts to comprehend organizations, organization theorists pay little attention to the epistemological and ideological overtone of the (ostensibly neutral) analytic concepts they employ, particularly 'rationality' and 'uncertainty'. The mechanical instrumental tenets of managerial rationality—the deus ex machina—are so pervasive that intersecting, impacting spheres such as political reforms, labor politics, and state action have become absorbed by the sovereignty of rationality's logic, content, and syntax.

Mary Douglas's (1992) criticism of Chester Barnard, a distinguished organization theorist, highlights this language game:

His classifications came from the world in which the organizations themselves function. This is using what anthropologists call actor's categories. In other words, he started with and stayed with the agents' own functioning classifications. These classifications impede theorising: The anthropologist ends up saying what the agent under study had been saying all along.

Douglas's critique points to an epistemological circularity which metaphorically can be described as a dog chasing its own tail.[2] Indeed, early rhetorical formulations created to justify the role of management are now presented in academic textbooks as building bricks of the theory of organizations (see, for example, March and Simon 1958; March and Olsen 1976; Scott 1987/1992). This is not surprising, given the fact that both the 'practice' and 'theory' of management can be traced back to the same origin: the systematization project during the period 1880s–1930s. The systematizers—the first to formulate maxims about organizations—were engaged in both describing and prescribing organizations with very little discrimination between these activities.

Most organizational theorists have argued that the literature on organizations started with a 'closed system' approach (focusing on internal administrative affairs of organizations), and was later replaced with an 'open system' perspective that took into consideration the broader environment (Scott 1987/1992).

Organization Theory (OT)—now widely accepted—starts with Scientific Management and describes it, together with the writing of Henry Fayol and Max Weber, as being concerned with organizations as closed systems. According to this narrative, it was only with the 'open systems perspective', introduced in the 1950s and the 1960s, that the broader environment entered in as a source of uncertainty. This transformation from 'closed systems' in the early 1900s to 'open systems' in mid-century provides OT with a clear-cut evolutionary account of theorizing and treating organizations. I argue, in contrast, that this narrative is the outcome of ideological boundary work of engineers in the early twentieth century. Engineers did not have the concepts of 'closed' and 'open' systems, but they talked about systems as though the entire management of organizations was an internal affair. Their theorizing thus created a rhetorical frame of mind that OT later appropriated.

What the linear narrative of OT does not take into account is that, prior to the rise of systems discourse, those concerned with business focused on issues such as tariffs, labor unions, labor markets, industrial unrest, and the relationship between business firms and the government. The main topics discussed were those of wages, cost of raw materials, and economic legislation. All these would be considered by contemporary OT standards as an 'open systems' approach to organizations. Yet it was edited out of the authorized, mainstream historiography. In actual terms, the task of the first systematizers was to define management as a separate domain by reorienting business thinking from open, political–economic, and macro-social domains into closed, internal, administrative affairs. This was what 'systematization' was all about. The perception of the firm as a unified whole that should be internally monitored, with efficiency and system as the main concerns, was a major invention of the engineers who worked to turn management into an autonomous endeavor. This actual shift from an 'open' system to a 'closed' system in the managerial discourse is contradictory to the evolution described in the canonical OT. The managerial discourse was actually open before it became closed by engineers.

Claiming that systematization strove to 'close down' the organization in the form of a system is in itself a rhetorical trope that should be clarified. To state without restriction that, before systematization, organizations were 'open' is to buy into the early engineering discourse that 'Systems . . . Shall replace Chaos' (Calvert 1967: 171). To be sure, the craft unions, subcontractors, and foremen of the pre-1870 period (the 'market', in OT parlance) all had their means of surveillance and routinization. When the engineers positioned their 'systems' as opposed to 'chaos'—rationality versus uncertainty—they did this in a particular ideological and sociological climate. Systematization claimed to take the industry beyond the "anarchy" that characterized the robber baron era on the one hand and labor unrest on the other. In the course of the nineteenth century, business ideology was legitimized by Social Darwinist philosophies, the Puritan ethic of hard work, and welfare capitalism. (See, for example, Henderson 1986, for a sociologist's point of view. See also Ross 1991, for a discussion on Sumner's ideology of capitalism.) At the turn of the century there was a growing desire, among social scientists as among professionals, to see the industry operated according to rational conduct, replacing religious and moral directives (for thorough discussions on this argument see Bendix 1956/1974; Guillen 1994). This was partly a reaction to the enormous and corrupt power of the large monopolies, partly a departure from the ideology of American Exceptionalism and the search for more universal models of business, partly a fascination with the undisputed success of American technology, and partly an outcome of the professional spirit of the Progressive era. All these forces placed mechanical engineering and its ideological claims at the epicentre of the new managerial ideology. OT later bought into this ideology and reproduced it by placing it in a linear narrative of transformation from 'closed' to 'open' systems and from 'markets' to 'hierarchies'. While rejecting that narrative, I agree with OT on one point: early systematization indeed strove to perfect a 'closed system', which should be read as an ever-growing regime of surveillance. Its scholarly program was to legitimize and authorize that 'closed system' approach by extending it to the social and the political realms. The engineering rhetoric was no less than a form of colonizing of the mind—the minds of employers and workers as well as of politicians, social scientists, and policy-makers. This book explored how this 'colonizing of the mind' was realized.

What were the key features that characterize the canonization of organization theory as a field of practice and discourse? I focus on three key characteristics: (*a*) the instrumental definition of rationality; (*b*) its symbiosis with 'systematic' and 'Scientific' management as well as its continuity and consistency with subsequent versions of administrative management; and (*c*) sociologist's tendency to assume their task to be social design.

Rationality, though a multifaceted concept implying values and maxims of thought, was reduced in organizational literature to its instrumental-technical dimension. Instrumental rationality is defined as complete knowledge of the consequences of choices that are predetermined by structural constraints (Simon 1957). In other words, rationality can be secured by structures that reduce uncertainty and ambiguity (see March and Simon 1958; Thompson 1967; Galbraith 1973; Pfeffer and Salancik 1978). In this view, human action is a subset of 'instrumental rationality' alone, as it is subordinated to unspecified and transient 'external' objectives. According to this definition, instrumental action is rooted in desired outcomes and in beliefs about cause and effect relationships (Thompson 1967: 14). The relevance of the instrumental version of rationality to the functioning of organizations is not disputed in organization theory. After all, there is no efficiency, effectiveness, order, and profits without planning, or in the absence of the process connecting means with ends.[3]

The legitimacy of instrumental rationality was reinforced by contrasting it with the threat associated with uncertainty. Organizations were conceptualized as instruments of uncertainty reduction in their ability to secure stability, predictability, and precision. According to this view, the prevalence of uncertainty creates irregularities and complications in planning, standardization, precision, consistency, and causal linkage between means and ends.[4] The concept of uncertainty assumed almost mythical and magical characteristics for organization theorists. For an organizational narrative constructed around the notion of rationality, uncertainty represented darkness and undesirability. It became a Pandora's box of threats: opportunism, labor unrest, short-sightedness, competition, and other enemies of the organizational order. The engineer, the manager, and the planner were set to the task of slaying the dragon of uncertainty. Their authority derived from their ability to cope with and reduce uncertainty.[5] 'Uncertainty' and 'uncertainty reduction' are used to legitimize the use of an instrumental definition of rationality. The root metaphor of uncertainty spawned a variety of strategies and frameworks to fight, reduce, or adapt to uncertainty. The most prominent are known as 'buffering' and 'bridging' strategies within the 'resource dependence' perspective (Pfeffer and Salancik 1978), and 'information processing' or 'information reduction' strategies within the structural contingency perspective (Galbraith 1973).

In a pattern of unquestioned historical continuity, organization theory adopted the language of early management engineers. The seeds for the 'uncertainty-reduction' and 'bounded-rationality' theory were sown in the nineteenth-century ideological view of management. For example, the editors of the *American Machinist* maintained that it was the role of engineers to 'serve humanity in the elimination of chance . . . [as] there are innumerable uncertainties to be cleared up' (*American Machinist*, 5 March 1914: 434). They conceptualized the business enterprise as a unified whole that needed to be controlled and coordinated in a systematic, rational fashion, in light of 'the chaotic state of factory practices' (Litterer 1963, 1986). They argued that systematization of organizations implied an attempt to transcend dependence upon the capacity of any single individual; its purpose was instead to build a solution into the formal system to achieve 'greater predictability in coordination' and 'forecasting'.

The rationale for systematization was made explicit in connection with the limitations of individual actors. In numerous articles, the system was portrayed as superior to individuals in handling uncertainty. Harrington Emerson, for example, suggested that 'the object of [organizational] records is to increase the scope and number of warnings, to give us more information than is usually received immediately through our senses' (*Engineering Magazine*, January 1911: 496–506). Systematizer Horace Arnold argued, 'If all men had absolutely infallible memories, and were incapable of making any statement at variance with those memories, it would be possible, perhaps, to carry on a successful and prosperous manufacturing business without the use of shop books or factory accounts.'[6] A related bounded-rationality argument can be found in the formulations of Alexander Hamilton Church. In Church's view, the justification for systematization in the newly developed factories of the late nineteenth century rested upon the limitation of the human mind faced with exploding complexity. He argued, 'The necessity for coordination is an inevitable result of the evolution of the factory, no one mind can grasp and hold all the details' (*Engineering Magazine*, June 1900: 392; cited in Jelinek 1980: 72). Hence,

It is hardly too much to say that the evolution of a science of management was inevitable as soon as the scale of industrial operations became so great that no single manager, however naturally gifted, could continue to control personally all the activities of the plant. (*Engineering Magazine*, April 1911: 97–102)

Canonical organization theory adopted and disseminated the rhetoric, logic, and epistemology that was produced by the agents under its study (see Chapter 3). Despite the ideological overtones embedded in 'uncertainty' and 'bounded rationality', these concepts were taken in organizational theory as neutral and universal, without reference to the specific cultural and historical conditions of their origin (e.g. Pfeffer and Salancik 1978; Williamson 1985). Furthermore, the theory of uncertainty and rationality became self-sufficient and circular. Uncertainty and rationality stand in a dialectical relation such that their opposition synthesizes one coherent scheme, while still maintaining the reproduction of the original binary pattern. Uncertainty and rationality validate each other's plausibility, constituting a single 'ideology-free' theoretical framework. Given this seductive framework, the 'uncertainty-reduction' argument and the definition of rationality as instrumental action became central elements in the professional ideology of management, and it served as one of the focal points in management education programs. These examples evidence no distance between the epistemology of sociologists (and other social science theorists) and the epistemology of the actors under study. Organizations encapsulating the ideology of instrumental rationality became the ultimate entities in the 'end of ideology' and 'end of history'.

Since organizational sociology serves here as an ally of managerial thought, I would like to go back to Lukács's suggestion to incorporate sociology itself in our—reflexive—analysis.

### 7.4 Sociology as an ally of management

The view of sociology as a science of social design—with an epistemology which is based on instrumental rationality—dates back to Auguste Comte. In Comte's philosophy, the chief dynamic force in history is the advancement of knowledge; scientific rationality, the most advanced form of knowledge, is thus the key to future progress. Comte's positivist project was based on the competency of experts who provide administrative, economic, and social planning. Any knowledge that would not follow the systematization and the generalization of the natural sciences must be excluded. After all, science is socially defined as a set of objective rules that appear to exist outside any particular social system. Such objective rules appear to be unaffected by power or resource allocations among the group of people that make up that society (Gouldner 1976: 40).

Comte's vision was incorporated into American academia as early as the 1890s by the first president of the ASA, Lester Ward. The second volume of Ward's *Dynamic Sociology* was devoted to the study of 'sociocracy' (analogous to 'technocracy'), the application of social laws to produce order and progress. Sociocracy was to replace politics as the mechanism of governing society (Ross 1991). In the late 1890s, Edward Ross published several articles in the *American Journal of Sociology*, in which he developed the idea of sociology as a mechanism of 'social control'. To maintain itself, society had to modify individual ideas, feelings, and behavior to conform, and to subordinate private interests, to the social interests. Consequently, William Graham Sumner, then the first vice-president of the ASA, stated in his 1906 book *Folkways* that sociology 'could lead up to an art of societal administration which should be intelligent, effective, and scientific' (quoted in Ross 1991: 221). Despite his controversial evolutionism, this statement placed Sumner within the sociological consensus of the time. It was a vision of science that promised prediction and control, tools that gave a technocratic spin to their conception of social roles and positions. Sociology as a form of social praxis sought to establish rational control over society and history.

The role of sociologists as agents of social control spilled over to industrial practice as well. In 1914, when Henry Ford faced grave organizational problems, he founded a Sociological Department that employed 250 people. Aiming to correct a daily absentee rate that exceeded 10 percent; a 370 percent yearly turnover rate, requiring nearly $2 million a year to train new workers; and negotiations with one of the most militant unions in the country (Marcus and Segal 1989), Ford designed a new program for loyalty and conformity. He decided to pay $5 a day to every 'qualified' employee. The Ford Sociological Department assumed the role of determining who was qualified to receive this bonus. These 'sociologists' visited homes and interviewed neighbors and priests to determine who conformed with the code of conduct stressing family and community values, thrift, and personal character. They used strict criteria for unsuitability: single young men, men who were engaged in divorce, those who did not spend evenings 'wisely', those who used alcohol, or those who did not speak English. They also gave lessons in home management to workers, taught them how to shop and how to preserve moral values (Marcus and Segal 1989: 236–8). The role of these experts in controlling the population of workers was a clear sociological experiment in social design. The department served as an agent in the moral bureaucracy of the Ford Motor Company. The legacy of Ford's sociologists reverses James Thompson's definition of organization science as the applied arm of sociology (see Thompson's definition in the inaugural issue of the *Administrative Science Quarterly*, 1956: 103). Rather, sociology is to be seen as the applied arm of organization science. This approach was severely criticized by American sociologists Alvin Gouldner in his *The Coming Crisis of Western*

*Sociology* and C. Wright Mills in his *White Collar,* as the latter said: 'intellectuals caught up in and overwhelmed by the managerial demiurge in a bureaucratic world of organized irresponsibility' (Mills 1951: 160; cited in Herman 1995).

In order to maintain the view of sociology as a science of social design (see Coleman 1993 for a contemporary example) historical contingencies need to have no role. The past needs to be forgotten, the future is an indefinite quantitative and qualitative multiplication, or some other formula, of the present. History is eventually tamed and incorporated into the analytic schemes of the sociologist. Since rationality is the last stage of evolution, idiographic analyses can be comfortably put to rest and become nomological knowledge, to use Weber's terminology. Jacoby explains the process by which forms of discourse lose their history and come to appear as if they have existed without a historical subject. He calls this process 'social amnesia':

It is social amnesia,—memory driven out of mind by the social and economic dynamic of this society . . . The social illusion works to preserve the status quo by presenting the human and social relationships of society as natural—and unchangeable—relations between things. The social loss of memory is a type of reification—better: It is the primal form of reification. All reification is forgetting. (Jacoby 1975: 4)

The argument against the naive scientific realism of organization theorists can be further substantiated by examining the relative nature of management practice and its cultural roots. In fact, management took different directions in various countries, an intriguing observation to which I now turn (in the following I refer to the Western experience. For management practices in the communist world see Bendix 1956/1974; Merkle 1980; Peteri 1984).

### 7.5 The cultural idiosyncrasy of the American case

Throughout the book I have emphasized the singularity of the American version in the development of an engineering ideology of management. Management, however, has also developed in and spread to other countries, and is currently enjoying an international career competing with national specificities (for cultural specificity arguments see Hickson 1993; Dobbin 1994). The international development of management, while relative and diverse, has unfolded along a converging path that produced isomorphism in both ideologies and actors (see Djelic 1998, for the forces behind the diffusion of the American model to European countries).

How did management become such a successful and dominant profession particularly in America? First, the engineering community in the United States, which emerged out of a 'shop culture', was the only one to develop a coherent voice of industrial management. At the turn of the century, the United States had the largest number of engineers per capita. Germany and France lagged behind, and their figures were three times as large as the British. The engineering ideology of rationality in US industry made a sharp transition from religious or national justifications to scientific justification for managerial ideas, a transition that differed from what occurred in Germany or Spain. Second, the United States experienced the largest increase in average firm size during the late nineteenth and early twentieth centuries. Consequently, it had the largest proportion of administrative workers per industrial employment worldwide. In 1900, manufacturing firms employed 8 administrative workers for each 100 production workers, a figure that rose to 18 in 1929. This ratio remained higher in the United States than in any other major capitalist country until 1950 (Guillen 1994: 36). Consequently, the United States experienced the strongest separation of ownership from control in industrial firms and the development of complex corporate structure. In the mid-nineteenth century, roughly half of the business elite in the United States were entrepreneurs. By the early twentieth century only 20 percent were in this category. That is, the justification of authority by reference to entrepreneurial success declined dramatically (Guillen 1994: 36, based on Bendix 1956/1974 and Fligstein 1990). Fourth, the United States experienced one of the most violent labor struggles compared with continental European countries. With the 'apolitical' spirit of Progressivism—very different from the political culture in Britain, France, and Germany—industrial violence could be 'solved' with the application of engineering techniques. Fifth, the United States government assumed a relatively passive role in regulating industrial practices. That is, the political ideology in the United States at the time characterized state intervention as undesired (see Dobbin 1994).[7] The engineering project of standardization and systematization was consistent with this conventional wisdom of the time. Employers who understood that price fixing and cartelization were unavailable—at least on the face of it—could more easily adopt standardization techniques than in other places (Kolko 1963).

This was not the case in other countries such as Britain, France, and Germany (see Bendix 1956/1974; Locke 1984; McCraw 1984; Gispen 1989; Hamilton and Sutton 1989; Dobbin 1994; Guillen 1994). As historian Charles Maier has argued, managerial capitalism was 'peculiarly American . . . Europeans remained more reserved: in Britain businessmen did not possess cultural hegemony . . . in France the state still claimed a major share of technocratic leadership, even in West Germany, where the American model might be received most congenially, the existence of a Social Democratic Party provided some counterweight' (Maier 1987: 67. Quoted in Locke 1996: 10. See also Maier 1970). Throughout the nineteenth century German engineers neglected management and organization ideas. They were infatuated with design for its own sake and abandoned issues such as cost, reliability, standardization, and systematization. As Gispen described Hermann Gruson, one of the most famous German mechanical engineers: 'an excellent designer, for whom . . . cost factors did not seem to play a role. Gruson tried to redesign from scratch every new locomotive that was ordered. Even true and tried designs were put aside' (Gispen 1989: 122).

Historical documents attest to a strong hostility that German managers and entrepreneurs felt for the general orientation of German engineering. Compared with American magazines *American Machinist* and *Engineering Magazine* (or the British *Engineering*), their German compatriots such as *Zeitschrift* were heavily weighted toward theoretical discussions and 'professional boasting', as one observer said (ibid.: 126). Gispen further suggests that the VDI, the German engineering society, and its leadership, were able 'to mute extreme versions of the managerial vision' (ibid.: 130). It was only at the turn of the century that German engineers shifted attention to the United States, and only in the late-1910s and throughout the 1920s were American engineering techniques imported to Germany. Guillen argues that, in contrast to the passive role of the US government, the German government—not an independent professional community—was instrumental in industrial rationalization through the National Board of Efficiency (RKW) and the German Normalization Committee (Guillen 1994). The German government provided a role model for industry to imitate and allocated resources to facilitate the adoption of organizational practices. The introduction of managerial ideas was initially based on models borrowed from the German army and state administration. Indeed, there was a widespread growth of offices including paperwork and card index systems and growth of organizational specialists (Lash and Urry 1987). But as Guillen emphasizes, the bureaucratization of the state and the army in Germany preceded that of industry, in sharp contrast to the American and the British experience. This fact is registered in the writing of management intellectuals in Germany (Guillen 1994: 93. See also Veblen 1915/1939). During the First World War, with the support of the government, German management theorists formulated the concept of *Rationalisierung* (rationalization), which included Scientific Management, Fordism, and state regulation (Guillen 1994: 100). Unlike in the United States, the German government was the provider of resources to facilitate and promote industrial rationalization. It offered industrialists the chance 'to maintain the national lead in competition with England and eventually to overtake the productive pre-eminence of America' (Rabinbach 1990: 240). But the German conversion to industrial systematization and engineering rationality was slow and adaptation to the American system was limited and partial in nature (Gispen 1989; Nolan 1994).

As argued above, in the United States the rationality of management was legitimized by the rhetoric of science. The truthfulness of 'modern management techniques' was determined by 'solid scientific experiments' conducted by trained engineers. The debate of scientific management centered around the reliability and validity of these experiments and their resemblance to other scientific fields. This was a science-based agenda in the engineering community lacking in Britain. Similar to American engineers, and unlike the German engineers, British engineers were trained on the job (McKinlay and Zeitlin 1989). Most of them came from the ranks of craftsmen and shop foremen (Locke 1984). However,

Britain lacked the 'enabling context' which made the nexus between engineering and management possible. Britain lacked an ideology of meritocracy and classless society that enabled the rise of a 'new class'; lacked the ideology of the American system; and lacked a political culture which would facilitate engineering-based management. Employers had no enthusiasm for engineering-based management techniques and the managerial community remained insulated and had very little effect on industrial practices (Anthony 1986). As Locke describes, at the turn of the century, American firms tried to capitalize on cheap labor and build factories in Europe. They took the machines but left the spirit behind. The result was unprofitable operations. It was estimated that American machine tools produced 10–30 percent less in European countries (Locke 1984: 90). Furthermore, British engineering periodicals showed a lack of curiosity, before the First World War, about the new management techniques perfected across the Atlantic. Of the three leading engineering journals (*Engineer*, *Engineering*, *Mechanical World*) only the *Engineer* had made reference to Taylor's first paper and his inventions. The editors were clear that 'too much science . . . is likely to lead to a decrease in efficiency rather than an increase' (25 April 1913: 413. Cited in Lash and Urry 1987: 179). Even as late as 1917, British engineers were still speaking of 'a man called Taylor . . . ' (Locke 1984: 99). A survey conducted in 1917 found that out of the 201 factories that introduced Taylorist schemes only four were in England (cited in Lash and Urry 1987). In the late 1920s, when the rationalization movement sprang up in Germany, engineering magazines in England did not publish a single article on the subject. Lacking supporting ideology, the management and engineering community in England rejected Scientific Management as inhuman and inadequate for the local conditions. The rejection of engineering management techniques in England was based on ideological and political grounds, not scientific ones (for the rejection of the American model in England see Lash and Urry 1987).

Dobbin has further argued that the French government took an active role in organizing national monopolies and in nationalizing the railroad industry while in the USA the ICC (Interstate Commerce Commission) was paralyzed for years. Dobbin suggested that distinct polities and institutional resources account for the different patterns of state involvement in industry. Until the First World War Taylorism in France remained limited to a few large firms in the automobile industry.[8] Until then French intellectuals defined the systems, introduced by Henry Le Chatelier and Henry Fayol, in extreme negative characterizations such as 'ferocious', 'barbaric', 'hopelessly regressive', and 'grotesquely childish' (Rabinbach 1990: 241, 242). They were concerned with systems' disregard for workers' well-being and defined Taylorism as a sort of 'scientific fetishism' (ibid.: 250). The gap in the implementation of such techniques, and management education, in France was evident in the 1940s. Americans visiting France following the Marshall plan were surprised not to find any French 'business administration' training (Boltanski 1990: 347, 1987).

In Sweden the introduction of engineering management was rather slow. From the beginning of the twentieth century there were efforts to encourage the rationalization of industry and to develop a 'forceful Swedish industrial policy'. Furthermore, the Swedish Industries Association pleaded in 1910 that the notion of *laissez-faire* should be replaced with a more responsible social order. However, there was little development of corporate structure, and multidivisional organizational forms did not appear there until after the Second World War. There was some enthusiasm regarding Taylorism, certainly more than in Britain, but the introduction of these methods started only in the 1920s. The main reason for this slow development, despite the favorable climate, was the slow development of autonomous technocrats and service classes. The growth of this 'new class' occurred only after the Second World War.

Japan provides perhaps the best example of both the relativity and isomorphism of management (see Locke 1996; Raz 1999). Originally, Taylorism had entered and influenced Japanese industry through the 'efficiency movement' of the 1920s, Depression-era 'industrial rationalization', the post-war drive for 'productivity', and later, Total Quality Management (Warner 1994; Tsutsui 1995). 'Japanese management', however, is better known for its arguably unique cultural blend of a seniority system, lifetime employment, and company unionism. This system appears to be essentially unlike early American management and is more easily associated with industrial relations. Management in Japan has been less of an independent project carried by mechanical engineers, and more of an aid to capitalists, with a strong and steady involvement of the state in the market. Notwithstanding, the 'art of Japanese management' developed—in a manner similar to its American counterpart—systems of work performance, authority, workflow, and payment as techniques for controlling labor (see Kelly 1982; Spender 1989, 1991). These techniques were implemented by Japanese employers who set up, in the inter-war period and following an upsurge of strikes, organizational cultures that involved high levels of worker commitment. Industrial stability was thus secured through 'seducing' workers with the 'enterprise as community' structure that included the seniority system, lifetime employment, and company unionism (see also Gordon 1985; Kinzley 1991; Kawanishi 1992).

The importation of management within modernization projects of nation-building can be illustrated in the cases of newly industrializing countries such as Israel and Spain. In pre-state Israel, management techniques did not emerge out of industrial engineering—as was the case in the United States—but from the broader ideological context within which industry was embedded (see Frenkel, Shenhav, and Herzog 1997). Even though industrialists were aware of Taylorism in the 1910s, it was not imported prior to the 1940s (see Frenkel 1992; Kalev 1998). However, Scientific Management could not be adopted openly since its premises contradicted the socialist collective nature of the Zionist rhetoric. To the extent that these practices were introduced they had to be synchronized with the narrative of nation-building, and to fit with its symbols, institutions, and practices.

Similarly in Spain, Suanzes, one of the supporters of Scientific Management, was an extreme nationalist who advanced Taylorism as an instrument for developing national economic forces (Guillen 1994). Spanish industrialists were exposed to Taylorism only in the 1910s and Guillen argues that 'had it not been for labor unrest, scientific management would have passed unnoticed before 1939' (ibid.: 152). Thus, it can be safely summarized that the effect of engineering techniques on the emergence of management in industry is mainly an American phenomenon that was later diffused—with the help of local engineering communities—to other European countries.

The singularity of the American case is therefore a combination of factors: the weak regulations of government over capitalism, the relative strength of the engineering-based 'managerial rationality', the magnitude of the labor struggle, the enormous economic and industrial growth, and the significant transition from nineteenth-century political culture to the spirit of Progressivism. It was the combination of these factors that constituted the uniqueness of the American case, of which the doctrine of American Exceptionalism was part and parcel. Paradoxically the outcome of this uniqueness was the birth of a worldwide, engineering-based project of industrial management.

## Notes

1. For example, Tomlinson argued that British employers were resistant to engineering bodies that had roles in initiating standards or enforcing them (1994: 177).
2. Known in modern philosophy as 'representing and intervening' (Hacking 1983/1992).
3. I invoke here Weber (1921/1968; 1949), when he said that instrumental rationality should be considered against its non-instrumental consequences and *vis-à-vis* its political and ideological context. Choosing one side of Weber's dualistic epistemological equation, as organization theorists have done, elevates instrumental rationality to a supreme position that gainsays attempts at critical assessment. This is exactly why Weber decided to keep the epistemological contradictions of 'instrumental' and 'substantial' rationality alive.
4. James Thompson paradigmatically links 'rationality' and 'uncertainty' as binary opposites: 'Uncertainty appears as the fundamental problem for complex organisations, and coping with uncertainty, as the essence of the administrative process. Just as complete uncertainty and randomness is the antithesis of purpose and of organisation, complete certainty is a figment of the imagination; but the tighter the norms of rationality, the more energy the organization will devote to moving toward certainty' (Thompson 1967: 159).
5. Oliver Williamson, a leading contemporary organizational economist, most explicitly elaborated the theoretical framework that adopted this ideological position.

According to Williamson's fourfold framework, uncertainty reduction and bounded rationality hold crucial importance for the understanding of 'market failures' (Williamson 1975, 1985). His scheme suggests that, given 'bounded rationality' (i.e. the limits of the human mind), it is very costly and sometimes impossible to determine all identifiable future contingencies (Simon 1957: 198). Transactions and long-term contracts may therefore be supplanted by hierarchies, which Williamson calls 'internal organization': 'Recourse to the latter, internal organization permits adaptations to uncertainty to be accomplished by administrative processes in a sequential fashion. Thus, rather than attempt to anticipate all possible contingencies from the outset, the future is permitted to unfold. Internal organization in this way economises on the bounded rationality attributes of decision makers in circumstances in which prices are not "sufficient statistics" and uncertainty is substantial.'

6. Horace Lucian Arnold, *The Complete Cost-Keeper* (1901), 9. Cited in Litterer 1986: 109.

7. Dobbin argued that the policy that the US government enforced was market enforcement: 'By the end of the nineteenth century, state policy had become oriented to the reinforcement of market mechanisms to ensure economic liberties and effect growth, and the prevention of other forms of government meddling with economic life' (1994: 24).

8. It was first introduced by Henry Le Chatelier during the Renault strike of 1913. See Rabinbach 1990: 244.

# APPENDIX

# Description of the Engineering-Management Literature

## 1. *AMERICAN MACHINIST*

*American Machinist* was founded in 1877 as a weekly. It was published in New York, with Horace Miller as its first owner, president, and publisher. It was the first and the longest-lived periodical in the post-1876 period, and probably the most important outlet of the mechanical engineering profession before 1905 (Calvert 1967: 136). The magazine focused on metal-working firms and the machine-building industry, where most of the industrial innovations as well as the revolution in management practices during the last two decades of the nineteenth century took place. *American Machinist* was an outlet to publicize information regarding professional conferences, cross-national comparisons of labor markets, 'modern management techniques', and methods of payment. The editors were firm supporters of the safety movement in industry and had a clear record of supporting the advancement of wages to labor (*American Machinist*, 15 November 1879: 8; *American Machinist*, 11 October 1879: 8; *American Machinist*, 26 June 1902: 917; see also *American Machinist*, 19 May 1927: 865). In 1896 John Hill—an ex-correspondent of *American Machinist* in Colorado—became proprietor and publisher of the magazine and McGraw-Hill took it over in 1917.

During the period under study, the *American Machinist* had nine editors, beginning with Jackson Bailey (1877–87), then Frank Hemenway (1887–95), Frederick J. Miller (1895–1907), Frederick H. Halsey (1907–11), Leon P. Alford (1911–17), John H. Van Deventer (1917–19), Ethan Viall (1919–20), and finally Frederick Colvin and Kenneth Condit as chief co-editors (1921–38) (for a full list of the individuals who had contributed to the *American Machinist* see: *American Machinist*, 19 May 1927: 822–3. See also 'Fifty Years of the *American Machinist*', *American Machinist*, 19 May 1927: 824). The publication sought to retain independence and not to accept payment for published materials except in the advertising columns (see also Ferguson 1989). In the first issue, Bailey stated that 'We shall always act independently, not holding ourselves under the least obligation to give "favorable notices" of anything under review, but rather to elicit the plain truth whether it be favorable or unfavorable.' James H. McGraw, president of the McGraw-Hill Publishing Company, recalled fifty years later that initially Bailey was thinking of a newspaper that would 'reflect accurately' events in the metal-working industry, but, realizing that being 'an accurate reflector' was an insufficient role in an evolving world, he also assumed leadership in the field (*American Machinist*, 19 May 1927: 824). Indeed, several editors of *American Machinist* were influential figures in the field of mechanical engineering; mainly Jackson Bailey, Fred Miller, Fred Halsey, Leon Alford, and Fred Colvin. The position taken by the first editors corroborates the phenomenological assumption undertaken in this study. The magazines provided, filtered, and constructed knowledge about their organizational and technical world.

The shop-culture orientation of the journal was apparent from the beginning. For example, in 1893, following a debate within ASME regarding the title 'engineer', *American Machinist* criticized those 'members of the ASME who would be ashamed of wearing overalls and of having greasy hands' (*American Machinist*, 9 March 1893: 8). To the editorial group, overalls and greasy hands in the shop were the nuts and bolts of engineering work. From early on, *American Machinist* employed traveling correspondents who made extended trips to machine shops around the country and facilitated the diffusion of innovations across the industry. For example, James Hobart, a special correspondent, made a lengthy trip from New York to Massachusetts, Missouri, Minnesota, Florida, and Philadelphia, where he searched for machine shops and documented his impressions. As Fred Colvin, chief editor of the periodical in the 1920s, recalled, James Hobart 'was a kind of nineteenth-century minnesinger of the lathe, a member of that now vanished band of traveling mechanicians who wandered from one town to another across the country . . . they helped considerably to spread new methods and new suggestions' (Colvin 1947: 47). In the 1880s this editorial policy was extended to include machine shops abroad. In the following I provide a brief description of the editors and their associates. This description brings to the surface a network of editors, writers, publishers, management consultants, and government bureaucrats who were central in the rising world of mechanical engineering.

Jackson Bailey, the first editor, was a mechanical engineer from Albany, New York. He was a veteran of the Civil War, and prior to becoming an editor of *American Machinist* he had some experience in publishing; he was the New York representative of *American Manufacturer* and *Iron World*. In 1879 he took the first steps in launching ASME by approaching John Sweet and facilitating a first meeting. After Bailey's death in 1887, Frank Hemenway, an authority on steam-engine performance, became editor, and in 1895 Fred Miller was appointed editor-in-chief of the publication and vice-president of the Hill Publishing Company.

Fred Miller was a machinist, a toolmaker, and later a foreman in Springfield, Ohio. He was recruited to *American Machinist* in 1887 as an associate editor in charge of the 'Tools' section. As part of the editorial policy he spent several months during 1897 touring European shops and studying the ways in which American machine tools were being used.[1] In 1907, John Hill and Fred Miller had differences on editorial matters which they 'gradually developed into a passage of arms' (Colvin 1947: 138). Miller had to leave his post, selling the stocks he had acquired to the company. Upon leaving, Miller was recruited to become a member of the Simplified Spelling Board, an organization established by Andrew Carnegie. In 1909, Miller became general manager of four typewriting factories in the Remington Co., where he took an active role in the development and introduction of management techniques. Miller hired Henry Gantt, a follower of Frederick Taylor and one of the pioneering figures in the modern management movement, as a consultant to aid the installation of Scientific Management in the company. For Gantt it was the largest consulting job he had ever undertaken. During the First World War, at the request of General William Crozier (head of the Ordnance Department), Miller helped in recruiting engineers to the service. In 1918 he set up machinery for war work in Bethlehem, Pennsylvania, and after the war he joined Henry Gantt's firm as a consulting engineer in management. Miller was an active member of the American Society of Mechanical Engineers. While still in the *American Machinist* office, he served on the publication committee that started the society's publication *Mechanical Engineering*, and in 1920 he became president of ASME.

Frederick Halsey took Miller's chair as editor-in-chief in 1907 and served in office until 1911. Halsey had a degree in mechanical engineering from Cornell, he had worked as a machinist, and was a superintendent of the Ingersoll-Rand Company's machine shop at Quebec. At Ingersoll-Rand he designed the earliest incentive plan to increase workers' productivity by allegedly dividing the benefits of increased production between owners and labor. The inauguration of his well-known 'Halsey Premium Plan' marked the first wage plan to break away from the rigid piecework system in American industry. Several years later, Taylor and Harrington in the United States, as well as Rowan in Scotland, proposed modifications to the plan. In 1894, Halsey became an associate editor for *American Machinist* and was notorious for his strong opposition to the movement that tried to make the metric system compulsory in the United States.

When Fred Halsey approached the age of retirement (in 1911), and was about to leave to become an associate professor of mechanical engineering at Cornell University, everybody in the *American Machinist* office assumed that the associate editor, Frank A. Stanley, would be the next editor-in-chief. However, Halsey felt that a college graduate could not handle the job properly and appointed a new man, Leon P. Alford, as editor-in-chief. For Halsey, Alford symbolized a new type of mechanical engineer, a person with a college degree who also had shop experience. After his graduation from college with a degree in electrical engineering, Alford worked as assistant machine-shop fore-man and later as a production superintendent in the McKay Shoe Machinery in Massachusetts. In 1906 he became head of the Mechanical Engineering Department at McKay. With this experience he fulfilled the requirements for the degree of mechanical engineer at Worcester Polytechnic Institute. Twenty-seven years later the same institute granted him an honorary doctoral degree in engineering (Jaffe 1957). As William Jaffe (Alford's biographer) suggested, at McKay Alford 'began to learn the lessons of stan-dardization' (Jaffe 1957: 9). Alford argued that his efforts to standardize screw machine parts for the shoe industry cut production costs by $150,000 per year. During his work at McKay he published articles in *American Machinist* about standardization in the machine-tool industry (e.g. *American Machinist*, 17 December 1914: 1062; *American Machinist*, 24 December 1914: 1112–15; *American Machinist*, 31 December 1914: 1148). In 1907 Fred Halsey and John Hill offered Alford the job of associate editor of *American Machinist*. In July 1910 Alford was sent by ASME to England to a joint conference with members of Britain's Institution of Mechanical Engineers. Alford there presented a paper ('Development of High-Speed Drilling Machines') that was based on articles and information presented previously in *American Machinist*. At the meeting he was first introduced to Frederick Taylor, who served as a discussant of the papers presented. Alford, however, never became attached to Taylor as he did to Henry Gantt. His criticism of Taylor's work became most apparent in the 1912 report on the status of industrial management that he crafted for ASME at the request of James Dodge and Fred Halsey (Jaffe 1957: 17). Alford served as an editor of *American Machinist* from 1910 to 1917 when he became an editor of *Engineering Magazine*. Later he was appointed dean of engineering at New York University. In 1934 he published a biography on Henry Gantt.[2]

During the war, John Van Deventer was the managing editor of *American Machinist* and in 1920 he was nominated as editor of *Industrial Management* (previously *Engineering Magazine*). Van Deventer attended technical schools in Switzerland and Germany, was a student at Yale, and became an instructor at the Sheffield Scientific School at Yale. In the late 1870s he worked at Midvale Steel Works in Philadelphia and ten years later at Bethlehem Steel, where he collaborated with Frederick Taylor on issues related to Scientific Management. Soon after the entry of the United States into the war, Deventer was asked by the Ordnance Department and the editorial staff of *American Machinist* to provide technical information to American munition-makers. The magazine published numerous articles on the Ordnance program written by the Secretary of War, the Assistant Secretary, and the Chief of Ordnance (e.g. *American Machinist*, 5 December 1918: 1013–17. See also *Industrial Management*, October 1920: 257–9). Furthermore, an army officer was given a desk at the editorial office of *American Machinist* to carry the details of forming an association of those who participated in munition manufacture. *American Machinist* also financed the newly established Army Ordnance Association during its first year (*American Machinist*, 19 May 1927: 825). After the war, the magazine supported the post-war plan for industrial mobilization and the macro-management of the economy.

Fred Colvin became editor in 1921 when Van Deventer went to co-edit *Industrial Management* with John Dunlap. Colvin was a mechanical engineer from Sterling, Massachusetts, who spent ten years with the Rue Manufacturing Company prior to joining *American Machinist* in 1907. Colvin knew Jackson Bailey and John Hill through his father Henry. He became a close friend of Mason Britton, who was one of Hill's right-hand men in the Hill Publishing Company and was a well-known figure in the machine-tool industry. Colvin also became a close friend of Frank Stanley, who was the senior associate editor of *American Machinist* when Colvin joined the staff. Both shared a New England background and they collaborated in publishing the *American Machinists' Handbook*. The handbook served as a reference material for machine-shop data and methods including a dictionary of shop terms. The first edition—published in 1908 by the Hill Publishing Company—sold 36,000 copies, rising to 600,000 in its eighth edition (1940s).

In 1916, during Alford's term as an editor, Colvin spent four months studying the manufacturing methods used in the Springfield Armory as an attempt to facilitate the war effort. In a few successive issues of *American Machinist*, Colvin criticized the organizational and technical procedures in rifle-making. According to Colvin, much of the machine equipment in Springfield was antiquated in comparison with contemporary standards, and the operation was conducted at a rather leisurely speed. The reports about the inefficiencies at the Springfield Armory resulted in a major clash with Maj. Gen. William Crozier who had been Chief of Ordnance and represented the War Department (see Petersen 1989 for a review of the efforts of Crozier in applying Scientific Management in the army arsenals). According to Colvin, the criticism—which was later published in a book form—hastened the retirement of Crozier as Chief of Ordnance (Jaffe 1957: 194). In 1921, after fourteen years in the *American Machinist* office and a significant contribution to the standardization of machine tools (*American Machinist*, 12

June 1919: 1143), Fred Colvin became editor of the journal. His co-editor, Kenneth H. Condit, was in aviation during the war, joined *American Machinist* as an associate editor as the war ended, and later became dean of engineering at Princeton University.

During the fifty-six years between 1879 and 1932, *American Machinist* published approximately 2,000 issues that I coded and analyzed (see *American Machinist*, 23 November 1932: 1164). The main contributors to management and organization issues during these years were principally machine-shop engineers, accountants, supervisors, and consultants. Articles about shop methods varied from metal-related technologies (e.g. 'cutting a coarse pitch screw', 'making thin threaded brass rings', 'making large holes on a small driller', 'case hardening for fine grain', 'putting a new cylinder on the tannery engine'), to engineering as a profession (e.g. 'the responsibilities of the educated engineer', 'early engineering reminiscences', 'the foundry trade school', 'The committee's report in congress on the metric system,' 'educating young machinists') and management issues (e.g. 'compensation of skilled labor', 'hanging workmen's coats', and 'The best weekly pay-day').

In assessing the materials published in the magazine it would be reasonable to ask to what extent the written text reflects upon the opinion of the editors. On 14 July 1910 the editors addressed this exact question. An editorial, probably written by Fred Halsey and/or his associates, explained 'What the *American Machinist* stands for' (*American Machinist*, 14 July 1910: 85). The editors suggested that given the wide range of opinions in the texts it is not always possible that *American Machinist* 'endorses or "stands for" everything that appears in its columns'. They explained that the magazine prints such 'widely differing views that it would be impossible to stand for them all' (ibid.).

It is probably safer to rely on editorials in order to get the 'official' line of the journal. But there, too, it is quite difficult to determine to what extent they were written by the editors or by their staff members, and how closely the latter were supervised. Robert Mawson, who was an associate editor from 1912 to 1917 under editor-in-chief Leon Alford, reported that he 'worked very closely with Mr. Alford' who 'was an engineer anxious at all times to assist the associate and assistant editors who worked with him, in presenting their findings in the best possible manner for the readers'.

## 2. ENGINEERING MAGAZINE

The New York monthly *Engineering Magazine* was founded in 1891 by John R. Dunlap and became the leading American magazine for shop management (a British edition was published from 1896 onward). It was also the first publication to represent the newly emerging field of 'industrial engineering' or 'industrial management'. The magazine started as a general purpose publication 'devoted to industrial progress'. From the first issues it devoted regular sections to civil engineering, architecture, electricity, mining and metallurgy, and mechanics. The format of the magazine and the structure of the sections changed frequently. The editorial department was composed of individuals from diverse fields: Franklin Pope stood for electricity; Leicester Allen for mechanics (later turned into mechanical engineering, a section edited by Henry Harrison Suplee); Barr Ferree for architecture; Albert Williams Jr. for mining and metallurgy; Thomas L. Greene for railways; and John C. Trautwine Jr. for civil engineering. From the very beginning Dunlap had an interest in railroad problems—an interest which he attributed to his experience on the engineer corps locating the Shenandoah Valley Railroad in 1873—and published a series of papers on railroad management.

Dunlap was perhaps the most active journalistic sponsor of the management move-ment (see Jenks 1961), as he himself recalled: 'political economy has been an absorbing study with me since boyhood'. He explained that 'when I founded The *Engineering Magazine* in 1891 I determined that industrial economy should be the central feature of the editorial policy' (*Engineering Magazine*, May 1915: 163–6). Dunlap's strong personal interest (see *Engineering Magazine*, May 1915: 165) in machine-shop management began in October 1894 with the publication of Oberlin Smith's[3] paper on 'Modern American Machine Tools: A Factor in our Industrial Growth' and of W. H. Wakeman's paper on 'Management of Men in Mills and Factories:—Rational Methods vs. Brute Force'. In December 1894, Dunlap accepted for publication a paper by James Brady titled 'Economy in Machine-Shop Management'. During the same year, 1894, Dunlap started a regular section on 'industrial sociology'; the section presented reviews of sociological subjects from other newspapers and magazines. The first issues covered such magazines as *Forum, Colliery Guardian, Iron Trade Review, Nineteenth Century, Bankers Magazine, Contemporary Review, Boston Journal of Commerce, Engineering and Mining Journal, American Journal of Sociology, Journal of Gas Lighting, Bulletin of the Department of Labor, American Magazine of Civics, World, Eagle, Fortnightly Review, Railroad Gazette, Iron Age,* and *Engineering Record*. The magazine also included excerpts from divers professional conferences on issues of industrial relations.

In January 1896, six months after Taylor's presentation in the Detroit meeting of ASME, Dunlap republished the paper entitled: 'A Piece Rate System: A Step Toward Partial Solution to the Labor Problem.' In the introductory notes, Dunlap stated that he regarded the paper 'as one of the most valuable contributions that have ever been given to technical literature'. This article established a firm link between 'technical literature' and the 'labor problem', a link that is at the core of this book and was made continuously by engineers. In April 1896 he invited Horace L. Arnold—also known as Henry Roland—to write a ('record breaking') series of six papers on 'Modern Machine-Shop Economics'. In 1901, Dunlap devoted the entire January issue to 'the works of manage-ment movement'. In 1901 James N. Gunn, a mining engineer and a lecturer at MIT, argued that 'industrial engineering' was 'a science which only awaits the creation of a literature to have its own existence recognized as a new department of engineering'. Dunlap objected and suggested an amendment where he substituted the word 'collation' for 'creation'. He explained that 'the creation of the literature has gone hand-in-hand with the development of the profession', and implied that the discipline was already under way. To demonstrate his point, his magazine carried in 1904 an annotated bibliography of several hundred titles, edited by Hugo Diemer, a former production engineer at Westinghouse and a professor of industrial engineering at Pennsylvania State College.[4] This collection was considered a distinct mark in the development of the 'new science' of management. Diemer himself wrote the first full text on management issues, entitled *Factory Organization and Administration* and published in 1910.

In 1905 Dunlap modified the magazine's title, adding the subtitle 'specially devoted to the interests of engineers, superintendents and managers'. He made a point in the December issue of 1905 of convincing the readers that the term 'engineer' must 'include the idea that the engineer is an economist' (*Engineering Magazine*, December 1905: 415). In 1915 Dunlap devoted an article to documenting the 'Historic events in the develop-ment of a new science' (*Engineering Magazine*, May 1915: 163–6). The first editor under

Dunlap's ownership was Charles Buxton Going. Going had a degree from the School of Mines at Columbia University, was a president of a manufacturing corporation in Cincinnati, became associate editor of *Engineering Magazine* in the autumn of 1896, and was appointed editor at the end of 1897 (see editorial in the *Engineering Magazine*, April 1916: 113). Going was an associate in mechanical engineering at Columbia University and was the author of a management text known as *Principles of Industrial Engineering*. He was concerned with the adequacy of engineering training to practical work. In a paper which he read in 1909 before the Society for the Promotion of Engineering Education, he made the recommendation that instructors in technical subjects should spend one year in every time-period (ideally three to five years) in the actual practice of the profession. According to Going, this should bring technical education more closely into touch with practical working conditions (*Review of the Engineering Press*, August 1909: 809).

Under Going's editorship, *Engineering Magazine* published articles by Gantt, Emerson, Church, Knoeppel, Day, Carpenter, and many other members of the management movement. Alexander Hamilton Church, a rival of Taylor in the movement, was for seven years a European manager for *Engineering Magazine*. Church was one of the chief speakers of the systematic management movement. He is relatively absent from the history of management, partly since he was less involved in promoting himself than Taylor was. He worked at the National Telephone Company in Britain as an electrical engineer, and in the 1890s became an assistant to J. Slater Lewis. Church refers, in his writing, to the significant influence Lewis had on him (Litterer 1986: 245). During the years 1898–1907 Henry Harrison Suplee served as a co-editor with Going and Dunlap. Suplee, a second generation machine-shop owner, had a degree in mechanical engineering from the University of Pennsylvania, served as an editor of *Mechanics* prior to the establishment of *Engineering Magazine,* and was an active member of ASME and the Franklin Institute. Dunlap occasionally appointed temporary co-editors, such as Charles T. Child in 1899 or Francis G. Wickware during 1909–11, to help him. In 1915, when Going's health became impaired, he resigned from his editorial duties and confined his work to industrial literature. He then selected, edited, and published the *Magazine*'s Library of Works Management (see *Engineering Magazine*, April 1916: 113).

*Engineering Magazine* was published regularly until November 1916, when—under the editorship of Dunlap, and with the assistance of Charles E. Funk—it changed to *Industrial Management*. When Funk decided to leave office in 1917, Dunlap searched for two candidates: one person to help promote the sales of the *Engineering Magazine* Company, and the other for the position of editor. He hired Erik Sellman for the first and Leon Alford, who was recommended by Henry Gantt, for the other. Leon Pratt Alford was unhappy at *American Machinist* after the death of John Hill in 1916. He was having disagreements with Arthur J. Baldwin, Hill's successor, and felt that it was time to leave. Alford was probably successful in his position. His biographer claims that Alford was able to extend *Engineering Magazine*'s list of subscribers during his first year in office from 7,253 in 1917 (of which two-thirds of the accounts were delinquents) to 18,750. One of his own notes suggested that in 1917 the magazine was 'practically bankrupt', and in 1920 'the net profit was some $70,000 after all obligations had been paid off' (Jaffe 1957: 86). Alford also helped establish *The Engineering Index*. Initially, it was a set of clippings from various periodicals. Under Alford, the clippings were classified, annotated, and sold to ASME (Jaffe 1957). In addition to his editorial work and his activities within

ASME, Alford was also a member of the American Engineering Council and contributed to its agenda on three major subjects: 'Elimination of Waste in Industry', 'The Twelve Hour Shift', and 'Safety and Production'. Alford is also known for his criticism of Scientific Management. He criticized it as too mechanistic and too eager to use the term 'science'. After spending three and a half years with *Industrial Management*, Alford decided to launch a new engineering periodical: *Management Engineering*. With the financial support of the Ronald Press Company, a publishing organization with a reputation in the field of business, the first issue of *Management Engineering* appeared in July 1921 with Alford as an editor. In 1922, Ronald added a subtitle: *Management Engineering: The Journal of Production*. In 1923 Ronald decided to consolidate the magazines and combined Alford's *Management Engineering* with *Administration,* which started in the same year. The magazine went through an additional series of changes, first as *Management and Administration in the Manufacturing Industries* in 1925 and then the title was contracted to *Manufacturing Industries* in 1926 (Jaffe 1957: 119; *Factory and Industrial Management*, January 1930).

In October 1920, John H. Van Deventer became Alford's successor as editor of *Industrial Management*. John Dunlap remained the owner of *Industrial Management* and edited it together with John Van Deventer until 1927, when it merged with *Factory*[5] to form a new magazine, titled *Factory and Industrial Management*. The new magazine was edited by John M. Carmody—an active figure in the New Deal of FDR—and was published as a joint venture of the McGraw-Shaw Company and the McGraw-Hill Publishing Company. In 1928 Ronald decided to leave the periodicals business and sold *Manufacturing Industries* to McGraw-Hill, who published it from March 1929. In 1933 *Factory and Industrial Management* merged with two additional magazines, *Maintenance Engineering* and *Manufacturing Industries,* to form a new periodical titled *Factory Management and Maintenance*. The editor-in-chief of *Factory Management and Maintenance* was Lester C. Morrow, formerly an associate editor of *American Machinist* and a close friend of Frederick Colvin. This period (1933 and later), however, is beyond the time-frame examined in this study.

*Engineering Magazine* published articles in engineering-related areas such as 'The European War from an Engineer Standpoint', as well as management issues (e.g. 'The Relation of the Railway to its Employees', 'American Railways and their Management') and labor issues ('Reflections on the Homestead Strike', 'The History of Strikes in America'). As was the case with *American Machinist*, from its inception *Engineering Magazine* was concerned with professional matters. Articles discussing pressing questions such as 'Who is an Engineer?', or 'Shall the Professions be Regulated?', were present from the very first issues. In 1901 the editors took a side in the internal professional battle over ASME dues. The battle was only a symptom of increasing discontent within the society particularly among junior members and 'out of town' members, those who did not belong to the inner circles of the New York oligarchy. Their resentment focused on what they perceived as the inefficiency and the extravagance of the New York City members. In this battle, different engineering publications took diverging sides (see Sinclair 1980: 66–71 for the background of the debate). For example, *American Machinist* and *Railway Age* gave voices to constituencies who were displeased with the actions of the society leadership (e.g. *American Machinist*, 21 November 1901: 1301. See Sinclair 1980: 69). The editors of *Engineering Magazine* had a different view. An editorial in December 1901 explained that 'there has arisen a curious opposition in certain quarters to the wise plans of the Council of ASME for the broadening of its scope in the true professional sense'. The editors sided with the older oligarchy and condemned this opposition: 'any efforts to oppose the plans of the administration cannot be considered as otherwise than detrimental and unadvised'. The editors believed that 'Such an organization as the ASME can not stand still; it must progress, and its advance must be upward as well as forward; Such an advance does not mean an accelerated increase in membership . . . The real progress must appear in its contribution to knowledge, in the results of its work as evidenced by the fame of its members and the importance and magnitude of their work.' According to the editors, 'It is evident that such a line of progress means increased expenditure as compared with the slower increase in resources . . . We regret to see, in some quarters, a short-sighted attempt to oppose such far-seeing plans, and to appeal to local and personal elements to hamper and hinder the obvious work which lies before the organization' ('Editorial', *Engineering Magazine*, December 1901: 423).

As early as 1897, a large number of articles on accountancy systems emerged, carrying such titles as 'Mine Accounts', 'Cost Keeping Methods in Machine Shops and Foundry', 'An Effective System of Finding and Keeping Shop Costs', or 'A Simple and Effective System of Shop Cost Keeping'. In 1899–1900, there was a growing number of articles on wage systems, production control, and inventory control. The main contributors to the development of these issues during 1891–1916 were (ordered by their quantity of contribution): C. E. Knoeppel (who was Taylor's disciple and worked with Emerson in his New York consulting firm), Harrington Emerson (who chaired the Efficiency Society), Charles U. Carpenter, Alexander Hamilton Church, Horace Lucian Arnold,[6] and Henry Gantt. Fewer contributions were made by Lewis Slater, Carl Barth, and Henry Towne. Some were active systematizers (e.g. Church), or efficiency engineers (e.g. Emerson), while others were writers in the technical press with an interest in management and labor (e.g. Arnold). In 1916, *Engineering Magazine* gradually turned into an exclusive management publication. Management was not conceived only as a technical matter but dealt with cultural issues as well. For example, an article entitled 'Negroes as a Source of Industrial Labor' was published in 1918. Under the sub-heading 'Irish Make Good Negro Bosses', the writer discussed the 'fitness' of blacks to the machine shop. He observed that 'an engine room full of negroes under an Irish boss would do quite as good work as a room full of German square-heads' (*Industrial Management*, August 1918: 123–9). The author emphasized the importance of the management function particularly given the lack of industrial habits among blacks. The writer suggests going 'easy on the negro: we accuse the negro of laziness. His ancestors picked their food from a bush, fished it out of a stream, or speared it in the next block. Why should he inherit a feverish desire to work?' The writer concluded with two suggestions for engineers practicing supervision: 'firmness [is] needed with the Negro' and 'someone must think for the Negro'. These statements attest to the then prevailing racist attitudes toward African-Americans within the American society.

### Notes

1.  In 1907 another staff member, J. Wallace Carrel, who subsequently became general manager of the Lodge and Shipley Company, made a similar survey for the *Machinist*.

2. L. P. Alford, *Henry Laurence Gantt* (1934).

3. Smith was an expert on drawing presses and a past president of ASME.

4. Hugo Diemer, 'A Bibliography of Works Management' with an editorial introduction, *Engineering Magazine*, July 1904: 626–42; and 'Index to the Periodical Literature of Industrial Engineering', *EngineeringMagazine*, July 1904: 643–53. See also Jenks 1961.

5. *Factory* or, more precisely, *Factory: The Magazine of Management* was started in 1907 by the A. W. Shaw Company.

6. Hounshell (1984) reports that Arnold used several pen names. The best-known ones were Henry Roland and Hugh Dolnar (personal communication). Arnold was a machinist in the railroads machine shops, superintendent, foreman, and designer. He wrote extensively on cost accounting and general management issues.

# References

ABBOTT, ANDREW (1988). *The System of Professions: An Essay on the Division of Expert Labor*. Chicago: Chicago University Press.

ABRAHAMSON, ERIC (1997). 'The Emergence and Prevalence of Employee Management Rhetorics: The Effects of Long Waves, Labor Unions, and Turnover, 1875 to 1992'. *Academy of Management Journal*, 40: 491–533.

ADAMIC, LOUIS (1983). *Dynamite: The Story of Class Violence in America*. New York: Chelsea House.

ADAMS, GRAHAM, Jr. (1966). *Age of Industrial Violence, 1910–1915: The Activities and Findings of the United States Commission on Industrial Relations*. New York: Columbia University Press.

AITKEN, HUGH G. H. (1960). *Taylorism at Watertown Arsenal: Scientific Management in Action, 1908–1915*. Cambridge, Mass.: Harvard University Press.

—— (1985). *Scientific Management in Action in the Watertown Arsenal 1908–1915*. Princeton: Princeton University Press.

ALBROW, MARTIN (1996). *The Global Age: State and Society beyond Modernity*. Cambridge, UK: Polity Press.

ALCHON, GUY (1985). *The Invisible Hand of Planning: Capitalism, Social Science, and the State in the 1920s*. Princeton: Princeton University Press.

ALDRICH, HOWARD E. (1979). *Organizations and Environments*. Englewood Cliffs, NJ: Prentice Hall.

ANTHONY, P. D. (1986). *The Foundation of Management*. London: Tavistock.

ASCE (American Society of Civil Engineers) (1972). *A Biographical Dictionary of American Civil Engineers*. New York: ASCE Historical Publications.

ASME (American Society of Mechanical Engineers) (1941). *Fred J. Miller*. New York: ASME.

—— (1980). Mechanical Engineers in America Born prior to 1861: *A Biographical Dictionary*. New York: ASME, History and Heritage Committee.

BARITZ, LOREN (1960). *The Servants of Power: A History of the Use of Social Science in American Industry*. Middletown, Conn.: Wesleyan University Press.

BARLEY, STEPHEN R., and KUNDA, GIDEON (1992). 'Design and Devotion: Surges of Rational and Normative Ideologies of Control in Managerial Discourse'. *Administrative Science Quarterly*, 37: 363–99.

BAUDRILLARD, JEAN (1989). *America*. London: Verso.

BAUMAN, ZYGMUNT (1989). *Modernity and the Holocaust*. Cambridge, UK: Polity Press.

—— (1992). *Mortality and Immortality and Other Life Strategies*. Cambridge, UK: Polity Press.

BELL, DANIEL (1973). *The Coming of Post-industrial Society: A Venture in Social Forecasting*. New York: Basic.

BENDIX, REINHARD (1956/1974). *Work and Authority in Industry*. Berkeley and Los Angeles: University of California Press.

BENSON, J. KENNETH (1975). 'The Interorganizational Field as a Political Economy'. *Administrative Science Quarterly*, 20: 229–49.

BERGER, PETER L., and LUCKMANN, THOMAS (1966). *The Social Construction of Reality*. New York: Doubleday.

BERLE, ADOLPH, Jr. (1959). *Power without Property*. New York: Harcourt Brace Jovanovich.

—— and MEANS, GARDINER (1932). *The Modern Corporation and Private Property*. New York: Macmillan.

BOLTANSKI, LUC (1987). *The Making of a Class: Cadres in French Society*. Cambridge: Cambridge University Press.

—— (1990). 'Visions of American Management in Post War France', in Sharon Zukin and Paul DiMaggio (eds.), *Structures of Capital: The Social Organization of the Economy*. Cambridge: Cambridge University Press: 343–72.

BOURDIEU, PIERRE (1992). 'The Purpose of Reflexive Sociology', in Pierre Bourdieu and Loic J. D. Wacquant (eds.), *An Invitation to Reflexive Sociology*. Chicago: University of Chicago Press: 60–215.

BRAVERMAN, HARRY (1974). *Labor and Monopoly Capital: The Degradation of Work in the Twentieth Century*. New York: Monthly Review Press.

BRESLAU, DANIEL (1998). *In Search of the Unequivocal: Political Economy of Measurement in U.S. Labor Market Policy*. New York: Praeger.

BURGOYNE, G. ARTHUR (1893/1982). *The Homestead Strike of 1892*. Pittsburgh: University of Pittsburgh Press.

BURNHAM, JAMES (1941/1960). *The Managerial Revolution*. Bloomington: Indiana University Press.

BURRELL, GIBSON (1988). 'Modernism, Post-modernism and Organizational Analysis 2: The Contribution of Michel Foucault'. *Organization Studies*, 9: 221–35.

BURSHALL, AUBREY F. (1965). *A History of Mechanical Engineering*. Cambridge, Mass.: MIT Press.

BURTON, HENDRICK J. (1919). *The Age of Big Business: A Chronicle of the Captains of Industry*. New Haven: Yale University Press.

BUTTRICK, JOHN (1952). 'The Inside Contract System'. *Journal of Economic History*, 14: 205–21.

CALHOUN, DANIEL H. (1960). *The American Civil Engineer: Origins and Conflict*. Cambridge, Mass.: Harvard University Press.

CALLON, MICHELE (1980). 'Struggles and Negotiations to Define What is Problematic and What is Not: The Sociological Translation', in Karin D. Knorr, Roger Krohn, and Richard Whitely (eds.), *The Social Process of Scientific Investigation*. Dordrecht: D. Reidel Publishing: 197–220.

CALVERT, MONTE A. (1967). *The Mechanical Engineer in America 1830–1910: Professional Cultures in Conflict*. Baltimore: Johns Hopkins Press.

CAPRA, FRITJOF (1982). *The Turning Point: Science, Society, and the Rising Culture*. New York: Simon & Schuster.

CARNEGIE, ANDREW (1886a/1992). 'An Employer's View of the Labor Question', in Joseph Frazier Wall (ed.), *The Andrew Carnegie Reader*. Pittsburgh: University of Pittsburgh Press: 91–101.

—— (1886b/1992). 'Results of the Labor Struggle', in Joseph Frazier Wall (ed.), *The Andrew Carnegie Reader*. Pittsburgh: University of Pittsburgh Press: 102–13.

CASSIRER, ERNEST (1951). *The Philosophy of Enlightenment*. Princeton: Princeton University Press.

CHANDLER, ALFRED D., Jr. (1956). *Henry Varnum Poor: Business Editor, Analyst and Reformer*. Cambridge, Mass.: Harvard University Press.

—— (1962). *Strategy and Structure: Chapters in the History of the American Industrial Enterprise*. Cambridge, Mass.: MIT Press.

—— (1977). *The Visible Hand: The Managerial Revolution in American Business*. Cambridge, Mass.: Harvard University Press.

—— (1984). 'Emergence of Managerial Capitalism'. *Business History Review*, 58: 473–503.

—— (1990). *Scale and Scope: The Dynamics of Industrial Capitalism*. Cambridge Mass.: Belknap.

CHASE, STUART (1929). *Men and Machines*. New York: Macmillan.

CLAWSON, DAN (1980). *Bureaucracy and the Labor Process: The Transformation of the U.S. Industry, 1860–1920*. New York: Monthly Review Press.

CLEGG, STEWART, and DUNKERLEY, DAVID (1980). *Organization, Class and Control*. London: Routledge & Kegan Paul.

COHEN, JERE, HAZELRIGG, LAWRENCE E., and POPE, WHITNEY (1975). 'De-Parsonizing Weber: A Critique of Parsons' Interpretation of Weber's Sociology'. *American Sociological Review*, 40: 229–41.

COLEMAN, JAMES (1993). 'Rational Reconstruction of Society'. *American Sociological Review*, 58: 1–15.

COLVIN, FRED H. (1947). *60 Years with Men and Machines: An Autobiography*. New York: McGraw-Hill Book Company Inc.

CREIGHTON, ANDREW L. (1990). 'The Emergence of Incorporation as a Legal Form for Organizations'. Unpublished Ph.D. dissertation, Stanford University.

CZARNIAWSKA, BARBARA AND SEVON, GUJE (1996) (eds.), *Translating Organizational Change*. Berlin: Walter de Gruyter.

DAHRENDORF, RALF (1968). *Essays in the Theory of Society*. Stanford, Calif.: Stanford University Press.

DAVIS, MICHAEl (1983). 'The Stop Watch and the Wooden Shoe: Scientific Management and the Industrial Workers of the World', in James Green (ed.), *Workers' Struggles: Past and Present. A 'Radical America' Reader*. Philadelphia: Temple University Press: 83–101.

DIGGINS, PATRICK J. (1992). *The Rise and Fall of the American Left*. New York: W. W. Norton & Company.

DiMAGGIO, PAUL J. (1991). 'Constructing an Organizational Field as a Professional Project: U.S. Art Museums, 1920–1940', in Walter W. Powell and Paul J. DiMaggio (eds.), *The New Institutionalism in Organizational Analysis*. Chicago: University of Chicago Press: 267–92.

—— and POWELL, WALTER W. (1983). 'The Iron Cage Revisited: Institutional Isomorphism and Collective Rationality in Organizational Fields'. *American Sociological Review*, 48: 147–60.

DJELIC, MARIE-LAURE (1998). *Exporting the American Model: The Postwar Transformation of European Business*. Oxford: Oxford University Press.

DOBBIN, FRANK (1994). *Forging Industrial Policy: The United States, Britain and France in the Railway Age*. Cambridge: Cambridge University Press.

DORAY, BERNARD (1988). *From Taylorism to Fordism: A Rational Madness*. London: Free Association Books.

DOUGLAS MARY (1992). *How Institutions Think*. London: Routledge & Kegan Paul.

DOUGLAS, PAUL H. (1923). 'An Analysis of Strike Statistics 1881–1921'. *Journal of the American Statistical Assocation*, 18: 866–77.

DRUCKER, PETER F. (1986). *The Practice of Management*. New York: Harper & Row.

DRURY, HORACE B. (1922). *Scientific Management: A History and Criticism*. New York: AMS Press.

DUBOFF, B. RICHARD, and HERMANN, EDWARD S. (1980). 'Alfred Chandler's New Business History: A Review'. *Politics and Society*, 10: 87–110.

DUBOFSKY, MELVYN (1967). *We Shall be All: History of the IWW*. Chicago: Quadrangle.

—— (1968). *When Workers Organize: New York City in the Progressive Era*. Amherst, Mass.: University of Massachusetts Press.

EDWARDS, PAUL K. (1981). *Strikes in the United States 1881–1974*. New York: St Martin's Press.

EDWARDS, RICHARD (1979). *Contested Terrain: The Transformation of the Workplace in the Twentieth Century*. New York: Basic Books.

EMERSON, HARRINGTON (1911). *Efficiency as a Basis for Operations and Wages*. New York: Engineering Magazine.

ENTEMAN, WILLARD (1993). *Managerialism*. Madison: University of Wisconsin Press.

FAMA, EUGENE (1980). 'Agency Problems and the Theory of the Firm'. *Journal of Political Economy*, 88: 288–307.

—— and JENSEN, MICHAEL C. (1983). 'Separation of Ownership and Control'. *Journal of Law and Economics*, 26: 301–25.

FAULKNER, HAROLD U. (1951). *The Decline of Laissez Faire*. New York: Holt, Rinehart & Winston.

FEENBERG, ANDREW, and HANNAY, ALASTAIR (1995). *Technology and the Politics of Knowledge*. Bloomington: Indiana University Press.

FERGUSON, EUGENE S. (1989). 'Technical Journals and the History of Technology', in Stephen H. Cutliffe and Robert C. Post (eds.), *In Context: History and the History of Technology*. Bethlehem, Pa.: Lehigh University Press.

FLIGSTEIN, NEIL (1990). *The Transformation of Corporate Control*. Cambridge, Mass.: Harvard University Press.

FONER, PHILIP S. (1947). *History of the Labor Movement in the U.S.* New York: International.

FOUCAULT, MICHEL (1975). *The Birth of the Clinic*. New York: Vintage.

—— (1977). *Madness and Civilization*. London: Tavistock.

—— (1979). *Discipline and Punish: The Birth of the Prison*. New York: Vintage Books.

FREELAND, ROBERT F. (1994). 'The Struggle for Control of the Modern Corporation: Organizational Change at General Motors, 1924–1958'. Unpublished Ph.D. dissertation, University of California, Berkeley.

FREIDSON, ELIOT (1986). *Professional Powers*. Chicago: University of Chicago Press.

FRENKEL, MICHAL (1992). 'Industrial Ideologies in Palestine between Industrialization and Nationalism'. Unpublished MA thesis, Department of Sociology and Anthropology, Tel-Aviv University.

—— SHENHAV, YEHOUDA, and HERZOG, HANNA (1997). 'The Political Embeddedness of Managerial Ideologies in Pre-state Israel: The Case of PPL 1920–1948'. *Journal of Management History*, 3: 120–44.

GALBRAITH, JAY (1973). *Designing Complex Organizations*. Reading, Mass.: Addison-Wesley.

GANTT, HENRY L. (1910). *Work, Wages, and Profit*. New York: Engineering Magazine.

GARNER, PAUL SAMUEL (1954). *Evolution of Cost Accounting to 1925*. Tuscaloosa: University of Alabama Press.

GEERTZ, CLIFFORD (1973). 'Ideology as Cultural System', in C. Geertz (ed.), *The Interpretation of Cultures*. New York: Basic Books: 193–233.

GIBSON, JAMES (1986). *The Perfect Way: Technowar in Vietnam*. Boston: Atlantic Monthly.

GILBRETH, FRANK B., and CAREY, ERNESTINE GILBRETH (1949). *Cheaper by the Dozen*. New York: Bantam Books.

GISPEN, KEES (1989). *New Profession, Old Order: Engineers and German Society, 1815–1914*. Cambridge, UK: Cambridge University Press.

GLOVER, JOHN D. (1980). *The Revolutionary Corporations: Engines of Plenty, Engines of Growth, Engines of Change*. Homewood, Ill.: Dow Jones-Irwin.

GOLDSTEIN, ROBERT J. (1978). *Political Repression in Modern America from 1870 to the Present*. Cambridge: Schenkman Publishing Company.

GORDON, ANDREW (1985). *The Evolution of Labor Relations in Japan: Heavy Industry, 1853–1955*. Cambridge, Mass.: Harvard University Press.

GORDON, M. DAVID, EDWARDS, RICHARD, and REICH, MICHAEL (1982). *Segmented Work, Divided Workers*. Cambridge, UK: Cambridge University Press.

GOULDNER, ALVIN W. (1970). *The Coming Crisis of Western Sociology*. New York: Basic Books.

—— (1976). *The Dialectics of Ideology and Technology*. New York: Oxford University Press.

—— (1979). *The Future of Intellectuals and the Rise of the New Class*. New York: The Seabury Press.

GRAMSCI, ANTONIO (1971). *Selection from the Prison Notebooks*. London: Lawrence & Wishart.

GRIFFIN, JOHN I. (1939). *Strikes: A Study in Quantitative Economics*. New York: Columbia University Press.

GUILLEN, MAURO F. (1994). *Models of Management: Work, Authority, and Organization in a Comparative Perspective*. Chicago: University of Chicago Press.

HABER, SAMUEL (1964). *Efficiency and Uplift: Scientific Management in the Progressive Era 1890–1920*. Chicago: University of Chicago Press.

HABERMAS, JURGEN (1970). *Toward a Rational Society*. Boston: Beacon.

HACKING, IAN (1983/1992). *Representing and Intervening*. Cambridge, UK: Cambridge University Press.

HALL, STUART (1982). 'The Rediscovery of Ideology: Return to Repressed in Media Studies', in M. Gurevich et al. (eds.), *Culture, Society and the Media*. London: Methuen: 56–90.

HAMILTON, GARY G., and SUTTON, JOHN R. (1989). 'The Problem of Control in the Weak State: Domination in the United States, 1880–1920'. *Theory and Society*, 18: 1–46.

HARRIS, HOWELL J. (1992). *The Right to Manage: Industrial Relations Policies of American Business in the 1940s*. Madison: University of Wisconsin Press.

HASSARD, JOHN (1993). *Sociology and Organization Theory: Positivism, Paradigms and Postmodernity*. Cambridge, UK: Cambridge University Press.

HAWLEY, ELLIS (1974). 'Herbert Hoover, the Commerce Secretariat, and the Vision of the "Associative State" '. *Journal of American History*, 61: 116–40.

HAWTHORN, GEOFFREY (1987). *Enlightenment and Despair: A History of Social Theory*. Cambridge: Cambridge University Press.

HAYEK, FRIEDRICH A. (1967). *Studies in Philosophy, Politics and Economics*. Chicago: University of Chicago Press.

HAYS, SAMUEL P. (1957). *The Response to Industrialism 1885–1914*. Chicago: University of Chicago Press.

—— (1959). *Conservation and the Gospel of Efficiency: The Progressive Conservation Movement, 1890–1920*. New York: Atheneum.

HENDERSON, C. R. (1896). 'Business Men and Social Theorists'. *American Journal of Sociology*, 1: 385–97.

HERMAN, ELLEN (1995). *The Romance of American Psychology: Political Culture in the Age of Experts*. Berkeley and Los Angeles: University of California Press.

HICKSON, D. (1993) (ed.). *Management in Western Europe*. Berlin: Walter de Gruyter.

HIRSCH, PAUL M. (1972). 'Processing Fads and Fashions: An Organization-Set Analysis of Cultural Industry Systems'. *American Journal of Sociology*, 77: 639–59.

HOFSTADTER, RICHARD (1955). *The Age of Reform*. New York: Vintage Books.

HOPWOOD, ANTHONY G. (1994). *Accounting as Social and Institutional Practice*. New York: Cambridge University Press.

HOUNSHELL, DAVID A. (1984). *From the American System to Mass Production 1800–1932: The Development of Manufacturing Technology in the United States*. Baltimore: Johns Hopkins University Press.

—— (1989). 'Rethinking the History of "American Technology" ', in Stephen H. Cutliffe and Robert C. Post (eds.), *In Context: History and the History of Technology*. Bethlehem, Pa.: Lehigh University Press: 216–29.

—— (1996). 'The Evolution of Industrial Research in the United States', in Richard S. Rosenbloom and William Spencer (eds.), *Engines of Innovation: U.S. Industrial Research at the End of an Era*. Cambridge, Mass.: Harvard Business School Press: 13–85.

HOWE, BARBARA (1980). 'The Emergence of Scientific Philanthropy, 1900–1920: Origins, Issues and Outcomes', in Robert F. Arnove (ed.), *Philanthropy and Cultural Imperialism: The Foundations at Home and Abroad*. Bloomington: Indiana University Press: 25–85.

HOWE, IRVING (1957). *Politics and the Novel: The Classic Study of the Impact of Ideology on Literature*. New York: Discus Books.

HOWELL, CHARLES (1995). 'Toward a History of Management Thought'. *Business and Economic History*, 24: 41–50.

HOXIE, R. F. (1921). *Scientific Management and Labor*. New York: D. Appleton Co.

HUGHES, THOMAS P. (1989*a*). 'Machines, Megamachines and Systems', in Stephen H. Cutliffe and Robert C. Post (eds.), *In Context: History and the History of Technology*. Bethlehem, Pa.: Lehigh University Press: 106–19.

HUGHES, THOMAS P. (1989*b*). *American Genesis: A Century of Invention and Technological Enthusiasm 1870–1970*. New York: Viking.

ISRAEL, PAUL (1992). *From Machine Shop to Industrial Laboratory*. Baltimore: Johns Hopkins University Press.

JACOBY, RUSSEL (1975). *Social Amnesia: A Critique of Contemporary Psychology From Adler to Laing*. Boston: Beacon Press.

JACOBY, SANFORD (1985). *Employing Bureaucracy: Managers, Unions, and the Transformation of Work in American Industry*. New York: Columbia University Press.

—— (1993). 'Comment'. *Industrial and Labor Relations Review*, 46: 399–403.

JACQUES, ROY (1996). *Manufacturing the Employee: Management Knowledge from the 19th to 21st Century*. London: Sage.

JAFFE, WILLIAM J. (1957). *L. P. Alford and the Evolution of Modern Industrial Management*. New York: New York University Press.

JELINEK, MARIANN (1980). 'Toward Systematic Management: Alexander Hamilton Church'. *Business History Review*, 45: 63–79.

JENKS, LELAND H. (1961). 'Early Phases of the Management Movement'. *Administrative Science Quarterly*, 5: 421–77.

JOHNSON, THOMAS H., and KAPLAN, ROBERT S. (1987). *Relevance Lost: The Rise and Fall of Management Accounting*. Boston: Harvard Business School Press.

JONES, PETER (1968) (ed.), *The Robber Barons Revisited*. Boston: D. C. Heath & Company.

JOSEPHSON, MATTHEW (1934/1995). *The Robber Barons: The Great American Capitalists 1861–1901*. San Diego: Harcourt Brace.

KALEV, ALEXANDRA (1998). 'The Institutionalization of Productivity Councils in Israeli Industry, 1945–1955'. Unpublished MA thesis, Department of Sociology and Anthropology, Tel Aviv University.

KANIGEL, ROBERT (1997). *The One Best Way: Frederick Winslow Taylor and the Enigma of Efficiency*. New York: Viking.

KANTER, ROSABETH M. (1977). *Men and Women of the Corporation*. New York: Basic Books.

KAUFMAN, ALLEN, and ZACHARIAS, LAWRENCE (1992). 'From Trust to Contract: The Legal Language of Managerial Ideology 1920–1980'. *Business History Review*, 66: 523–53.

——and KARSON, MARVIN (1995). *Managers vs. Owners: The Struggle for Corporate Control in American Democracy*. New York: Oxford University Press.

KAUFMAN, BRUCE E. (1993). *The Origins and Evolution of the Field of Industrial Relations*. Ithaca, NY: ILR Press.

KAWANISHI, HIROSUKE (1992). *Enterprise Unionism in Japan*. London: Kogan Page.

KELLY, JOHN (1982). *Scientific Management, Job Design, and Work Performance*. London: Academic Press.

KINZLEY, DEAN W. (1991). *Industrial Harmony in Modern Japan: The Invention of a Tradition*. London: Routledge.

KJIR, PETER (1998). 'Field Creation: The Danish Productivity Drive 1945–1955'. Paper prepared for the EGOS 14th Colloquium, Maastricht, 9–11 July 1998.

KLOPPENBERG, JAMES T. (1986). *Uncertain Victory: Social Democracy and Progressivism in European and American Thought 1870–1920*. Oxford: Oxford University Press.

KNORR-CETINA, KARIN D. (1983). *The Manufacture of Knowledge: An Essay on the Constructivist and Contextual Nature of Science.* Oxford: Pergamon Press.

KOLKO, GABRIEL (1963). *The Triumph of Conservatism: A Reinterpretation of American History, 1900–1916.* New York: Free Press.

KRAUSE, ELLIOTT A. (1996). *Death of the Guilds: Professions, States, and the Advance of Capitalism 1930 to the Present.* New Haven: Yale University Press.

LANDES, DAVID S. (1969). *The Unbounded Prometheus: Technological Change and Industrial Development in Western Europe from 1750 to the Present.* Cambridge: Cambridge University Press.

LARNER, ROBERT J. (1970). *Managerial Control and the Large Corporations.* New York: Dunellen.

LARSON, MAGALI S. (1977). *The Rise of Professionalism: A Sociological Analysis.* Berkeley and Los Angeles: University of California Press.

LASH, SCOTT, and URRY, JOHN (1987). *The End of Organized Capitalism.* New York: Polity Press.

LATOUR, BRUNO (1986). 'The Powers of Associations', in John Law (ed.), *Power, Action and Belief.* London: Routledge & Kegan Paul: 264–80.

—— (1987). *Science in Action.* Cambridge, Mass.: Harvard University Press.

—— and WOOLGAR, STEVE (1979). *Laboratory Life: The Social Construction of Scientific Facts.* London: Sage.

LAYTON, EDWIN T. (1971). *The Revolt of the Engineers: Social Responsibility and the American Engineering Profession.* Cleveland: Press of Case Western Reserve University.

LEIBY, JAMES (1960). *Carroll Wright and Labor Reform: The Origin of Labor Statistics.* Cambridge, Mass.: Harvard University Press.

LILIENFELD, ROBERT (1978). *The Rise of Systems Theory: An Ideological Analysis.* New York: John Wiley.

LIPSET, SEYMOUR MARTIN (1996). *American Exceptionalism: Double-Edged Sword.* New York: W. W. Norton & Company.

LITTERER, JOSEPH A. (1961*a*). 'Systematic Management: The Search for Order and Integration'. *Business History Review,* 35: 461–476.

—— (1961*b*). 'Alexander Hamilton Church and the Development of Modern Management'. *Business History Review,* 35: 211–25.

—— (1963). 'Systematic Management: Design for Organizational Recoupling in American Manufacturing Firms'. *Business History Review,* 37: 369–86.

—— (1986). *The Emergence of Systematic Management as Shown by the Literature of Management from 1870–1900.* New York: Garland Publishing Inc.

LOCKE, ROBERT R. (1984). *The End of the Practical Man: Entrepreneurship and Higher Education in Germany, France, and Great Britain, 1880–1940.* London: JAI Press Inc.

—— (1996). *The Collapse of American Management Mystique.* Oxford: Oxford University Press.

LORWIN, LEWIS (1933). *The American Federation of Labor.* Washington: Brookings Institution.

LUKÁCS, GEORG (1923/1971). *History and Class Consciousness.* Cambridge, Mass.: MIT Press.

LYOTARD, J. F. (1984). *The Postmodern Condition: A Report on Knowledge.* Manchester: Manchester University Press.

McCraw, Thomas K. (1984). 'Business & Government: The Origins of the Adversary Relationship'. *California Management Review*, 26: 33–52.

McKenna, Christopher D. (1995). 'The Origins of Modern Management Consulting'. *Business and Economic History*, 24: 51–8.

McKinlay, Alan, and Zeitlin, Jonathan (1989). 'The Meanings of Managerial Prerogative: Industrial Relations and the Organisation of Work in British Engineering, 1880–1939'. *Business History*, 31: 32–47.

Maier, Charles S. (1970). 'Between Taylorism and Technocracy: European Ideologies and the Vision of Industrial Productivity in the 1920s'. *Journal of Contemporary History*, 5: 27–61.

—— (1987). *In Search of Stability: Explorations in Historical Political Economy*. Cambridge, Mass.: Harvard University Press.

—— March, James G., and Olsen, Johan P. (1976). *Ambiguity and Choice in Organizations*. Bergen: Universitetsforlaget.

—— and Simon, Herbert A. (1958). *Organizations*. New York: John Wiley.

Marcus, Alan, and Segal, Howard P. (1989). *Technology in America*. New York: Harcourt Brace Jovanovich.

Marglin, Stephen A. (1974). 'What Do Bosses Do? The Origins and Functions of Hierarchy in Capitalist Production'. *Review of Radical Political Economics*, 6: 60–112.

Mason, E. S. (1931). 'Saint-Simonism and the Rationalization of Industry'. *Quarterly Journal of Economics*: 640–83.

Mayr, Otto, and Post, Robert C. (1982) (eds.), *Yankee Enterprise: The Rise of the American System of Manufacturers*. Washington: Smithsonian Institution Press.

Merkle, Judith A. (1980). *Management and Ideology*. Berkeley and Los Angeles: University of California Press.

Merrick, Charles M. (1980) (ed.). *ASME Management History Division 1886–1980*. New York: American Society of Mechanical Engineers.

Meyer, John W. (1988). 'Society without Culture: A Nineteenth-Century Legacy', in Francisco O. Ramirez (ed.), *Rethinking the Nineteenth Century: Contradictions and Movements*. New York: Greenwood Press: 193–202.

—— (1994). 'The Evolution of Modern Stratification Systems', in David Grusky (ed.), *Social Stratification: Class, Race, and Gender in Sociological Perspective*. Boulder, Colo.: Westview Press: 730–7.

—— and Rowan, Brian, (1977). 'Institutionalized Organizations: Formal Structure as Myth and Ceremony'. *American Journal of Sociology*, 83: 340–63.

—— and Scott, W. Richard (1983). *Organizational Environments: Ritual and Rationality*. Beverly Hills, Calif.: Sage.

Miller, Peter, and O'Leary, Ted (1989). 'Hierarchies and American Ideals, 1900–1940'. *Academy of Management Review*, 14: 250–65.

Mills, C. Wright (1951). *White Collar: The American Middle Classes*. New York: Oxford University Press.

Miranti, Paul J. (1990). *Accounting Comes of Age: The Development of an American Profession, 1886–1940*. Chapel Hill: University of North Carolina Press.

Mizruchi, Mark S. (1987). 'Managerialism: Another Reassessment', in Michael Schwartz (ed.), *The Structure of Power in America: The Corporate Elite as a Ruling Class*. New York: Holmes & Meier: 7–15.

MONTGOMERY, DAVID (1974). 'The New Unionism and the Transformation of Workers' Consciousness in America, 1909–22'. *Journal of Social History*, 7: 509–29.

—— (1987). *The Fall of the House of Labor: The Workplace, the State, and American Labor Activism, 1865–1925*. Cambridge: Cambridge University Press.

MORGAN, GARETH (1986). *Images of Organization*. Newbury Park, Calif.: Sage.

MOTT, LUTHER FRANK (1957). *A History of American Magazines 1865–1885*. Cambridge, Mass.: Harvard University Press.

MUMFORD, LEWIS (1970). *The Myth of the Machine: The Pentagon of Power*. New York: Harcourt Brace Jovanovich, Inc.

MUSIL, ROBERT (1953/1979). *The Man without Qualities*. London: Secker & Warburg.

NADWORNY, MILTON (1955). *Scientific Management and the Unions*. Cambridge, Mass.: Harvard University Press.

NELSON, DANIEL (1974). 'Scientific Management, Systematic Management and Labor, 1880–1915'. *Business History Review*, 48: 479–500.

—— (1975). *Managers and Workers: Origins of the New Factory System in the United States, 1880–1920*. Madison: University of Wisconsin Press.

NOBLE, DAVID F. (1977). *America by Design: Science, Technology, and the Rise of Corporate Capitalism*. New York: Oxford University Press.

NOLAN, MARY (1994). *Visions of Modernity: American Business and the Modernization of Germany*. New York: Oxford University Press.

OAKES, LESLIE S. (1988). 'Organizational Implications of Accounting-Based Incentive Plans: An Historical Examination of Accounting in the Labor Process'. Unpublished Ph.D. dissertation, University of Wisconsin-Madison.

PERROW, CHARLES (1986). *Complex Organizations: A Critical Essay*. New York: Random House.

PETERI, GYORGY (1984). *Effects of World War I: War Communism in Hungary*. New York: Brooklyn College Press.

PETERSEN, PETER B. (1989). 'The Pioneering Efforts of Major General William Crozier (1855–1942) in the Field of Management'. *Journal of Management*, 15: 503–16.

PETERSON, FLORENCE (1937). 'Methods Used in Strike Statistics'. *Journal of the American Statistical Association*, 197: 90–6.

—— (1938). *Strikes in the United States 1880–1936*. United States Department of Labor Bulletin No. 651. Washington: United States Printing Office.

PFEFFER, JEFFREY, and SALANCIK, GERALD R. (1978). *The External Control of Organizations*. New York: Harper & Row.

PIPPIN, ROBERT B. (1991). *Modernism as a Philosophical Problem: On the Dissatisfactions of European High Culture*. Oxford: Basil Blackwell.

POLANYI, KARL (1944/1963). *The Great Transformation: The Political and Economic Origins of our Time*. Boston: Beacon Press.

POLLARD, SIDNEY (1965). *The Genesis of Modern Management: A Study of the Industrial Revolution in Great Britain*. Cambridge, Mass.: Harvard University Press.

PORTER, THEODORE M. (1994). 'Objectivity as Standardization: The Rhetoric of Impersonality in Measurement, Statistics, and Cost-Benefit Analysis', in Allan Megill (ed.), *Rethinking Objectivity*. Durham, NC: Duke University Press: 197–238.

QUIGEL, JAMES P. (1992). 'The Business of Selling Efficiency: Harrington Emerson and the Emerson Efficiency Engineers'. Unpublished Ph.D dissertation, Pennsylvania State University.

RABINBACH, ANSON (1990). *The Human Motor: Energy Fatigue and the Origin of Modernity.* New York: Basic Books.

RAZ, E. AVIAD (1999). *Riding the Black Ship: Japan and Tokyo Disneyland.* Cambridge, Mass.: Harvard University Press.

ROE, JOSEPH W. (1916). *English and American Tool Builders.* New Haven: Yale University Press.

ROSS, DOROTHY (1991). *The Origins of American Social Science.* Cambridge: Cambridge University Press.

—— (1993). 'An Historian's View of American Social Science'. *Journal of the History of the Behavioral Sciences,* 29: 99–112.

ROY, WILLIAM G. (1990). 'Functional and Historical Logics in Explaining the Rise of the American Industrial Corporation'. *Comparative Social Research,* 12: 19–44.

—— (1997). *Socializing Capital: The Rise of Large Industrial Corporation in America.* Princeton: Princeton University Press.

SASS, STEVEN A. (1982). *The Pragmatic Imagination: A History of the Wharton School 1881–1981.* Philadelphia: University of Pennsylvania Press.

SCHUMPETER, JOSEPH A. (1943/1966). *Capitalism, Socialism and Democracy.* London: Unwin University Books.

SCHWARTZ, MICHAEL (1987). *The Structure of Power in America: The Corporate Elite as a Ruling Class.* New York: Holmes & Meier.

SCOTT, RICHARD W. (1987). 'The Adolescence of Institutional Theory'. *Administrative Science Quarterly,* 32: 493–511.

—— (1987/1992). *Organizations: Rational, Natural and Open Systems.* Englewood Cliffs, NJ: Prentice-Hall.

—— and MEYER, JOHN W. (1994). 'Environmental Linkages and Organizational Complexity: Public and Private Schools', in W. R. Scott and J. W. Meyer (eds.), *Institutional Environments and Organizations: Structural Complexity and Individualism.* Thousand Oaks, Calif.: Sage.

SHAFER, BAYRON E. (1991) (ed.). *Is America Different? A New Look at American Exceptionalism.* Oxford: Oxford University Press.

SHALEV, MICHAEL (1992). *Labour and the Political Economy in Israel.* Oxford: Oxford University Press.

SHELEFF, LEON S. (1997). *Social Cohesion and Legal Coercion: A Critique of Weber, Durkheim and Marx.* Amsterdam: Rodopi.

SHENHAV, YEHOUDA (1994). 'Manufacturing Uncertainty and Uncertainty in Manufacturing: Managerial Discourse and the Rhetoric of Organizational Theory'. *Science in Context,* 7: 275–305.

—— (1995). 'From Chaos to Systems: The Engineering Foundations of Organization Theory'. *Administrative Science Quarterly,* 40: 557–85.

SHORTER, E., and TILLY, CHARLES (1971). 'The Shape of Strikes in France, 1830–1960'. *Comparative Studies in Society and History,* 13: 60–86.

SIMON, HERBERT A. (1957). *Administrative Behavior.* New York: Macmillan.

SINCLAIR, BRUCE (1980). *A Centennial History of the American Society of Mechanical Engineers 1880–1980.* Toronto: University of Toronto Press.

SKLAR, MARTIN J. (1988). *The Corporate Reconstruction of American Capitalism, 1890–1916: The Market, the Law, and Politics.* Cambridge: Cambridge University Press.

SLAUGHTER, SHEILA, and SILVA, EDWARD (1980). 'Looking Backwards: How Foundations Formulated Ideology in the Progressive Period', in Robert F. Arnove (ed.), *Philanthropy and Cultural Imperialism: The Foundations at Home and Abroad.* Bloomington: Indiana University Press: 55–86.

SMITH, ADAM (1937). *An Inquiry into the Nature and Causes of the Wealth of Nations.* New York: Random House.

SMITH, LAURENCE D. (1986). *Behaviorism and Logical Positivism.* Stanford, Calif.: Stanford University Press.

SPENDER, CHRISTOPHER JOHN (1989). *Industry Recipes: The Nature and Sources of Managerial Judgement.* Oxford: Blackwell.

—— (1991). 'Villain, Victim or Visionary: F. W. Taylor's Contribution to Organization Theory'. Working paper. Newark, NJ: Rutgers University.

STARK, DAVID (1980). 'Class Struggle and the Transformation of the Labor Process'. *Theory and Society,* 9: 89–130.

STEVEN, KREIS (1993). 'The Diffusion of Scientific Management: The Bedaux Company in America and Britain, 1926–1945', in Daniel Nelson (ed.), *A Mental Revolution: Scientific Management since Taylor.* Columbus: Ohio State University Press: 156–77.

STIGLER, GEORGE J. and FRIEDLAND, CLAIRE (1983). 'The Literature of Economics: The Case of Berle and Means'. *Journal of Law and Economics,* 26: 237–68.

STONE, KATHERINE (1974). 'The Origins of Job Structures in the Steel Industry'. *Review of Radical Political Economics,* 2: 113–73.

SUTTON, FRANCIS., HARRIS, S., KAYSEN C., and TOBIN, J. (1956). *The American Business Creed.* Cambridge, Mass.: Harvard University Press.

SZELENYI, IVAN, and MARTIN, BILL (1988). 'The Three Waves of New Class Theories'. *Theory and Society,* 17: 645–67.

TAFT, PHILIP, and ROSS, PHILIP (1969). 'American Labor Violence: Its Causes, Character, and Outcome', in Hugh Davis Graham (ed.), *Violence in America: Historical and Comparative Perspectives.* New York: Bantam Books: 221–303.

TAYLOR, FREDERICK W. (1895). 'A Piece Rate System: A Step toward Partial Solution to the Labor Problem'. *Transactions of the ASME,* 16: 856–93.

—— (1903). *Shop Management.* New York: Harper.

—— (1911). *Principles of Scientific Management.* New York: Harper.

THOMPSON, JAMES D. (1956). 'On Building an Administrative Science'. *Administrative Science Quarterly,* 1: 102–11.

—— (1967). *Organizations in Action.* New York: McGraw-Hill.

TICHI, CECELIA (1987). *Shifting Gears: Technology, Literature, Culture in Modernist America.* Chapel Hill: The University of North Carolina Press.

TILLY, CHRIS, and TILLY, CHARLES (1998). *Work under Capitalism.* Boulder, Colo: Westview.

TOCQUEVILLE, ALEXIS DE (1945). *Democracy in America.* New York: Vintage Books.

TOLMINS, CRISTOPHER L. (1985). *The State and the Unions: Labor Relations, Law and the Organized Labor Movement in America, 1960–1980.* Cambridge, UK: Cambridge University Press.

TOMLINSON, JIM (1994). 'The Politics of Economic Measurement: The Rise of the "Productivity Problem" in the 1940s', in Anthony Hopwood and Peter Miller (eds.), *Accounting as Social and Institutional Practice*. Cambridge, UK: Cambridge University Press: 168–89.

TOULMIN, STEPHEN (1990). *Cosmopolis: The Hidden Agenda of Modernity*. New York: Free Press.

TRAHAIR, RICHARD C. S. (1984). *The Humanist Temper: The Life and Work of Elton Mayo*. New Brunswick, NJ: Transaction books.

TREGOING, JOHN (1891). *A Treatise on Factory Management*. Lynn, Mass.: Press of Thomas P. Nichols.

TSUTSUI, MINORU WILLIAM (1995). 'From Taylorism to Quality Control: Scientific Management in 20th Century Japan'. Unpublished Ph.D. dissertation, Department of History, Princeton University.

TYACK, DAVID B. (1974). *The One Best System: A History of American Urban Education*. Cambridge, Mass.: Harvard University Press.

TYRRELL, IAN (1991). 'American Exceptionalism in an Age of International History'. *American Historical Review*, 96: 1031–55

URWICK, L. (1929). *The Meaning of Rationalisation*. London: Nisbet.

US Department of Commerce (1975). *Historical Statistics of the United States: Colonial Times to 1970*. Washington: Bureau of the Census.

VEBLEN, THORSTEIN (1915/1939). *Imperial Germany and the Industrial Revolution*. New York: Viking.

—— (1919/1963). *The Engineers and the Price System*. New York: Harcourt & Brace.

VOLTAIRE (1947/1970). *Candide*. New York: Penguin Books.

VOSS, KIM (1993). *The Making of American Exceptionalism: The Knights of Labor and Class Formation in the Nineteenth Century*. Ithaca, NY: Cornell University Press.

WACQUANT, LOIC J. D. (1992). 'Towards a Social Praxeology: The Structure and Logic of Bourdieu's Sociology', in Pierre Bourdieu and Loic J. D. Wacquant (eds.), *An Invitation to Reflexive Sociology*. Chicago: University of Chicago Press: 1–59.

WARD, JOHN WILLIAM (1964). 'The Ideal of Individualism and the Reality of Organization', in Earl F. Cheit (ed.), *The Business Establishment*. New York: John Wiley: 37–76.

WARING, STEPHEN P. (1991). *Taylorism Transformed: Scientific Management Theory since 1945*. Chapel Hill: University of North Carolina Press.

WARNER, MALCOLM (1994). 'Japanese Culture, Western Management: Taylorism and Human Resource in Japan'. *Organization Studies*, 15: 509–33.

WEBER, MAX (1921/1968). *Economy and Society*. Vol i, ed. Guenther Roth and Claus Wittich. New York: Bedminster Press.

—— (1949). *The Methodology of the Social Sciences*. New York: Free Press.

WEISS, RICHARD (1983). 'Weber on Bureaucracy: Management Consultant or Political Theorist?' *Academy of Management Review*, 8: 242–8.

WEITZ, ELY (1997). 'The Institutionalization of Uncertainty in Organization Theory'. Unpublished Ph.D dissertation, Tel Aviv University.

WHITELY, RICHARD (1992) (ed.). *European Business Systems*. London: Sage Publications.

WIEBE, ROBERT H. (1967). *The Search for Order, 1877–1920*. New York: Hill & Wang.

WILLIAMSON, OLIVER E. (1975). *Markets and Hierarchies: Analysis and Antitrust Implications.* New York: Free Press.

—— (1985). *The Economic Institutions of Capitalism.* New York: Free Press.

WILSON, ARTHUR M. (1957). *Diderot: The Testing Years.* New York: Oxford University Press.

WREN, DANIEL A. (1972). *The Evolution of Management Thought.* New York: Ronald Press Company.

WUNDERLIN, CLARENCE E. (1992). *Visions of a New Industrial Order: Social Science and Labor Theory in America's Progressive Era.* New York: Columbia University Press.

YATES, JOANNE (1989). *Control through Communication: The Rise of System in American Management.* Baltimore: Johns Hopkins University Press.

YONAY, YUVAL (1998). *The Struggle over the Soul of Economics: Institutional and Neoclassical Economists in America between the Wars.* Princeton: Princeton University Press.

ZEITLIN, MAURICE (1974). 'Corporate Ownership and Control: The Large Corporation and the Capitalist Class'. *American Journal of Sociology*, 79: 1073–119.

ZIEGER, ROBERT H. (1986). *American Workers, American Unions, 1920–1985.* Baltimore: Johns Hopkins University Press.

ZUCKER, G. LYNN (1987). 'Institutional Theories of Organization'. *Annual Review of Sociology*, 13: 443–64.

# Index